THE KRILOV

The Guardians BOOK 1

CONTINUUM

J. M. H. Lovegrove

D0812889

MILLENNIUM

A Millennium Paperback Original
First published in Great Britain in 1998 by Millennium,
a division of Orion Books Ltd,
Orion House, 5 Upper St Martin's Lane,
London WC2H 9EA

A CIP catalogue record for this book
is available from the British Library.

ISBN: 1 85798 536 2

Typeset by Deltatype Ltd, Birkenhead, Merseyside
Printed and bound in Great Britain by
Clays Ltd, St Ives plc.

For Simon Spanton
A rock of an editor

A tree cannot find out, as it were, how to blossom until comes blossom time. A social growth cannot find out the use of steam engines until comes steam engine time.

– Charles Fort, *Lo!*

Prologue

The woman rode out on to the edge of the plain, where the taiga thinned, dense coniferous forest giving way to coiling ground shrubs and grasses. Still just within the cover of the trees, she halted her horse and raised a hand to shield her eyes against the setting sun, which hung low above the jagged mountain range on the horizon. Renko, refractory as ever, snorted and stamped. Like her, he was impatient for the journey to be over. Ahead, a mile distant, lay their destination: a cluster of wooden farm buildings, black against the greens and greys of the tundra, set beside a sinuous silvery rivulet.

The woman smiled a weary smile and dismounted, the sabre and rifle that were slung crosswise over her back jangling as her bootheel struck the ground. It would be dark soon. Another hour at most. She would wait until then before moving in. For now, she was simply glad to be out of the forest, out of the heat and the humidity, away from the cloying smell of pine sap and the swarming flies. It was good to be able to take pleasure in a view again, after three days of having nothing to look at but trees and more trees.

While Renko set to browsing the grass, she took a canteen from her saddlebag and sipped the last of the water it contained. Drawn from a small lake she had passed yesterday, the water tasted disgusting – brackish and marshy – but she consoled herself with the thought that, if all went well, this and the many other deprivations she had had to endure over the past three years would soon be at an end.

Three years? Sometimes it felt as though she had been pursuing him for ever. For three years, across the length and breadth of the land, she had been following a trail of rumours and sightings and leads both false and firm, making the occasional wrong turn thanks to bad advice or a paid lie, and invariably arriving a month or a week or sometimes just a couple of days too late, to find an empty house or apartment, rooms strewn with a few scattered pieces of scientific apparatus, evidence of his recent tenancy and even more recent departure, left there as though to taunt her, to mock her efforts.

For three long years he had remained constantly one step ahead of her, like an unkind partner in a dance. Always he had seemed to know precisely how long to stay in one place and exactly when to move on, taking with him several hundredweight of equipment, much of it bulky, some of it delicate, transporting it lock, stock and barrel to another destination, there to begin his experiments anew. A remarkable feat, really. But then he was a remarkable man, and with every near-miss, every failed attempt to overtake him, her respect for him had grown ... and so had her determination to catch him.

The closest she had come to doing that had been in St Petersburg, where she had learned from a reliable source that, under a false name, he was using the laboratory and engineering facilities at the Imperial Academy of Sciences, his Alma Mater, to further his research and oversee the machine-tooling of components for his invention. It was a brazen but clever place for him to hide. Where better for a professor to lose himself but among professors? Not only that, but he must have known that it would be difficult for her, as a woman, to penetrate the ranks of that male-dominated establishment. Never mind that during the reign of Catherine the Great the Academy had had a female president. Those days were long gone, and the faculty and administration were all one close-knit

2

fraternity now, prone to secrecy, protective of their own. Thus he was shielded from her by an extra layer of defence considerably more impenetrable than that provided by the two burly bodyguards who accompanied him at all times: a stockade of scholastic sodality.

From her preliminary investigations she had learned that he never ventured beyond the boundaries of the Academy, but which of the campus buildings he frequented and which contained his lodgings she was unable to ascertain, and these things she had to know if she was to isolate and invalidate him stealthily and with the minimum risk of discovery. She had debated whether she might be able to glean any further information by donning a gown, a patched pair of trousers, a false beard and an earnest expression, and passing herself off as a student. (On more than one occasion in the past her stocky physique and the somewhat masculine cast to her features had enabled her to pull off a male disguise convincingly.) In the end, she had decided that a less direct approach might be equally effective, namely working her wiles on one of the undergraduates and using him, first for reconnaissance, then as a means of access.

In this scheme, unfortunately, she proved rather too successful. The dog-like devotion she aroused in poor young Yevgeny, a pupil of the famous behaviourist Ivan Pavlov, led to an ugly scene one evening at the boarding house where she was staying, when, in the throes of a depressive fit doubtless brought on by reading too much Dostoevsky, Yevgeny had come in brandishing a cutthroat razor, demanding to see her and threatening that he would slit his own wrists if she did not, then and there, declare undying love for him. Since she had, admittedly, toyed with Yevgeny's affections, she could not in all conscience allow him to kill himself for no good reason, and so, having first disarmed him, she then set about trying to convince him that life without her would be worth living. At this point the landlord had appeared and said that the other tenants were complaining about the disturbance and that the police had been summoned.

3

She could not risk a run-in with the police, because they would ask too many questions to which she had no good answers, and so she was forced to flee the city and, by the time she returned, her quarry, of course, had got wind that she was on to him again and had disappeared.

Bad luck aside, there was something not a little uncanny about the way her quarry seemed to know whenever she was getting close. It was almost as though, like some animal prey, he could sense the proximity of the hunter, although in his case this was more likely due to intellect rather than instinct. His was one of the keenest minds in Russia, perhaps in the entire world. No befuddled, unworldly academic he, but a sharp-witted thinker, a man who could observe the tangled skein of events, discern patterns and trends, and deduce the most likely outcome – a talent he exercised both in the laboratory and beyond. Little wonder, then, that his invisible masters had chosen him as the unwitting vessel through which to carry out their plans. She knew of perhaps one other man alive who was his mental equal. A man she admired, desired ... and had steeled herself to forget.

And so through season after season the chase had continued, from the steppes to the Caucasus, from the Urals to the shores of the Black Sea. She had endured the very bitterest of the winters that her native country had to offer, and also the very fiercest of the summers. She had ridden for weeks on end until her backside had felt as leathery as the saddle beneath it, with Renko balking almost every step of the way and she in turn cursing him, calling him a son of a mule and other, coarser biological impossibilities. She had purchased Renko at the outset of her mission, and he had perhaps, in retrospect, been a poor choice of steed. Over the three years, however, she had developed a grudging tolerance of his foibles that was almost an affection, and therefore insulting him was a liberty only she was allowed to take. When, at one point during the course of her travels, she had overheard a count refer to him – in French, the preferred language

4

of Russian nobility – as an ill-tempered nag good for nothing but peasant stew and glue, she had immediately challenged that worthy gentleman to a duel, and had won, leaving the fellow with a scar on his forehead that would serve as a constant reminder to think twice before disparaging someone else's choice of mount, even in a language he did not think the other person could speak. On another occasion, it was her own virtue she had been obliged to defend, when an amorous Cossack at a tavern had refused to take *nyet* for an answer – although he had understood the non-verbal negative of a knee in the groin well enough.

And in all that time, although she had often entertained doubts that she would ever complete her mission, not once had she wavered from her task or questioned the rightness of what she was doing. She had forged on relentlessly, her jaw regally set, through hardship and trial and tribulation, drawing strength, if ever she needed it, from the brooch that she wore upon her person at all times, either attached to the breast of her double-buttoned overcoat or fastened to her sable hat as a kind of cockade. The brooch was a gold egg, reminiscent in appearance of something Fabergé himself might have fashioned, perhaps less finely wrought, but possessed of properties of which that great jeweller could not even begin to conceive. Composed of tightly interlocking parts, like a Chinese puzzle, the egg was the talismanic symbol of the clandestine international cabal, the Popechitli, to which she belonged and in joining which she had forgone (some sacrifice!) any chance she might have had of leading a normal, sedate, respectable life.

Then, six months ago, at the beginning of the year, the trail had gone cold again. Stone cold. She had tried every one of her contacts, her nationwide network of allies, interested parties and informants. Not a thing. Everywhere she had looked, she had drawn a blank. For a while she had staked out her quarry's family home in Moscow, but his wife and son did not receive a visit from the husband and father who had all but abandoned them.

He had gone to ground, and for him to disappear like that, to drop out of sight without a trace, could mean only one thing: that he was close to success, and needed to be somewhere where he could see his work through its final stages without fear of being distracted or, more importantly, discovered.

It occurred to her that he might have gone abroad, although this seemed unlikely. He was canny enough to realise that in a foreign country a Russian would stand out, would be remarked upon, would be easy to find. Why take that risk when he had the whole of his vast homeland to hide in? She made enquiries at all the major ports anyway, simply so as to be doing *something*, but even as she looked over countless carnets and bills of lading she knew she was wasting her time. The same at border crossings: no one matching his description had passed that way. It was almost too frustrating to bear. Just when it was more imperative than ever that she locate him, she had not the least clue where he was.

Then, at the beginning of spring, she had struck lucky. A fellow Popechitel in Novosibirsk got in touch with her, telling her that he had met a bargee at an inn in Krasnoyarsk who had boasted, when in his cups, of a passenger he had recently taken down the Yenisey river, a well-educated, well-spoken man who had paid well over the going rate for his passage. It sounded, the Popechitel said, very much like the man she was seeking.

Straight away she had travelled to Krasnoyarsk and tracked down the bargee. He was reluctant to talk at first. The extra roubles her quarry had given him had clearly doubled as hush-money, but in return for a modest outlay of her own, in the form of vodka, it was not long before the bargee was telling her all about the man he referred to as 'the doctor', and about the two large companions and the several dozen large crates that the doctor had had with him, and about the polite evasions with which the doctor had met questions concerning the contents of the crates and his reasons for wishing to transport them into one of the country's remoter regions.

Where had this 'doctor' put in, she asked the bargee. At Osinovo, she was told. Showing him a sheaf of roubles, a sum at least as great as that which her target had paid him, she said she would like to hire his barge, too. The bargee's eyes lit up. She could see him mentally translating the notes into bottles. A deal was struck.

Renko, confined to the barge's hold, where the floor had been covered in straw to form a makeshift stable, had hated every minute of the journey downriver, and she had not much enjoyed it either. The Yenisey itself was both a sombre and a spectacular sight, immense and wide and lead-grey, its deceptively placid surface here and there disturbed by the wrinkles and swirls that indicated powerful currents roiling away below, for the river was swollen with late-spring meltwater and its breadth disguised the speed of its flow. Spectacle, however, was no compensation for tedium, and the swift current did not translate into a swift journey, because the bargee insisted on putting ashore at every town, village and landing on the way, ostensibly to buy supplies but in fact to go and get drunk.

Though she was glad of these stopovers, in as much as they gave her an opportunity to exercise Renko and so prevent him from going completely insane with cabin fever, they also cost her precious time. Frequently the bargee's trips ashore left him too incapacitated to steer, and he would stagger back aboard only to head straight belowdecks, collapse on to his bunk and fall fast asleep. She then had nothing to do but pace the deck while he snored. She would have commandeered the boat herself, but she knew that parts of the river were treacherous and required the hand of a skilled pilot to navigate them. The delays chafed, but somehow she managed to curb her impatience. If nothing else, she had a purpose once more. Her period of casting vainly around for her quarry's scent was over. She was on his trail again.

Finally they reached Osinovo, and there the bargee

introduced her to a friend of his, a coarse-complexioned, mad-bearded old fellow who scratched a living as a fur trapper and whose living, to judge by the numerous scars that crosshatched his face and the backs of his hands, often scratched him back. At first the fur trapper would not even admit to having met any 'doctor', but discretion bought by money was once again undone by vodka. Soon she had established that her quarry had paid the fur trapper to hire him several troikas and teams of horses, and had then asked to be escorted to some form of accommodation far from civilisation, but still habitable, where he and his companions might stay. The fur trapper had taken him to an abandoned farm roughly three days' journey from Osinovo, a place where he himself sometimes took shelter during blizzards.

In return for a handsome bribe the fur trapper had marked the location of the farm for her on a map. He had then offered his services as guide. 'After all,' he said, 'in these parts, a woman on her own –'

'Is far safer than a woman in the company of one such as yourself,' she replied, softening the rejoinder with a genial laugh so that he would not take offence.

She had left Osinovo at first light the next morning, and, on the evening of the following day, had come upon a small Tungus settlement, deep in the forest. There she had bought dried reindeer meat and, having some knowledge of the Tungusic language, had been able to confirm that some months previously four men *had* passed that way with troikas piled high with crates, and that one of the men had returned alone, on horseback, a couple of days later. The villagers, delighted at finding a Russian who spoke their tongue, insisted she stay the night and showed her great hospitality. From past experience she had developed an affinity for the Tungus lifestyle – its raw, natural, season-driven simplicity presented an alluring alternative to the complexities and many-layered subterfuges of her own existence – and she would willingly have stayed longer, but duty called. She left the village the following morning, promising to return, and it was a promise she fully intended to keep, even if it meant she would have to face another barrage of marriage proposals from the male villagers, all of whom were desperate to add her to their bevies of wives.

And now, a day later, here she was, about to confront – finally – the man who had led her such a merry chase these past three years. After all this time, she and he would have much to talk about ... before she killed him.

As the sun descended behind the mountains and long purple shadows filtered across the plain, a thin, uncertain thread of smoke began to rise from the chimney of the main farm building, quickly thickening to a steady plume. Not long after, a light came on in a window. Seeing this, she unbuttoned the flap of a leather case attached to her belt and took out a pair of binoculars. Housed in burnished brass, and as compact as a pair of opera glasses, but five times as heavy and twenty-five times as powerful, the binoculars were a gift from her own invisible masters. When she removed the caps that covered the lenses, the dilated irises within contracted automatically upon exposure to light, in fluent, eerie mimicry of their living equivalent, and to the accompaniment of a faint grinding whirr. Raising the binoculars to her eyes and bringing them to bear on the farm, she saw the distant buildings come jerkily into focus, blurred outlines resolving themselves by degrees to pin-sharp clarity. There was no need for her to adjust the depth of field manually. The binoculars did that for themselves, courtesy of a mechanism she did not understand and did not *want* to understand. She homed in on the lit window, and there she perceived the silhouette of a man, standing, peering out, his profile delineated by the glow from a kerosene lantern.

Him.

What she felt then was excitement, to be sure, but, greater than that, and somehow strangely dismaying, a sense of inevitability, as if it had been preordained all along that her pursuit of him would end here, in this desolate spot on the western fringes of the Central

Siberian Plateau. Probably he sensed this, too, and that was why he had taken up position at the window, like the host of a party anticipating the arrival of the first guest, the light an open invitation. Either that or he had fallen into the habit of looking out for her, no matter where he was or how unlikely it was that she might appear – a thought which filled some small dark corner of her heart with satisfaction.

She scanned the rest of the farm, and ascertained that one of the bodyguards was on sentry duty in the courtyard while the other was roving further afield, patrolling the perimeter of the buildings. Both were armed with rifles.

She tethered Renko to a tree, silencing his huffs of protest by stroking his neck and whispering in his ear that she wouldn't be long. She then divested herself of all her weapons except her revolver and boot-knife. The latter, like the binoculars, was a gift, its blade fashioned of an iridescent metal that maintained its sharpness by sometimes, visibly, *flowing*. Then she hunkered down on a rock and waited for nightfall.

The sky was massed with stars – there were more stars up there, it seemed, than blackness – and the moon was jaundiced and full, so there was enough light to see by as she crept across the plain towards the farm. She slit the throat of the first bodyguard while he was relieving himself against the side of one of the outbuildings. The second died equally silently, and as she lowered his body to the hard-packed mud of the courtyard she felt the handle of her knife purr joyously as its blade absorbed the bloodstains, renewing its lethal cleanliness.

Passing a stable where, to judge by the soft snorts and whinnies coming from inside, the horses her quarry had hired were being kept, she approached the farmhouse. It occurred to her, as she reached the front door, that perhaps she ought to knock. Some kind of formality, she felt, was in order. She decided against it, though. Her quarry was hardly a man of action, but why risk alerting him?

Drawing her revolver, she silently raised the latch and nudged the door inward. She found herself looking in at a spacious but dingy kitchen that reeked of damp, wood-smoke and cooked meat. On a large, rough-hewn, age-blackened table in the centre of the room lay several meals' worth of dirty eating utensils: enamel dishes haphazardly stacked, cutlery handles sticking out between them like tongues. Three bedrolls were unfurled on the floor beside the hearth, where smouldering pine logs crackled and spat.

Her quarry was seated at the table with his back to her and his feet to the fire, lost in a meditation so profound that he did not notice that anyone had entered until the draught coming in through the open door caught the flames and set them flickering wildly.

'Sergei?' he said, turning.

His look of surprise was disappointingly short-lived, yielding so swiftly to a look of resignation that she could only assume that she *had* been expected. But then he must have realised that neither the bargee nor the fur trapper could be relied upon to stay silent for long. Maybe he had been counting on that, in order to lure her here. But if so, why? She dismissed the thought. Having gone to so much trouble to elude her for so long, it would have been perverse of him, to say the least, suddenly to want to make it easy for her to find him.

'Valentina Aleksandrovna,' he said, with exaggerated politeness.

'Anton Mikhailovich,' she replied.

He gestured around the kitchen. 'Please forgive the mess,' he said. 'Had I but known I was to have company, I would have made an effort to tidy up. Living with a pair of apes like Oleg and Sergei ...' He caught himself. 'Ah. Yes. Of course. Poor Oleg. Poor Sergei.'

She drew up a chair opposite him and set the revolver down on the table between them, within her reach, just out of his.

He was a slight man, smaller than she had imagined he would be from his photographs. His hair was going grey and, on top, had that coarse, clumpy look that denoted the onset of thinning. His nose was broad at the bridge, narrowing to a point at its tip. His gaze was steady and penetrating. For a man who must have known that he was shortly to die, his manner was admirably calm.

'Would you care for something to eat?' he enquired. 'You must be famished after all your travels. There's some lemming meat left over. It's tough but not untasty.'

She shook her head.

'No? Later then, perhaps.' He clasped his hands together. 'So. At last we meet. You're quite the spitting image of your father, you know. But it can't be the first time you've been told that. You have his eyes, his jawline. Very distinguished, and on you not unattractive.'

'I do not know who my father was,' she said, refusing to rise to the bait.

'Oh, come, come, Valentina Aleksandrovna! *Everyone* who knows anything about you knows who your father was. How are things with your half-brother's family, anyway? I understand that that peasant charismatic has complete sway over the Empress's mind now. Her body, too, if the rumours are to be believed. A dangerous fellow. Perhaps he's next on your list, after me?'

'Why should he be?'

'Because he is bringing the royal family into disrepute.'

'If you ask me, the royal family have been managing that for several years now without anyone's help.'

He chuckled. 'So what *is* it, Valentina Aleksandrovna, that makes me a marked man and not someone like that debauchee Rasputin or any of the Marxist agitators currently stirring up trouble? This has been puzzling me. What has humble Professor Anton Krilov done to deserve being hounded back and forth across the country? Never given a chance to settle anywhere for longer than a few months? Cut adrift from his beloved family – his wife, his son? Barely allowed to catch his breath before he has to up stakes and move on again?' He pointed to his chest, the gesture self-consciously theatrical. 'Do I plot to overthrow monarchies? Do I lust to gain political power by fair means or foul? On the contrary. All I wish to do is push back the frontiers of knowledge a little, and whatever scientific advances I might make will be of benefit to everyone; may even, perhaps, help to unite this rapidly fragmenting nation of ours by giving us all an achievement to be proud of. Does that make me a threat? And if so, a threat to what?'

The questions were disingenuous and she did not answer them. Krilov was no fool. From the very start he must have had his suspicions about the institute that had agreed to fund him so generously and so unquestioningly in his scientific endeavours, the Moscow Engineering Foundation. He had surely done his research and found out that that institute was owned outright by another, larger institute, which in turn was owned outright by another, yet larger institute, and so on, like a nest of dolls, each contained by a shell one size up, and the shells becoming more nebulous, more expansive, their limits harder to trace and define, with every increment. And while no doubt it was necessary for him, in order to be able to concentrate on his work, not to ponder too deeply on these things (among scientists, such acts of moral self-blinkering were not uncommon), he none the less could not be entirely ignorant that he, like her, was being used as a pawn in a much larger game – a game of symmetry and equilibrium, of checks and balances.

And in that moment she felt compassion for him – a twinge of it, not enough to deter her from what she had to do, but enough to make the prospect of doing it just that much more difficult to contemplate.

The shrewd Professor Krilov perceived this; had possibly been counting on this. 'Valentina Aleksandrovna,' he said, 'it's obvious that you are here to destroy my invention. Doubtless you have brought some dynamite with you for that task.'

She nodded. After she had invalidated Krilov, she would go back and fetch it from one of Renko's panniers. Dynamite, or something very similar.

'It's obvious, too,' Krilov went on, 'that you are here to

13

kill me. Because of I don't know what reason, I must die and my work must die with me. All this I realise. And I realise also that I possess neither the physical wherewithal to prevent you from carrying out your mission nor the rhetorical powers to dissuade you from it. However, I would beg of you the one favour traditionally permitted all condemned men. My device is nearly finished, a few turns of the screw away from completion, and I would like to be allowed to run one last practical test, so that I may at least die with the satisfaction of knowing that my life's work has not been in vain.' He offered her a plaintive smile. 'A reasonable enough request, wouldn't you agree?'

Under the circumstances, she could hardly refuse.

She kept the revolver trained on him as he led her out across the courtyard to the biggest of the outbuildings, a large double-doored barn. The sight of the dead bodyguard perturbed him, but only a little. He swung the barn doors wide, then held up the lantern so that she could look inside.

At first, beyond the lantern's glow, which had become the nucleus for a swiftly growing cloud of winged insects, she could see nothing but darkness. Then gradually she discerned a hulking cylindrical shape, somewhat like a locomotive, but flatter, sleeker, more streamlined, and with a bulging, breast-like nosecone that reminded her of an airship's. Two slender triangular fins ran along the cylinder on either side, aligned with its horizontal axis, starting narrow and broadening out the further back they went. In all, the bizarre-looking vehicle was some thirty feet in length from stem to stern, and at its rear was a cabin large enough to accommodate two people, fitted with a row of portholes all around. The entirety was made from sections of iron riveted together, and rested on a specially constructed wooden cradle.

'And there she is,' said Professor Krilov. 'The one and only working model in existence of the Krilov Gravitational Annulment Engine.' He lowered his voice, as though confiding a secret. 'Ever since, as a little boy, I saw an engraving in a picture book of the Montgolfiers' balloon, Valentina, I have known that this is what I was born to do. To take their invention one step further. To create a method of shrugging off the fetters of the earth that will allow unrestricted, directionable flight.'

'I hate to point this out to you,' said Valentina, 'but the Wright brothers have already achieved that.'

'Pfah! Their clumsy canvas contraption has no future. It can barely carry one man more than a hundred yards. Eventually, Gravitational Annulment Engines will be able to transport hundreds, perhaps even thousands, of people untold distances, along with untold quantities of cargo. Packet steamers of the sky, requiring not tons of coal but just a relatively small amount of electrical energy in order to cleave through the air at fantastic speeds.'

Carried away by the rapture of his dream, Krilov seemed to have forgotten Valentina's reason for being there. Then he remembered.

'Well,' he said glumly, 'perhaps one day that is how it will be. And perhaps one day I will be acknowledged as the true originator of such craft, even if history forgets me for now.'

Directing an aggrieved scowl at Valentina over his shoulder, Krilov entered the barn. The lantern's light revealed dozens of empty crates lying around in a disordered jumble with their lids half on and shallow drifts of packing sawdust on the floor around them. He hung the lantern from a hook on a beam and lit another two. In the combined radiance of the three sources of light, the Gravitational Annulment Engine's smooth iron contours pulsed with reflected golden lambency.

Collecting a spanner and a large screwdriver from a manger that had been pressed into service as a makeshift workbench, Krilov leapt nimbly up the three rungs of the ladder that led to the cabin. He opened a hatch and ducked inside. A moment later his head reappeared in the hatchway. 'I have no idea how long this is going to take,' he said.

'That's fine,' said Valentina, resecuring the lid of one of

the crates. 'I am a patient woman.' She clambered on top of the crate and seated herself there cross-legged, resting the revolver on one thigh and wriggling her backside around until she was comfortable.

'Yes,' said Krilov. 'Yes, that you are.'

He worked hard through the night – checking, adjusting, fine-tuning, tightening up, lubricating here and there with a dab of oil, moving over and under and around the machine, and sometimes disappearing deep into its bowels for anything up to half an hour. He worked like a man hypnotised, dreamily absorbed in his labours, scarcely aware of the passage of time or of Valentina's presence. She could probably have left him there, crossed back to the farmhouse, curled up in front of the fire, slept for a few hours, and returned to find him still busy toiling away, unaware that she had even been absent – but she thought it wise not to take the chance. She sat on the crate, now and then stifling a yawn, now and then climbing off in order to stretch the stiffness out of her limbs, but for the most part content to watch Krilov minister to his iron invention. She had to admit to a certain curiosity. Would it actually work or not? The few aircraft she had hitherto seen, fragile constructs of wood and canvas, at least *looked* sufficiently light and birdlike to take flight. This – this was something else altogether. This was a fantasy lifted straight from the pages of a scientific romance. And, she reminded herself, her job was to ensure that that was where it remained: in the realm of speculation.

Dawn was just beginning to silver the sky when Krilov stepped down from the cabin, wiping oil from his hands with a cloth. 'She's ready.' He looked exhausted but excited. 'No doubt you'll be wanting to accompany me on her maiden voyage.'

'I don't see that I have a choice. If your machine does fly and I'm not aboard with you, what's to prevent you making a bid for freedom?'

'Quite, quite.' Krilov peered out through the doors at the sky. 'Well, we have the light. Shall we get started?'

The interior of the cabin sported a bewildering profusion of controls. There were no seats. Space was at a premium, comfort a luxury. Valentina kept out of Krilov's way as he set about throwing switches, turning dials, consulting gauges, manipulating levers. A hum began to emanate from the main body of the craft. She felt it first as a vibration through the soles of her feet, then as pressure in her ears.

'There will, I believe, be some disorientation,' Krilov announced. 'An unavoidable side-effect. We're interfering with the force that keeps us stuck to the planet's surface. You can't argue with Mother Nature and not expect to suffer for it.'

As if on cue, the pressure in Valentina's ears intensified and she began to feel faint and vertiginous. She reached out with her left hand, the one that was not holding the revolver, and grasped one of the cabin's reinforcing inner ribs for support.

The air seemed to grow thicker and harder to breathe as the hum further increased in volume. She checked to see whether Krilov was affected, too, and noted, with grim approval, that he was; otherwise she would have suspected a trick and would have put a bullet in him. Despite evident discomfort he continued to operate the controls, at the same time throwing comments her way, explaining how his invention worked with the furrow-browed enthusiasm of a small boy showing off his collection of clockwork automata. 'Electromagnets – that's what it's all about, Valentina. Electromagnets triggered in precessional sequence. The Gravitational Annulment Engine is, even as I speak, generating a motional gravity field around itself. Its own private gravity field, counter to that of the Earth. The result should be acceleration in a plane perpendicular to the – Ah! And there we have it!'

The Gravitational Annulment Engine gave a little leap, then settled back down onto the cradle again. The hum was near-deafening now. The cabin trembled, and again the machine leapt up into the air ... and this time stayed there. Glancing out of the nearest porthole, Valentina saw that there was a gap of at least two feet between the base of the cabin and the cradle. The sawdust, agitated by unseen forces, was swirling up around it in a vortex. The machine swayed a little from side to side, a ton of metal buoyant as a hot-air balloon. It was hard not to be awed.

'And now,' said Krilov, shouting to be heard above the din, 'forward motion.' He clasped a large brass dial that was at the top of a ring of eight such dials and turned it a few degrees clockwise. 'It's simply a question of increasing the resistance to gravity' – he similarly rotated the two dials that flanked the top one – 'in whichever direction you want to go.'

The Gravitational Annulment Engine tipped forwards at a slight angle and began juddering ponderously towards the open doorway. As the machine emerged clear of the barn, Krilov brought it to a standstill by restoring the same three dials to their original positions. He then grasped the handle of a wheel that was situated above a plaque marked 'Vertical Disposition' and began spinning it. Valentina thought about stopping him – as far as she was concerned, the Gravitational Annulment Engine was a success and the test was at an end – but she decided there would be no harm in letting Krilov put the machine through its paces. As he himself said: 'It's not enough to hover. We must fly!'

And no sooner had he said this, and given the wheel a further spin, than the machine began to rise, slowly at first, but gradually gathering speed. Valentina began to feel her body being pressed down, her cheeks sagging on her face, her back bowing as though someone had placed a yoke across her shoulders and was pouring gravel into its buckets. The craft's upward acceleration increased until her legs seemed in danger of buckling beneath her, but, just when she thought she could withstand it no longer and she was ready to collapse to the floor, Krilov spun the Vertical Disposition wheel anticlockwise, and abruptly their ascent was halted.

The Gravitational Annulment Engine hung suspended

in the air half a mile above the earth, swaying, shudder-ing and thrumming with the effort of its achievement. The roofs of the farm were far below, and the whole breadth of the plain was in view. There was the stream, and there, to the west, was the mountain range, and visible beyond it now a second range; and there, to the east, lay the expanse of forest she had trekked through, a dense, dark-green furze that extended to the horizon; and there, at the forest's edge, was Renko, toy-sized, fretting at his tether and gazing up at the machine in alarm.

'Valentina Aleksandrovna.' Krilov moved close to her so that he would not have to shout too loudly. 'I can honestly say that of all the men and women I have met over the course of a lifetime, I cannot think of anyone I would rather have shared this moment of triumph with than you.'

Flattered in spite of herself, she gave him a gracious nod.

'I have come to despise you over these past three years,' he went on. 'You have kept me from those I love. You have turned an innocent man into a fugitive. But I have also, perversely, come to admire you. Your resourcefulness, your intelligence, your tenacity ...'

Again, she acknowledged the compliments with a nod. It was strange how, in such exceptional circumstances, Krilov's words seemed neither inappropriate nor improper.

'And if I am to die today,' he said, 'in the hour of my greatest glory, then who better to join me in death than the woman who has done everything she can to prevent me realising my vision?'

She reacted just a fraction of a second too late to stop him. A thrust of a lever, a twist of a dial, and all of a sudden the Gravitational Annulment Engine was hurtling forwards. Krilov, having known what was about to happen, had braced himself. She had not, and, losing her footing, was thrown backwards against the rear of the cabin. Her head struck the wall with stunning force, and she slithered to the floor. Somehow she managed not to

let go of the revolver. The machine continued to acceler-
ate, its hum mounting to a howling shriek, the cabin
rocking about as though in the grip of some child-god's
tantrum.

Valentina hauled herself to her feet, shaking her head
to dispel the sparkling lights that were spiralling across
her vision. Out of one porthole she caught a glimpse of
treetops rushing by below. Such speed! Shouldering
Krilov aside, she groped for the controls. There had to be
some way of slowing the machine down. But what to
press? What to push? The instruments were a foreign
language to her. The needles of the gauges were shivering
blurs. The vibration of the machine was too intense for
her even to read any of the inscriptions beside the
controls.

She spun round and levelled the revolver at Krilov.
'Make it stop!' she demanded. 'Now!'

Krilov smiled scornfully at the gun. 'Can't be done, my
little princess. What do you think I was up to all last
night? She was ready to fly the day before yesterday, but I
knew you'd be coming. I wanted you with me. This is the
only way it can end, my dear Valentina. Sabotage!
Revenge for three years of persecution!'

Valentina reiterated, with the addition of several oaths,
her demand that Krilov halt the machine.

'Or what? Or you'll kill me?' Krilov uttered a hoarse,
hollow laugh – fractured but gloating, the sound of
Pyrrhic victory. 'We are dead already, Valentina! We are
going to crash at a speed of, I should say, two hundred
knots, and when we do … well, I doubt there'll be much
left either of us or of this craft.'

'Bastard,' she spat.

'An epithet, my dear, which, coming from you, loses
much of its sting.'

She was tempted to shoot him then and there, out of
sheer spite, but instead she merely glared at him, then
lowered the revolver. Outside, the rim of the craft had
begun to give off a pinkish glow. The cabin was growing
hot. One gauge cracked and shattered, then another, and

another. The machine was starting to leave a trail of vapour behind it.

So this is it, she thought. This is how it all ends.

And with that thought came sudden, sweet, acquiescent serenity. Hatred, fear, the wailing of the doomed machine, the oven heat in the cabin that was becoming suffocating, the imminence of her own death – suddenly none of these things mattered any more. All she could think of was the man she had loved and left in Salzburg. She had vowed to herself that one day she would return to him, although she had not made the same promise to him. Now she would never have the chance.

And that was all she felt as Professor Anton Krilov's Gravitational Annulment Engine hurtled across the sky in a long, incandescent arc that would take it to an impact point some 200 miles north-east of the farm.

Regret, not for anything she had said or done, but for things she had *not* said or done.

Sorrow, not for herself, but for what might have been.

PART 1

1

That morning, as she did every alternate Monday morning, Ruth Byrne prepared her husband his favourite breakfast of sausage links and scrambled eggs with a heap of buckwheat pancakes on the side. Though his midriff was not getting any thinner or his blood pressure any lower, still this fortnightly ritual was one she felt she could not fail to observe – a small wifely token of fondness and farewell.

And while Ruth was downstairs cooking, Tony Byrne, as he did every alternate Monday morning, was taking his time in the shower, revelling in the decent water pressure and in the mingled aromas of his wife's choice of body gel and shampoo. For twelve days out of every fourteen he had to make do with slow-dribbling faucets and unscented, poorly lathering government-issue toiletries that fulfilled their function of cleaning and little more. Thus, on the two weekends a month he was able to spend at home, he made the most of the domestic luxuries available to him.

He lingered beneath the jet of water until his fingertips started to prune. Then, having dried and dressed, he headed downstairs. In the kitchen, he came up behind Ruth at the range, slipped his arms around her waist and nuzzled her ear. She kissed him on the cheek and waved a spatula in the direction of the breakfast nook. 'Go sit down. Breakfast'll be along in a minute.'

Ant was already at the table, with a spiral-bound pad

of drawing paper in front of him and, beside it, a *Spawn* comic-book flattened open. In between shovelling spoonfuls of rainbow-coloured cereal into his mouth, he was drawing a picture, using a set of coloured pencils. It was not until Byrne sat down next to him that Ant even registered that his father had entered the room. The ability to close his mind to all external distractions while he was concentrating on something was a character trait Ant had inherited from his father, along with the physical traits of auburn hair, pale skin and a smattering of freckles.

The picture Ant was labouring over so intently was of the comic book's titular character, Spawn himself, who sat crouched on the edge of a rooftop amid swirls of cape and chain, gazing balefully down with his fluorescent green eyes on the city streets below. A gibbous moon glowered over the skyscrapers in the background, highlighting them and the contours of Spawn's body with tinges of yellow. Ant was not, however, copying directly from one of the panels on the comic-book page. The comic book was there for costume reference only. Spawn's pose, surroundings, indeed the entire composition of the picture, were of Ant's own devising. And although Byrne did not know much about art, he knew that his son's technique and grasp of perspective were way in advance of the average nine-year-old's. Ant's art-class teacher repeatedly intimated as much. She often whispered about scholarships to art colleges, and on one occasion she had even mentioned, with circumspection, the word 'genius'.

Where this artistic talent had come from was not immediately apparent to Byrne, since no one on Ruth's side of the family had any ability in that direction, and neither did he. It may well have come from his own father, but since he had never known the man and his mother had never told him who he was, this was something he could only guess at. It was, perhaps, a little disappointing to Byrne that Ant showed no particular propensity for his own discipline, theoretical physics, but

Byrne reckoned one significant talent was better than no talent at all, and could not have been any prouder of his son.

Ruth arrived with his breakfast, and Byrne, with a loud murmur of appreciation, drenched his pancakes in maple syrup and tucked in.

At last Ant looked up from his labours. He stared at Byrne's meal with grave disapproval and announced, 'Daddy's death breakfast.' He was quoting his mother almost verbatim. 'Too much salt, too much cholesterol.'

'Hey, you can talk,' Byrne retorted. 'That sugary goop you're shoving down your throat – I'll bet there isn't a single natural ingredient in that stuff.'

'Bleaahhh!' said Ant, displaying a multicoloured tongue. He knew that on the Monday mornings when his father was leaving, a certain level of bad behaviour would be indulged.

Ruth joined them at the table with her customary bowl of granola and cup of decaffeinated coffee, both with 2 per cent milk, and for the rest of the meal the family chatted about things that had little or no relevance to Byrne's imminent departure. If they did happen to mention it, they talked about it as if he was returning next weekend and not the weekend after, a form of verbal shorthand they all, Ant included, had learned to employ in order to make Byrne's periods of absence seem less long. During their infrequent conversational pauses, the silence was filled by the kindly hiss of the sprinklers in the backyard jetting out their prismatic parabolas of water as they burnished the lawn to the gleaming green lustre of Astroturf.

Breakfast finished, the dishwasher loaded, and with the time getting on for a quarter to eight, Byrne reversed his Mazda Protégé out of the garage on to the driveway. Clambering out of the car, he paused for a moment to look around. He and his family lived in a cul-de-sac that ended in a turning circle, the street's shape resembling a crude diagram of a thermometer such as a teacher might draw on a blackboard. It was a busy hour of the day.

Outside each house something was happening. Cars were pulling out of garages, kids were using the time until they had to go and catch the school bus to get in some hoop-shooting practice, a pair of workmen were about to commence retarring the Cleggs' drive at number 2048, Wanda Flugel at number 2057 was out tending to her bedding plants, which, in the relentless desert sunshine, needed all the care and attention they could get ... and here, jogging along the sidewalk, came old Mr Crabtree from number 2078, red-faced, sweat stains darkening his running vest and bandanna headband, gangsta rap screeching in his Walkman headphones. As the scrawny, energetic octogenarian huffed past the end of the Byrnes' driveway, Byrne raised a hand in greeting, and Mr Crabtree, without averting his gaze from the road ahead, waved back.

The sights and sounds and smells of a typical street in a typical American suburb on a typical Monday morning – and Byrne thought to himself, None of my neighbours know it, but soon all this is going to change. Soon the entire *world* is going to change.

He inhaled a deep breath through his nostrils. The morning air was tinged with the bitter odour of exhaust fumes and the sweeter scent of melting tar. Craning his neck, he could make out all of Carson City, including its old quarter, which hunkered down at the foot of the mountains. Above the city's rooftops hung a faint fringe of petrochemical brown, fading into the poster-paint blue of the sky.

He exhaled the breath and turned and strolled back to the front doorstep, where Ruth and Ant were standing, waiting for him. His policy was always to play down their partings by acting cheerful and nonchalant, as though he were any dad, off downtown to the office for the day, sure to be home by five-thirty, six at the latest. But the act convinced none of them, least of all himself, and his heart, as usual, seemed to shrivel inside him as he picked up Ant for a goodbye hug. He told Ant he was getting too big for this – the rate he was growing, he soon would not be able to lift him at all – and then told him how much he loved him and how he was going to miss him over the next twelve days. He felt the dampness of Ant's tears on his neck, and it was all he could do to keep from crying himself. It was at moments like this that he would willingly have sacrificed his entire career, abandoned the pursuit of his dream and the benefit to the world (and the personal renown) which achieving that dream was sure to bring, and taken a job, any job, even stacking shelves at a grocery store or flipping burgers at Mickey D's, so that he could come home each evening and be with his wife and son; could enjoy what almost every other husband and father on the planet took for granted.

He set Ant down. Ruth's eyes were glistening as she stepped forward to embrace him. They held each other tightly, reminding each other, through the warmth and proximity of their clothed bodies, of the deeper intimacy they had shared the night before, when they had lingeringly made love. With their kiss they told each other, without words, that to be apart was painful but endurable, because they knew they would be together again twelve short days from now.

'This won't be for much longer,' Byrne whispered to her. 'I swear.'

'I guess I'll just have to take your word on that, won't I?' Ruth replied, without bitterness.

Byrne climbed into the Mazda, started up the engine and backed the car down the driveway. As he reached the foot of the driveway he hit the sunroof switch and poked his hand up through the aperture for a quick parting wave. Ruth and Ant waved back. Then he reversed on to the street, shifted into first gear and accelerated away. He knew his wife and son were still waving to him, but he could not risk a look back, not even a quick glance in the rearview mirror. If he looked back, he might hesitate about going, and if he hesitated about going, even for just a second, then he might not go at all.

Ruth slid an arm around her son's shoulder and drew

him close. Ant leaned his head against her ribs, and together they continued to wave to the small black car until it reached the end of the street and made the turn. Then Ruth spun Ant around and shooed him indoors. It was time to get ready for school.

As Byrne put Carson City behind him, heading eastwards into the desert on US 50, the pang of parting slowly faded, to be replaced by the first faint tinglings of the old familiar excitement. Much though he loved his family, loved *being* with his family, the prospect of returning to the laboratory after a weekend away and getting back down to work was always an enticing one, particularly now, with the project so near completion. Success was probably just a matter of days away. Posterity, and his name in the history books, was sure to follow. Maybe even a Nobel, too. But most importantly of all, a new beginning for the human race. A chance to put the old ways aside and embrace the new.

The 120-mile journey from Carson City to the research facility took, on average, two and a half hours. It had been a conscious decision on Byrne's part to put a significant geographical distance between his family and his work. Ruth and Ant could have lived with him on-site, but Byrne wanted Ant to have as normal an upbringing as possible, and the facility was anything but a normal place. Though Carson City, like every town in Nevada, was in part given over to the gambling industry, at least it had schools, shopping malls, movie theatres, neighbourhoods, subdivisions filled with ordinary houses filled with ordinary people, kids Ant's own age for Ant to play with.

From the day Ant was born Byrne had vowed that his son would have the stable family background that he himself had been denied. His own childhood had been, to say the least, eccentric. His mother – a gossamer woman, filled with more good intentions than she knew what to do with – had drifted from place to place during the sixties and seventies, his formative years, going wherever the whim took her, to this commune, to that ashram, trying out one alternative lifestyle after another, seldom settling anywhere for long, always moving on when she became bored or things did not work out, and he, of course, having to move on with her. She had been trust-funded by her well-to-do parents, so money had never been a problem for them, but until Byrne turned thirteen, when, at his grandparents' insistence, he had been sent away to boarding school, he had yearned for steady friendships and a consistent education. Those Ant now had. He also had a father who was absent most of the time, which was not perfect, but at least it was an improvement on Byrne's own paternal situation.

Not that Byrne had not enjoyed his peripatetic child-hood. It had been constantly exciting and interesting, and it had exposed him, at an early age, to what he considered to be good influences, and had inculcated in him various worthy characteristics. A respect for nature was one of them, a zeal to improve the world another. He had learned to trust strangers and look for the best in everyone. He was, in a sense, a closet hippie. A free spirit in conservative clothing. He saw no shame in that.

At the intersection with Route 95 at Fallon, Byrne turned south. The landscape was consistent and unchanging: parallel mountain ranges alternating with broad basins, like a sheet of corrugated iron laid down by a titan long ago and gone rusty in the sun. The desert vegetation consisted primarily of shad scale and sage-brush – scrubby, stunted, sparse. Higher up, and sparser still, there were piñon and juniper trees, and the occasional bristlecone pine, its squat tangle of trunks like the tower-blocks of some miniature arboreal city. Nevada was not the most beautiful state in the union, but there was something about its barren, intimidating, Martian ugliness that was oddly beguiling.

Byrne settled back in his seat to enjoy the view and the drive, and began idly mulling over the theoretical concepts on which the project he was working on was based, re-examining them from every possible angle. *Fluctuations of electrical field energy embedded within the fabric of space ... A magnetic field forced to move along its field lines at right angles to an electric field within a toroid ... Applying Lorentz forces to the charged plasma particles around the hull ...* Since all the fundamental bugs had been ironed out long ago, this was more of a mental warm-up exercise than anything. He was looking for flaws in well-polished pebbles of abstract thought, flaws he knew did not exist because countless computer-model and practical tests had proved so. By allowing his brain to limber up in this way, he would be ready to get back down to work as soon as he reached his destination.

He stopped to fill up with gas on the outskirts of Goldfield, one of the many towns that had sprung up in the region following the discovery of the Comstock Lode back in 1859. (Back then, prospectors had other things on their minds than dreaming up imaginative place-names.) Ten miles further down the freeway, he turned off on to an unprepossessing sideroad, a long, straight splat of blacktop that ribboned into the emptiness.

Far off, a wavering smear of discoloration heat-shimmered amid the volcanic orange of the landscape. Squinting, it was just possible to make out the shapes of the handful of buildings that made up the town of Nowhere, Nevada.

Byrne drove towards the town for twenty minutes, during which time it seemed to come no nearer. Then he crested a shallow rise and suddenly it was there, in front of him, less than a mile away.

From this distance, the collection of trailer homes and single-storey, aluminium-sided houses looked half-dead, like some sort of junkyard/cemetery hybrid. Here and there the odd patch of greenery was visible where someone was trying to raise tomatoes or beans in their backyard, and here and there could be seen movement – the slowly circling vanes of a well-windmill, a pick-up truck trundling along a street – but for the most part all was dust-clogged and still. The impression was of a town crusted with neglect, corroded with apathy and lethargy; a town whose inhabitants would have abandoned it, had they been able to summon up the willpower; a town that did not welcome visitors, mainly because it was not expecting any.

Which was precisely the impression it was *meant* to give.

As the road began flattening out to become Nowhere's main drag, there was a roadside sign demarcating the town limits and providing the casual passer-by (assuming such a creature existed) with two morsels of information: the name of the town and its population, which currently stood at 136. In truth the total was closer to 150, but for various reasons the dozen or so extra residents remained unaccounted for on official records.

Half a minute later, Byrne was driving along Nowhere's main street. Up close, there was even less to suggest that here was a town inclined to look favourably on visits from outsiders. Many of the trailer-home lots were enclosed by low chickenwire fences, and most of those fences were crowned with loops of barbed wire. Windowpanes were cracked or, where absent, replaced with cut-to-fit pieces of cardboard. The sheets of tarpaper covering the roofs of slumped outhouses had curled up at the edges and corners. Dogs on chains tethered to posts embedded in the ground emerged from the shade of their kennels to snap and snarl at the Mazda as it went by. Stocky, stern-jawed men sitting out on their front porches simply stared, heads swivelling slowly to track the progress of the car, like satellite dishes locked on to a signal. A bony old woman in dungarees and a Marlboro baseball cap, walking with arthritic slowness along the uneven concrete sidewalk, paused long enough to fix Byrne with a glare before resuming her painful, uncertain journey; her eyes were like two beetles pressed into thumbholes in dough. Had Byrne been an unwary traveller, drawn here perhaps out of curiosity to learn what kind of a place would be facetious enough to call itself Nowhere, he would not have needed much further persuasion to turn his car around and head back to the highway.

At the centre of town lay that essential triumvirate without which no smalltown American community can be considered complete: chapel, drugstore and diner. The chapel's peppermint-green paintwork was flaking away like eczematous skin, the wooden cross that sat atop its belltower was askew, and its doors were padlocked. The drugstore, too, was closed, and the battered soda machine out front had an out-of-order notice pinned to it. The notice in the window of the diner, however, said, 'Open for Business'.

The diner was called The Brilliant Bagel. The name, though it had been Byrne's idea, nevertheless always brought a smile to his face. He found himself a space in the parking lot and went in.

Inside there were a dozen patrons seated in the Naugahyde-upholstered booths or on the chrome-legged stools along the main counter. All of them were elderly, and all of them turned to look at Byrne as he entered. Conversations dwindled away to nothing. Suddenly Byrne was the focal point of an intense and aggressive scrutiny. It was remarkable how they could pretend not to recognise him even though they knew perfectly well who he was. The temptation to offer him some small sign of acknowledgement – a wink, a quick grin – must have been great, but they were self-disciplined enough to resist it. Everyone who came into town had to be treated like a complete stranger, no exceptions. The illusion had to be total. All the same, to be blanked by people who had seen you dozens of times before was just a little too *Twilight Zone* for comfort.

Byrne walked up to the counter. The blowsy waitress in her yellow nylon uniform ignored him for a full minute, absentmindedly twirling a lock of her dyed-black, bouffant hair and staring off into space, before finally, with a sigh, deigning to acknowledge his exist-ence. She came over and, with a surly curl of her upper lip, flipped open her order pad and slid out a pencil from behind her ear. Her name-badge said that she was called Phyllis and that it was her pleasure to serve him.

'Yeah?'

Byrne cleared his throat. This part always made him nervous. The penalty for a screw-up was steep.

'Coffee, please,' he said, speaking slowly and with precision. 'Three sugars. Non-dairy creamer.'

The waitress fixed him with a look of contempt. 'We don't do no "non-dairy creamer" here.'

Someone, on cue, laughed.

'Milk'll do fine,' said Byrne. 'And a' – he hesitated briefly – 'a blueberry muffin, please.' It was the second week of the month, therefore blueberry.

The waitress shook her head and gestured with her pencil at the menu fixed to the wall behind her, one of those ribbed boards into which can be stuck pronged plastic letters. 'Just what it says up there.'

'All right,' said Byrne. A bead of sweat trickled down his forehead from his hairline, diverted around his eye socket and headed rapidly down his cheek. 'Just the coffee, then. And can you tell me where the restrooms are?'

The waitress pointed to a doorway over in the corner.

'Thank you,' said Byrne, and relaxed. Had he got wrong a single syllable of his side of the foregoing exchange of dialogue, he would now be lying face down on the floor with several cocked sidearms aimed at his head. Ten seconds after that, if he had failed to blurt out the emergency error codephrase correctly, he would have been dead.

The toilet facilities in the men's room comprised one sink, two urinals and a lavatory cubicle which, like the soda machine outside the drugstore, was labelled OUT OF ORDER. Byrne entered the cubicle regardless, and sat down. He slid the door bolt to, then reached around and depressed the flush lever.

From underneath him came a mighty, resounding clunk, followed by a sonorous reverberation. The walls and ceiling of the men's room began to rise, or so it seemed; in fact, it was the floor that was descending, and Byrne, his porcelain perch and the cubicle partitions were descending with it, while the sink, the urinals and even the toilet-roll dispenser, being fixed to the walls, stayed where they were. He was tempted, as he had been on countless previous occasions, to grab the end of the toilet-roll and watch it unspool as he went down. He managed to resist the urge this time, though he had not been so self-restrained in the past.

Beneath the level of the floor, wall-tiles gave way to blank steel. The room-sized elevator sank smoothly. After twenty seconds, it slowed and sighed to a halt. Byrne got up, exited the cubicle and crossed to a corridor entrance many feet below the door he had used to get into the men's room. The elevator began to rise again, hydraulics whining as its huge, lubricated central pole lifted it up to rejoin the adjacent women's-room elevator at ground level.

Byrne walked along a short corridor, at the end of which was a code-locked door. He tapped a five-digit number into the alphanumeric keypad. The door slid open and Byrne passed through.

The subterranean research complex was laid out all on one level, and occupied roughly a tenth of the acreage of Nowhere overhead. A couple of colleagues greeted Byrne respectfully as he passed through the sleeping quarters on his way to Lab 1. He fielded their enquiries after the well-being of his family politely but without enthusiasm. He showed greater eagerness when it came to tackling their questions concerning a few minor technical matters. He was transforming into Tony Byrne, Scientist, sloughing off the mantle of Tony Byrne, Doting Husband And Father. It was somewhat shaming that he found it so easy to switch from one mode to the other, not to mention so necessary. More shaming still was how keen he was to see his other 'child' again, the one he had birthed virtually by himself, the one that had sprung from his brain rather than his loins.

Hansen, chief engineer on the project, was already at

her terminal in Lab 1, hunched in front of the screen, on which a virtual diagnostic was running. Overweight, thickly bespectacled, with lank, mud-brown hair which she wore pinned clumsily back from her face with two barettes, and dressed in shapeless sweatpants and an unironed T-shirt, Hansen was, self-evidently, one of those people for whom outward appearance comes low on the list of priorities. Her principal index of character was intellectual rigour. She could not abide an uninformed and unenquiring mind, which made her, in most social situations, hard to bear. In the company of other engineers, discussing different ways of making abstract concepts concrete, was where she was at her happiest.

'Checking the microwave shielding on the AMF generator?' he asked her, having glanced at the screen.

'Uh-huh,' replied Hansen, with a vague nod.

She obviously did not want to be disturbed. Byrne crossed the laboratory to the row of blind-covered windows that, along with a door marked with a radiation-hazard symbol, occupied one wall. At the touch of a button the blinds retracted upwards.

As Byrne peered through the windows' thick glass into the next chamber, he broke into a smile – a smile that could not have been broader if he had been a proud father who had just picked out his newborn baby asleep in its cot through the windows of a maternity ward.

2

Cecil Evans was not listening to Mr L. Brain. Oh no. Not listening to anything Mr L. Brain had to show-tell him in his picture-word voice.

On the apron of pavement outside the Palace Theatre in London's Cambridge Circus, where *Les Misérables* was showing, Cecil was standing with his fingers in his ears, singing loudly to himself. Not holding a tune, just randomly la-la-la-ing, as though auditioning – badly – for a part in the musical as a ragged *sans-culottes*.

Singing was not going to keep Mr L. Brain quiet, Cecil knew that. Once Mr L. Brain piped up, there was no shutting him up until he had said his piece. But still Cecil continued with his impromptu, melody-free recitation, refusing to give in without a struggle.

An image spiked into his brain with the force of a hammered tent peg.

a forest – a fiery streak in the sky like a comet – a vast, billowing explosion, too bright to look at – around it, a forest catching fire – pine needles burning

'No!' yelled Cecil, startling several passers-by, who glanced at this large, stoop-shouldered man in shabby army-surplus greatcoat and unlaced brogues, with his fingers in his ears and his eyelids tight shut, and quickened their pace, at the same time averting their gazes and acting as if they had not seen him.

'No,' Cecil moaned, more softly, and slid his hands forward to clutch his cheeks. Cecil had not heard from

Mr L. Brain in over six months, and had dared to hope that Mr L. Brain might have gone away for ever, and in hoping this had dared to feel that he might have a chance, at last, of leading the kind of life most people led. He should have known better.

Another image.

the years stretching back like increments on a ruler – counting off nine groups of ten on this measure of time – and a pair of crimson threads, twisted and tangled

'Shut! Up!' Cecil roared, alarming everyone within a ten-yard radius except a couple of tourists from New York.

But Mr L. Brain was not some jabbering bar-room bore you could simply cow into silence.

Cecil turned and ran. He sprinted across Shaftesbury Avenue, heedless of the traffic. A motorcycle courier had to brake sharply to avoid colliding with him, and raised his helmet visor to deliver a package of choice epithets at Cecil's retreating back.

Just as you could not quieten Mr L. Brain's voice by shouting, so you could not escape from him by running – not when Mr L. Brain actually lived inside your head. None the less Cecil shambled onwards in his lumbering, long-legged way, over Charing Cross Road, then down narrow Litchfield Street, not looking where he was going, not really caring either, simply fleeing in order to demonstrate to Mr L. Brain that he was not prepared to stand there and *accept* his unwelcome intrusions.

And, as if to show contempt for this futile gesture of defiance, the next image Mr L. Brain slammed into Cecil's mind was of such vivid, widescreen, Technicolor intensity that, for a brief, dizzying moment, Cecil was no longer on the streets of London; he had been transported to a location thousands of miles, and tens of years, away.

a desert – mesas like mountains sheared of their peaks by God's scythe – night-time – boiling black clouds riven by lightning – a storm raging, and something silver and disc-shaped, something buffeted by violent winds and rain, seesawing through the air, descending, coming

39

*closer and closer to the ground, and finally hitting with a
violent, bellyflop impact – bouncing up again to continue
its erratic journey for some distance, then gradually
coming back down again, to land amid a spray of dirt
and slither to an ungainly rest – and then detonating into
smoke and flames – and again that pair of crimson
threads, wound around each other, running through the
decades like the name of a seaside town through a stick
of rock*

Cecil lost his footing, stumbled off the kerb on to the
road, and collapsed to his knees in the gutter. He used a
parking meter to help haul himself upright, then tottered
on in the direction of the St Martin's Theatre where, for
what seemed like aeons, *The Mousetrap* had been luring
in punters with its cheesy melodramatics.

*and those two red lines continuing to now, and
projecting beyond, into the near future*

Dazedly Cecil wandered on to West Street, which
intersected with Litchfield Street at a sharp angle.

and a sense of inevitability, of repetition

And by the steps of a tall, shiny-white building on the
corner of West Street and Upper St Martin's Lane he
halted, wavering like a weathervane in a contrary wind.

and a name

Cecil was lost, both internally and geographically. All
he knew was the picture-voice that was image-speaking
to him in his mind's eye. His stare was blank and
unseeing. He had become a hulking, straw-brained
scarecrow of a man, his own thoughts and feelings
temporarily ousted from his head.

*a silhouette of a man with wings instead of arms –
white bird's wings, outstretched as if in readiness for
flight, or crucifixion*

Everything Mr L. Brain vision-said was imprinting
itself on Cecil's memory, like a seal stamped into soft
wax.

*and another name – a man aflame – standing calm,
motionless, as fire licked and rippled up his featureless
body*

And with that, Mr L. Brain was done, and Cecil felt an inner unclenching and the dizzying relief of his own consciousness returning like blood to a numb limb.

Fading, faint, fast, down a long tunnel into emptiness, Mr L. Brain withdrew, and as he withdrew left behind one last ghostly image: what Cecil thought of as his signature-symbol.

a small, stern mouth, its corners fractionally upturned – a mouth that seemed just on the point of breaking into a smile – a parental sort of smile, sternly affectionate – and behind this mouth, slightly to the side, like a shadow cast against a wall immediately behind: another mouth – this one without the hint of fondness promised by the other – narrow, tight, hard – malicious, disapproving, inimical

This, too, faded, and Cecil was fully himself again.

And then the nausea came, as it always did, and he doubled over and vomited. Out came the contents of his stomach in a heaving, gelatinous rush – the mixed grill he had eaten for breakfast that morning at the hostel, the sandwich and the can of 7-Up he had had for lunch – spattering the pristine white steps at his feet.

He vomited until his retches were dry. Then, panting, he straightened up. Running his tongue around his teeth, he collected a few lumpy morsels of digested food, which he spat out. He wiped his mouth on his coat sleeve, then delved a hand into his trouser pocket to see how much he had on him in loose change. A palmful of coppers. With a resigned sigh he turned and shambled off towards Leicester Square, which was the best place to try and scrounge up cash for the payphone. It was going to take him some time, because the number he was going to call was a mobile phone and he would need at least fifty pence.

And just as he was about to curse cellular telecommunications and whoever had invented it, Cecil had to stop and laugh.

Because what was he himself, essentially, but a living, breathing, one-way mobile phone?

41

3

Rattray steepled his fingers and pressed them to his upper lip, his expression betraying nothing as he watched Cecil bite a chunk out of his burger and follow it up with a thrust fistful of french fries. In front of him a cup of tea was growing cold. He had ordered the tea solely to keep Cecil company and had no intention of drinking it. Rattray was extremely partial to tea, Earl Grey in particular, but the scalding-hot brown liquid served at fast-food restaurants did not find favour with him. In his opinion, it barely qualified as a beverage.

The former Detective Inspector John Rattray of Her Majesty's Metropolitan Police was a smooth-faced man with tidily trimmed fingernails and a head of snow-white hair which he wore in a conventional short-back-and-sides. His forehead was broad and pronounced, casting his eyes into perpetual half-shadow, and his jaw, though firm, tapered to a chin that was pointed and oddly delicate. Estimating his age at a glance, you might put him in his late thirties. A closer look at his eyes might lead you to revise your estimate upwards. Though they were without significant bags or wrinkles, there was something about Rattray's eyes that spoke of the wisdom and suffering that comes only with great age. They did not fit the face that framed them.

He was dressed smartly but soberly in a simple dark suit, a narrow-collared white shirt and a plain tie. His velvet-lapelled overcoat had been folded neatly over the back of one of the spare chairs at the table which he and Cecil were sharing. He looked incongruous, sitting there in the Oxford Street branch of an internationally renowned and reviled burger chain, amid primary colours and glossy, striplight-reflecting surfaces of fake wood and Formica, while on every side raucous, sugar-hyped children argued with their parents and overseas-exchange students jabbered, all to the accompaniment of piped music pitched aggravatingly at the precise threshold of human hearing so that it could be neither ignored nor enjoyed. Sitting opposite shabby, bedraggled Cecil, he seemed even more out of place. Two more dissimilar dining companions, and a less likely venue for them to choose for their rendezvous, you would be hard pressed to imagine. Yet while the one munched and gobbled, and the other looked patiently on, it was clear that a bond of some kind existed between them, a strong one, forged of necessity, tempered by empathy.

Cecil popped his last few french fries into his mouth and took a final, rattling slurp of his vanilla milkshake, then licked his fingers clean and looked up at Rattray.

'That's better,' he said. 'Thanks.'

'My pleasure,' said Rattray.

'I hate that. The way I always throw up after I have one of my … you know.'

'Episodes.'

'Episodes. Waste of good food, it is. Not that that's the only thing I hate about them, of course,' he added.

'I understand,' said Rattray. 'Now, you told me on the phone that this particular vision –'

'It happens every bloody time,' Cecil continued. 'Just when I think I'm getting better, just when I feel like I'm getting my life back on track …' He snapped his fingers. 'Bam! I'm knocked back to square one again. I was lucky this time, though. Last time it happened, a cop spotted me. You remember?'

'I remember.'

'Bastard ran me in. Reported me to the hostel. Told them I'd been drinking, and I hadn't been, but of course they believed him and not me. Lost my bed. Bastard police.' He nodded apologetically to Rattray. 'Nothing personal.'

'That's all right,' said Rattray. 'I haven't been a policeman in a very long time. It's a whole different profession these days. Now, this vision of yours ...'

'You having that?'

Cecil gestured at Rattray's tea with his right hand. As he did so, his forearm extended from the frayed sleeve of his greatcoat and an ugly-looking scar was exposed, located just above his wrist. At first glance, the scar looked like it might have been the result of an accident, perhaps a mishap with boiling water, but on closer inspection it became apparent that it was a design. Depicted, in waxy ridges of healed tissue, was an oval divided up into irregular geometrical shapes. This Cecil had etched into his own skin when he was a teenager, using one of his father's spare razor blades.

Rattray made a be-my-guest gesture, and Cecil grabbed the cup, uncapped the plastic lid and took a long and appreciative swig.

'Ahh!' he said. 'Nothing like a good cup of tea.'

'And that's *nothing* like a good cup of tea,' Rattray deadpanned.

Cecil laughed. 'The old music-hall standbys, eh?'

'A good joke never ages.'

'Like you, you mean?'

'If I'm a joke,' said Rattray, half-smiling, 'I'm not convinced I'm necessarily a good one.'

'Don't be so hard on yourself.' Cecil patted his dining companion solicitously on the arm and took another sip of tea. 'You're dying for me to get on and tell you what I saw, aren't you?'

'Regrettably, yes. So often in these cases time is of the essence. The Librans seldom see fit to give us much advance warning, and deciphering their instructions isn't always a simple task.'

'Well ...' Cecil finished the tea, took a deep breath to steady himself, and began.

He recounted to Rattray everything that Mr L. Brain had shown him: the explosion and the crash-landing; the different environments in which each occurred; the decades separating the events; and the crimson lines which seemed to link them and give them continuity. Rattray, having produced a pen and a small pad of paper from an inner pocket, took down careful notes in shorthand, interrupting Cecil occasionally to pump him for further descriptive details and, if Cecil was unable to furnish these, asking for sensory impressions instead. Rattray knew that it was hard to encapsulate visions in words, particularly visions as imprecise as Mr L. Brain's messages typically were, but any response Cecil could remember having – emotional, intellectual, instinctual – was useful and pertinent.

To illustrate the crimson lines, Cecil fetched several sachets of tomato ketchup from the area of the restaurant where such condiments were available. Biting the sachets open, he painstakingly squeezed out a pair of regularly overlapping trails of thick red sauce across the tabletop. Rattray, managing to look both amused and disapproving, copied down the pattern into his pad.

'And that's it?' he asked.

Cecil nodded.

'Not much to go on there.' A brief, grim twist of Rattray's lips seemed to indicate that this was not an unusual state of affairs.

'Any ideas what it might all be about?'

Rattray cast an eye back over his notes. 'Off the top of my head, I'd say we're looking at references to the Tunguska explosion and the Roswell crash.'

'The what explosion?'

'Tunguska. A remote Siberian province where, on the morning of July thirtieth, 1908, a burning fireball was seen streaking across the sky, followed by an explosion which flattened several hundred acres of forest. The shockwaves were felt as far away as London.'

'And what was it, this burning fireball?'

'It's generally thought to have been a meteor.'

'But you're a Guardian. To you, everything is more than it seems.'

'Sometimes things just are what they are. And Cecil, you're a Guardian, too.'

'Yeah, well, maybe so, but I'm a conscript, not a volunteer. There's a big difference.'

'I don't know how many of us would describe ourselves as volunteers,' Rattray observed. 'As for the Roswell crash …'

'Even I know about that,' said Cecil. 'A UFO that came down in the Mexico desert in 1947.'

'Alleged UFO. And it was in *New* Mexico.'

'And that was a meteor, too?'

'No,' said Rattray. 'That, I know for a fact, was a Guardian action-to-suppress.'

'You were involved?'

'Not directly.'

'Oh, hold on!' Cecil slapped his forehead. 'I forgot. There *was* one other thing.'

Rattray raised his eyebrows encouragingly and licked the tip of his pencil.

'A name,' said Cecil, frowning in concentration. 'Only, of course, Mr L. Brain isn't too hot on names. With him it has to be a sort of cryptic clue, like one of those children's picture puzzles.'

'A rebus.'

'That's the one. In this case, it was a man with wings.'

'Wings?'

'Yeah. You know, flap flap.' He mimed flight.

Rattray said nothing. Somewhere deep in the recesses of his mind, something had stirred. Something that wasn't clear enough or well focused enough to be called a memory, at least not yet. Something that was more of an instinct, a hunch, a foreshadowing of a certainty. To which part of Cecil's vision this nascent revelation was connected, Rattray was unsure, but he knew that to try and grasp at it right away would be to risk losing it altogether. Left alone, and given time, like a maggot it would work its own way up to the surface.

The trouble with being 150 years old was that, with two lifetimes' worth of accumulated incidents and sensations and facts and fictions and reactions and reflections crowded inside his head, sifting through them for a specific recollection took a while. Many portions of his past Rattray had lost for ever. But this, he sensed, was not one of them.

On the pavement outside the restaurant, amid the dusk-driven rush of workers making for the Tube and entertainment-seekers bound for the West End, the two Guardians tendered their goodbyes. As they shook hands, Cecil felt a small wad of folded paper being pressed into his palm. With a mumbled thanks, he turned and joined the milling flow of bodies, heading east toward Holborn. The fifty-pound note Rattray had given him was not some conscience-salving charitable offering. Both he and Cecil considered it to be fair and just payment for the service Cecil had performed as an 'oracle,' a vehicle for communications from the Guardians' otherworldly employers.

Rattray set off in the opposite direction.

Oxford Street was nose-to-tail taxis and buses, their exhaust fumes adding to the heavy brown haze that was descending over the city with the night. For all the appurtenances of Progress – the combustion engine, neon lighting, in-store stereo systems, tar macadam – little had changed in the century and a half since Rattray had first walked down this thoroughfare as a small boy. The essence of Oxford Street remained immutable; its commerce and the modes of transport that plied its length had merely found faster and flashier ways of disporting themselves.

Faster transport? Rattray had read somewhere recently that the average speed of traffic in London was eleven miles per hour, no quicker than it had been in the age of the horse-drawn carriage. Some improvement!

It was fully dark by the time he reached Marble Arch. The most direct route to his Kensington flat, and the one he preferred to take rather than head south alongside the motorway that was Park Lane and then turn right down Knightsbridge, was to cross Hyde Park diagonally. He entered the park at Speakers' Corner, and soon had left the fuss and bustle of the city behind him. The sound of traffic was dimmed to a dull rumble, and all was sodium-lit stillness, the pathways empty except for the occasional jogger, roller-blader or dog-exerciser.

He walked, brooding. The stark, sky-cracking winter silhouettes of the trees were only just beginning to be softened by the arrival of spring buds and blossom. The air was still brisk enough to draw a wisp of vapour from his mouth every time he exhaled.

Though most of its pathways had been asphalted over, little else about the park had visibly altered over the course of Rattray's long life. It was here that he, as a raw constable, aged barely twenty, had once pounded his beat. He knew every trail and dell and twist and turn by heart.

Just north of the Serpentine, on a section of pathway screened from the rest of the park by trees, he came across a young Scandinavian couple, who were standing in the middle of the pathway, looking lost. The man was tall and broad-shouldered, with an uneven gingery beard. The woman was shorter, with rounded, maternal features. Both had ash-blonde hair, both wore matching purple anoraks, and both nodded to Rattray with the wary politeness of strangers in a strange land. He, though preoccupied, returned the greeting with a friendly-native smile.

The young man asked him for the time, and Rattray, slowing his pace fractionally, consulted his watch and replied that it was getting on for half past seven.

'Thank you,' said the man, and reached inside his anorak. At the same time, the woman unzipped the canvas pouch that was slung around her waist.

Rattray reacted almost without thinking. Spinning around, he launched himself at the man, who was the closer of the two. The man just managed to withdraw what he had been reaching for as Rattray tackled him. Rattray glimpsed a dull grey metallic cylinder, ribbed and studded and with rounded ends, like some kind of sinister sex-toy. Then he was driving his shoulder into the man's sternum, and together they crashed down on to the pathway.

More by luck than design the man managed to depress one of the studs on the cylinder, and a blinding blue two-inch tongue of pure voltage sprang from either end, licking and coruscating like liquid flame. He brought the knife-like weapon around, aiming for Rattray's head, but Rattray caught his wrist and braced his arm away.

The two men remained locked in this position for several seconds, the weapon's twin arcs of electricity fizzing and crackling between them, casting their faces into chiaroscuro relief, every feature, every furrow of effort and determination, sharply delineated in scorching-blue highlights and deep-black shadows.

Rattray, being on top, had the slight advantage, and by adding his body weight to his strength was able to force the weapon, millimetre by millimetre, closer to his opponent's face. Its electric flame-tongues curved down-ward, seeking to be earthed. There was a smell of singeing skin. The man grunt-screamed.

Then: a slash of flaring agony across Rattray's back. He spasmed, losing his grip on the man's wrist, rolling off him in a silent, arching ecstasy of pain.

The woman. Standing, legs apart, in an expert stance. And in her hands, a thin steely whip that twitched and writhed of its own volition, like an angry cat's tail.

Rattray's back had been flayed open clean to the spine. Swiftly the pain dimmed, relieved by a localised, auto-nomic rush-release of endorphins. A simultaneous squirt of adrenaline galvanised him into leaping to his feet to face the woman, just as she drew back her arm.

The whip came streaking towards him, a mercurial blur. Rather than attempt to avoid it, Rattray threw himself, left shoulder first, into its path. His deltoid and biceps muscles took the brunt of the scourging, flesh gashing open, spraying blood, but his impetus carried him forward, straight at the woman, inside the arc of her swing. Up close her weapon would be useless, although it took her a second or two to realise this.

His left arm having been disabled, Rattray used his right hand to seize the whip while it was engaged in re-coiling itself. The woman had been trained in the use of her weapon but was no natural-born fighter. Before she could put up a concerted resistance, Rattray had entwined the whip once, twice, three times around her throat. Pulling it taut, he kicked her legs from under her so that she fell forward. A sort of choked gargle was forced out from her windpipe as the whip snapped tight, embedding itself deep in her neck. He pressed a heel between her shoulderblades and raised his arm to increase the tension on the whip. She clawed at the impromptu noose but could not get her fingernails under it. Her feet scrabbled on the path, toecaps unable to find a purchase.

The intervention of her companion saved her from death by garrotting. He came charging at Rattray, electric-flame knife held high. One of his cheeks was blackened and blistered, half his beard reduced to tarry stubble.

Rattray let go of the whip and got his arm up just in time to meet the attack. Using the man's own momentum against him, he spun him around, forcing him to trip over his prone accomplice. Reaching down with both hands to break his fall, a reflex action, the man inadvertently touched his weapon to the woman's back. There was a blinding, deafening *snap* as the electric-flame knife, with a seemingly sentient glee, discharged a powerful blue bolt into her body. A pork-barbecue stench filled the air.

The man looked down, bewildered, at the body beneath him, twitching in its death throes. Then, with an inarticulate yell of anger, he propelled himself to his feet and at Rattray again.

Rattray was ready for him. A punch to the gut. An elbow to the nose. Stiff fingers to the throat. The man collapsed to the ground, the weapon tumbling from his hand and rolling to the edge of the pathway. Rattray delivered a savage, debilitating kick to his assailant's kidneys. The man screeched and slumped on to his side.

Rattray squatted down beside him.

Interrogation would be futile. Mercy was not an option.

He hauled the whimpering man up by his collar, braced his neck across his thigh, laid his forearm across the man's head, and with a swift downward thrust parted two of his cervical vertebrae.

The man died with a guttural gurgle and a sigh.

Grimacing, Rattray released the corpse and sat back on the pathway. A wave of exhaustion swept over him as his body, now that the danger was past, set to repairing itself, drawing heavily on his reserves of physical energy in order to stem the flow of blood and seal the wounds in his back and shoulder, reknitting flesh and skin. Lassitude enveloped him. All of a sudden he could not think of anything he would rather do than lie down, curl up and go to sleep.

'Come on, Rattray,' he urged himself. He could hardly afford to sit there beside a pair of dead bodies and let some unsuspecting passer-by, or, worse, a member of the Parks constabulary, come across him. What would he say? How would he explain away the situation?

He could always tell the truth, he supposed. But not only would he not be believed, there was every chance that someone might try to have him sectioned and locked away.

A fresh adrenal surge brought him back to his feet. He knew he was going to pay for all this heightened physiological activity later.

Using his one good arm, he dragged the young man and woman into the bushes, making sure both bodies were tucked well out of sight. As he did this, he experienced a vague pang of pity for them. They had been gulled into becoming cannon-fodder in a war they could not hope to fathom. He could imagine the lies they had been told: that this man John Rattray was evil, that he was someone without whom the world would be a much better place, that killing him would not be murder but an act of heroism. Subtle subliminal stressors would have been brought to bear on them (patriotism, parents, politics). Immunity from the law would have been guaranteed. Having undergone a crash-course in the use of their highly advanced weapons, they would have boarded a ferry bound for England, telling friends and family that they were going on holiday. The conviction they had felt as they had waited for him in the park, the sense of mission and rightness, would have been all-consuming. Young people made the best Anarch dupes. They were naïve, uncynical, and filled with idealism … and idealism could so easily be perverted.

Rattray retrieved his jacket and coat. Taking a mobile phone from his jacket pocket, he keyed one of the preset numbers. A tuneful sequence of bleeps in the earpiece was followed by the sound of ringing.

A youthful voice answered. 'Hello?'

'Hello. Is that Daisy or Alice?'

'Daisy. Is that Uncle John?'

'It is.'

'Hi, Uncle John. How are you doing?'

'Fine. May I have a word with your mother?'

'No problem. She's in the studio. I'll go and get her.'

'Thanks.'

Cradling the phone to his ear with his shoulder while Daisy Holman-Fisk went to fetch her mother, Rattray circumspectly approached the whip and the electric-flame knife, both of which were still active, the whip rolling and lashing across the pathway like a snake with a broken back, its counterpart fizzing like a double-ended firework. After a moment's study he determined which was the shut-off button on each, and bent down and deactivated them. Inert, the weapons still looked anything but harmless. It was strange how 'lethal' could be a design feature. Rattray removed his ruined overcoat and, one-handed, furled the weapons up carefully inside it.

From the other end of the line came the sound of footsteps approaching and the receiver being picked up.

'Good evening, John. To what do I owe the pleasure?'

'Hello, Lucretia. I'm afraid I've just had a little run-in with a couple of Anarch operatives.'

'God. Are you all right?'

'Fine. Mostly unharmed. It was my fault, really. I should vary my routes home a bit more. Too much a creature of habit.'

'Want the Domestic?'

'Please.'

'I'll send her over. Did you say two?'

'That's right. One male, one female.'

'Where are you?'

'Hyde Park. I'll leave a transponder with them.'

'Good. John, Anarch attacks don't just happen out of the blue. Something must be up.'

'Something is, but I'm not yet sure what. Kim will be able to help. I'll call you again as soon as I have any further information.'

'You take care, John.'

'You too.'

Rattray closed the phone and stowed it away, then detached from the waistband of his trousers a small device that looked to all intents and purposes like a common-or-garden pager, and indeed was a common-or-garden pager, although it doubled as a locating transmitter/receiver. Crawling into the rhododendrons again, he attached the pager to the dead man's belt and activated its transponder mode, then scrambled back out to the pathway, brushed himself down, smoothed out his hair and clothing, and walked briskly away from the scene, his injured left arm hanging by his side.

The Domestic seldom took long to arrive, and it was wise not to be in the vicinity when she got there.

4

At his flat, a maisonette that occupied the top two floors of a five-storey terraced Georgian house, Rattray left the weapons bundled up in his overcoat in the hallway. Going into the bedroom, he undressed, laid his torn, bloodied jacket aside to be dry-cleaned and mended, threw his similarly besmirched shirt (not worth repairing) into the bin, showered, put on a towelling bathrobe, and went into the kitchen to make himself a pot of Earl Grey, which he carried, along with a mug and a small jug of milk, on a tray into his study.

The study was furnished in a classic style, with a large teak desk, a leather-upholstered desk chair that clutched its castors with eagle's feet, bookshelves laden with old, leather-bound volumes, a wing-backed reading chair, and a table lamp the base of which was a replica of a blue and white Chinese vase. Only the Hewlett Packard computer, which sat on the desktop surrounded by cables and assorted peripherals, was state-of-the-art, bang-up-to-date modern.

Rattray hit the power switch and, while the Hewlett Packard booted up, running through its routine of chattering self-analysis, poured himself a mugful of tea. The computer announced with a chime that it was ready and offered him a prompt-box inviting him to enter his password. He typed in 'Methuselah', and when his digital desktop appeared, double-clicked on the word-processing icon. A blank white page filled the screen. He paused a moment to collect his thoughts, sipping the tea and gazing out of the study's tall windows at the darkened trees and shrubbery of the communal rear garden shared by all the houses on this side of the street. His back and his left shoulder itched aggravatingly, yet he resisted the urge to scratch, which would only protract the healing process. He needed food and he needed sleep, but could not permit himself either yet.

Setting down the mug, he opened his notebook and set to transcribing his notes on Cecil's vision on to the screen.

He was careful to keep the transcript as simple and succinct as possible. Policemen had a tendency to use a florid, unnatural form of English when it came to filing reports, for example employing verbs like 'proceed' and 'apprehend' where 'go' and 'catch' would do, and stretching the limits of grammar with convoluted circumlocution. Rattray had managed to wean himself off this practice, but often found himself lapsing back into it when he was tired and not concentrating.

The text of the transcript, when completed, ran to three pages. He checked it over, weeding out a few extraneous adjectives and adverbs. The essence of Cecil's vision seemed to be there.

He went online, and in the mail composition editor tapped out a quick message of greeting to Kim, then e-mailed her the file containing what he had just written. He logged off and, yawning and rubbing his eyes, shut down the Hewlett Packard.

In the kitchen he prepared and ate a cheese sandwich, his movements somnambulist-slow. By the time he got around to shuffling to his bedroom, he was nearly asleep. It was all he could do to stretch himself out on the bed. Crawling beneath the covers would simply have been too much of an effort. Warm oblivion beckoned, a welcoming, gently sucking vortex. He plunged willingly in.

5

'*Ohayō gozaimasu*, Kim!' trilled Haiiro No from the screen of the terminal on Kim's bedside cabinet, while, in the adjoining room, a fly's eye of TV screens ignited one after another into cathode life.

The Guardians' intelligence co-ordinator groaned and stirred. The bedside terminal's infra-red sensor detected the movement, and so Haiiro No continued with his cheery, singsong reveille. 'The time is oh-seven-hundred hours!' the animated sprite said. His voice was Kim's own, frequency-modulated so that it sounded weird and alien. 'You have forty-two new items of e-mail!' Haiiro No stumbled slightly over the numbers, hopping tonal registers as he plucked each digit from his library of samples and slotted it into the preformatted sentences. 'You have one priority encrypted message, callsign "Methuselah"!' Haiiro No's text-recognition software could cope with the name only by breaking it down into its component syllables: Me. Thus. El. Ah.

'Repeat,' said Kim, raising her head from the pillows.

Haiiro No dutifully reiterated the three statements, although the only one Kim was interested in was the last.

No sooner had she heard the fractured 'Methuselah' again than she hurled back the covers, swung her legs out of bed, grabbed a zigzag-patterned kimono off the floor and flung it on. Pausing only to perch her spectacles on the bridge of her nose, she headed into the main room.

The wall of screens was by now fully operational. The

sets, perched on modular shelving, ranged in size from an eight-inch black and white security monitor to a wide-screen anamorphic television. No two were of the same dimensions, and their mismatched Mondrian rectangles formed a multicoloured, multistorey collage of images from dozens of different sources: international news channels, network role-playing games in progress, MUDs, intercepted chunks of raw, unedited reportage from various trouble-spots around the world, NHK, broadcasts from weather satellites, but principally Web sites, newsgroups and homepages, including the chat room Kim herself moderated, Kawai Kim's Koven. The volume on every set had been turned down to zero, leaving only the busy, tinnitus whine of their scanning coils to fill the room. The light reflecting off the ceiling and other walls shifted constantly, luridly, kaleidoscopi-cally. LEDs on stacks of hard drives and signal decoders winked and stuttered. Thick plaits of gaffa-taped cables festooned the floor.

Kim wheeled back her chair, sat down at her control desk, and drew her ergonomic, RSI-minimising split-keyboard towards her on its slide-out shelf.

The largest of the screens, the central mother-unit, was capable of pulling a feed from any of the surrounding subsidiary screens. Using a remote control handset, Kim selected the channel for her CPU mainframe and upped the volume on the mother-screen.

Haiiro No's password puzzle was waiting for her. He introduced it with a wave of one slender-fingered hand, saying, 'Here is your lovable little egg!' A set of twenty jigsaw-like shapes appeared onscreen, arranged around an empty oval outline. Kim had half a minute, from the moment she first moved the mouse on its pad, to guide the shapes correctly into the oval until they fitted. If she failed twice, Haiiro No would deny her access to her mainframe. A third time, and a series of small plastique charges would be detonated, destroying every scrap of hardware in the room. Kim had installed this somewhat drastic precautionary measure in order to foil any attempt to break into her files, or coerce her into doing so, via this terminal. But the puzzle was a nice mental challenge, too, a good way of sharpening up the brain first thing in the morning. The pieces were randomly generated, so the solution was different each time, but she never failed to complete the puzzle in under twenty-five seconds. Her record, noted at the top of the screen, stood at 15.73 seconds.

Today, in a series of swift, deft mouse-manoeuvres, she managed 22.35 seconds – 'Not bad!' was Haiiro No's assessment – and was granted access. Immediately she logged on to her service provider and retrieved the e-mail from Rattray. As the message decrypted itself, Haiiro No offered her the choice between original text or translated. Being fluent in English, the international language of computing, Kim selected the former.

The e-mail began, 'My dear Kim-san …'

Kim smiled. The Japanese were famed for their politeness, but the English were at least their equals in that regard. Perhaps it was something to do with coming from a densely populated island-nation. Manners were all the more important when people were constantly rubbing shoulders with one another.

She pictured Rattray mouthing the greeting – 'My dear Kim-san …' – perhaps accompanying it with a little forward bob of the head. She and Rattray had yet to meet F2F, but she knew what he looked like from his file-photograph. A handsome face, though his eyes, even in the photograph, spoke of great suffering.

She read on.

'Once again,' ran the e-mail, 'there is call for your talents as an, if you'll pardon the pun, "IT-girl". I need to establish a link between the Tunguska explosion and the Roswell crash, with possible consequences for an event happening now or soon to happen. See attached file below. It is, needless to say, a matter of some urgency. Regards, John Rattray.'

Kim studied the contents of the attached file carefully, and got down to work.

Tunguska and Roswell were the obvious starting-points, but they were easily researched. The Internet teemed with facts, fictions and theories about those two particular incidents.

The names were more problematic, and not for the first time Kim found herself resenting the obliqueness of the Librans' modus operandi. She understood that there were restrictions on how much help the Librans could give the Guardians, but sometimes she wished the instructions they provided via oracles such as Cecil Evans were not composed of hints and images, were more straight-forward and specific. The Librans reminded her of schoolteachers who know the answers but want their pupils to have the satisfaction of working things out for themselves. She could not help but feel that such an attitude was patronising.

A winged man and a man on fire. The winged man – an angel? Angel was a common Spanish forename. What about the wings? Wing was a Chinese surname. She would prime a 'Net-agent to collect all possible variants on names to do with wings and angels in the principle languages. As for the man on fire, a reference to Alfred Bester perhaps? No, she should think more literally. Laterally. Flame. Fire. Burning. Burns? Again, a properly programmed 'Net-agent would turn up something.

She tuned every set in front of her to a different computer channel, until she was facing what was pre-dominantly a wall of text, interspersed here and there with graphics and scanned-in images of varying quality, from crystal clear to smoky smear. Then she called up several 'Net-agents, heuristic, autonomous programs far more intelligent and sophisticated than the average search engine. Entering key-words and key-phrases in every permutation she could think of, she prepared her hard drives for a worldwide 'Net-trawl. Onscreen, Haiiro No jumped up and down eagerly, his big, black, insectile eyes gleaming like almond-shaped slivers of jet. The hard drives, in their racks, growled their readiness like hounds straining at the leash. Hitting 'Enter', she let them slip.

Kim stood up, wandered, poured herself coffee, drank it, sat again, while all across the planet digital libraries were consulted, encyclopaedia databases were plundered, archives were mined for useful nuggets, and helpful 'Net-users fired off responses to enquiries by non-existent research students at non-existent colleges in far-flung locations. Her search engines roamed Gopherspace and ftp sites, retrieving relevant files. Chains of hypertext links were established, reaching into the furthest corners of the Web, and as reams of binary and ASCII text came rattling back into her hard drives, the information was superimposed and analysed by comparison software in order to eliminate duplication. Her tiny two-tatami room in an apartment in a large condominium in the Hibiya district of Tokyo became the focus for a thousand threads of input, which her main CPU picked through, discarding those that were clearly irrelevant and storing those that were not.

As the first few megabytes of cached data began accumulating on her screens, Kim made herself comfortable in her chair, closed her eyes and reached inward for that still, quiet place that resides in all of us, the eye of our personal storms.

At first, trivia. Mental white noise. A nascent grocery list, the imminent release date of the new Iggy Pop album, her period (regular as clockwork, due in two days' time), a recently received electricity utilities bill (yet another bank-breaker) ... A crust of quotidian concerns, easily penetrated.

Then down into the shallows of thought, the haunt of hopes and anxieties, like a school of koi carp mingling with a school of piranha, the alluring side-by-side with the repellent, somehow managing to coexist.

Through this and plunging deeper now, into an inner dark beset with traps, the traps being sprung by the pressure-wave of her descent ...

A plain child. Thick-framed glasses. Buck teeth. Eye-brows so heavy they nearly joined in the middle, which led her classmates to call her 'Ainu', which she knew she

*should not resent, but did anyway, because the Ainu,
Japan's indigenous race, were generally thought of as
unsophisticated throwbacks. Her classmates teased her,
too, about the fact that her parents were away most of
the time, off on some campaign or other to protect the
rights of whales or prevent the rainforests of Borneo
from being turned into chopsticks, chipboard and disposable frames for house-building. About the fact that she
sometimes had to live with her grandmother (whom she
loved). About all these things and anything else they
could find, simply because some people, for no reason,
are victims, there to be picked on.*

The classmates were always there, taunting.

*A fight in the schoolyard, just one of many. Names
called. Pigtails pulled. Shins skinned. Uniforms torn.
Bruises. A teacher, Miss Ikegami, arrived to break it up.
The blame was laid, by majority consent, on the wrong
person: her. She tried to protest her innocence, but could
only stammer tearfully, rendered inarticulate by her
outrage. Miss Ikegami sent her to see the headmaster. He
expressed his disappointment. Her parents were contacted. They, too, were disappointed. Only her grandmother was prepared to listen and understand, and that
ought to have been enough, but on this occasion was not.*

Miss Ikegami was always there, missing the point.

*An ungainly teenager, trying to make the best of the
poor hand nature had dealt her looks-wise, but the boys
were not interested. Jun Shirow in particular, the school
baseball star, was not interested, though she would have
done anything short of martyring herself to get his
attention. Her supposed friend Michiko, sworn to secrecy
about the crush on Jun, blabbed. His indifference turned
to contempt. The only way he could save face with his
friends was to reject her openly and absolutely. This he
did in Ueno-Kōen Park one afternoon during the late-
March Hanami, the public holiday celebrating the annual
arrival of the cherry blossom, when all of Tokyo was out
picnicking and getting blind drunk. Before an audience of*

a dozen of their peers Jun casually, mercilessly destroyed her with words. Called her a hideous hag-face, among many other things. Then spun on his heel, leaving her weeping.

Jun Shirow was always there, humiliating her.

The time her grandmother fell seriously ill, and she went to the Meiji-Jingū and wrote a wish on the back of an ema *and hung the votive plaque up on the board outside the shrine. A wish for her grandmother's speedy recovery, and a cry from the heart to the one person who really cared about her: Don't leave me. And a week later her grandmother was dead, and because Shintō was not so much a religion as an expression of Japaneseness, she felt that she had been let down not by some distant, indifferent gods but by everyone around her, by an entire way of life.*

The *ema* was always there, just a piece of wood painted with words.

The traps popping open one after another, a history of slights, insults, rejections, dismissals, deceits, betrayals and losses, all calling out to her, cooing and competing for her attention like a gaggle of side-street whores ...

But she, descending, immune.

Not listening.

Heart closed.

Mouth stopped.

Into silence.

Selfhood.

Zen.

Kim's eyes snapped open and immediately began imbibing the information in front of her, darting from screen to screen, subliminising facts, figures, thoughts, opinions. A stream of data, data, data flowing into her, and she prospector-panning for nuggets.

Her hands skittered over the keyboard like a pair of demented spiders, her right occasionally darting off to one side to nudge the mouse, her left off to the other side to utilise the remote control.

Line after line of text scrolling up on the screens, and Kim instinctively assessing and skimming and highlighting and sorting and storing and evaluating, her breathing controlled and steady, her eyelids blinking at regular intervals, her pulse below forty beats per minute, her face alert yet impassive.

Everything sinking in, being filtered and the filterings being refiltered through a finer mesh, and then filtered again through a yet finer.

Time stretching eliptically, like an elastic band. From outside, street noises: commuters, traffic, trains. Could be moving time-lapse quick; could be moving apocalypse-slow.

Gradually, an impression forming. Certain facts, certain names recurring. Some of them falling by the wayside, but a few lingering, catching. Pachinko tactics: a swarm of steel balls being winnowed down, by a combination of chance and skill, to just a handful.

A pattern emerging.

Dates, places, events, names.

Lines of coincidence appearing, converging, connecting.

Kim, Otaku Queen, the calm centre of a universe of possibilities, drawing order from the chaos.

And at last, there it was. Coherent. Entire. The answer that laced together two separate incidents divided by half a century, and pointed to a third. The overall shape of events, of which Cecil had been given just glimpses.

Kim sat back in her chair and reviewed what she had uncovered. She could, to her satisfaction, find no fault with her conclusions.

The onscreen clock read half past midday. She had been hard at it for a little over five hours, although it felt as if it could have been five minutes or, equally, five days.

She rolled her shoulders and neck to ease out some of the stiffness. Cracked her knuckles. Got up and went to the kitchen nook to reheat the remains of last night's miso soup in the microwave, because she was starving hungry. Then returned to her desk, and, taking occasional slurps of the soup from a delicate china bowl, composed a reply to Rattray.

'My dear Mr Rattray,' she began, reciprocating Rattray's tone of ironic formality.

It was nearly half past one by the time she finished setting out, in as clear and concise a manner as possible, all the facts she had gleaned. Nine hours' time difference between Tokyo and London – Rattray would be able to peruse her findings over his corn flakes and toast.

Her part in the proceedings, for now, was almost done, and she felt a machine's contentment at having efficiently discharged the function for which she had been, as it were, hardwired. She also felt some relief that the responsibility for formulating an appropriate response to the information she had unearthed was not hers. Such things were not in her remit. She merely did as she was asked, with a compliance that had nothing to do with race or gender and everything to do with her desire to please others – a desire which had been nurtured in her by her grandmother and manured by the sufferings of her unhappy youth.

With a flourish of keystrokes, Kim transmitted the fruits of her labours to Rattray.

6

Xavier Barraud had been poised so long to make the swipe that he nearly missed it. Ever since his watchdog program had alerted him to the transmission of the encrypted e-mail to the *Japonaise* the previous evening, he had been waiting, using every trick in the book to keep himself awake and alert: chain-smoking Gauloises, chain-drinking coffee, dunking his face in a basin of cold water, slapping himself, even pricking the ball of his thumb with a drawing pin. Sleep repeatedly kept trying to snare him. Repeatedly, and with increasing determination but diminishing success, Xavier resisted.

The crucial moment came just as dawn was gilding the crumbling white flanks of the apartment blocks of the low-rent Parisian *banlieue* that Xavier, reluctantly, called home. Xavier was on the point of succumbing to the relentless dragging undertow of tiredness when the Apple Macintosh sitting on his desk suddenly chittered, for all the world as though a cicada had sprung to life inside its casing. After that, things happened very quickly.

The Apple Mac had been set up to detect the arrival of the *Japonaise*'s reply at its destination at a London-based service provider and then download a duplicate in response to a manual command, which Xavier now entered as fast as his fingers could type. A copy of the e-mail peeled off on to the Mac. Drawing a deep breath, Xavier clicked it open.

A prompt-box appeared, warning him, in English, that

he had ten seconds to enter the correct password or risk having the contents of his hard drive entirely erased. The *Japonaise* had, as Xavier knew only too well from experience, developed a remora virus of chip-blowing toxicity that was activated by the unauthorised opening of her e-mails. The software she had access to was an order of magnitude more sophisticated than anything Xavier had ever used or seen himself, and he had hacked into some of the most advanced systems in the world. Kim styled herself Otaku Queen – Queen of the Cyber-Fanatics – and in Xavier's opinion this was no idle boast. But that only made what he was doing all the more exciting.

Instead of entering a password, Xavier spent the ten seconds transferring as much of the e-mail data as he could on to diskette. The Mac's floppy drive whirred with staccato urgency, as if aware that time was short. The onscreen percentile bar that traced the progress of the transfer crept from zero towards a hundred with agonising slowness, or so it seemed to Xavier.

He managed to duplicate 68 per cent of the e-mail before he ran out of time. The screen-image started to smear and drip like a water-colour in a rainstorm – a cheap shot, this; unnecessary and malicious – and the computer went down with a bronchial rattle.

Stabbing the eject button, Xavier extracted the diskette and took a quick-smart step backwards away from the Mac, half-expecting smoke and flames to burst forth from its cooling vents. Such was his respect for the awesome programming skills of the *Japonaise* that it did not seem to him beyond the realms of possibility that she might be able to induce the violent destruction of hardware as well as software, despite the fact that such a feat was technically unfeasible.

When the Mac failed to spontaneously combust before his very eyes, Xavier relaxed. With a hand that was no longer trembling he held up the diskette to examine it, and then he uttered a low, throaty chuckle of victory, and clenched his other hand into a fist, and did a little dance about his apartment.

The text the diskette contained would be most of it irrecoverably corrupted, and what was not corrupted would be garbled and in need of painstaking unscrambling. None the less he was holding a small, black, square, wafer-thin symbol of success. Gérard de Sade was going to be exceedingly pleased with him, and consequently much less grudging when it came to stumping up Xavier's fee.

7

Screaming out of the black cloud, things that had once been men, but were not now. Disrupted-pattern-material combat gear stretched tight-to-bursting over impossible musculature. Eyeballs scarlet with bloodlust. And his legs knee-deep in the sand, stuck fast. Unable to run, unable to move, able only to stand and watch their remorseless approach. Coming towards him, closer, ever closer ...

MacGowan awoke from the dream, knowing from the very moment he broke the surface of consciousness and his eyelids snapped open that it *had* been a dream (knowing this, deep down, even as he had been dreaming it), but all the same believing, for the space of several thunderous, skull-straining pulsebeats, that *they* were still coming for him. Beyond the walls of the unfamiliar bedroom, making their hideous charge. About to burst through the door and curtained windows.

Christ!

With a concerted effort MacGowan slowed his breathing, counting out his inhalations and exhalations, increasing the intervals each time. Panic management, just as he had learned back at Stirling Lines. Gradually he regained control of his lungs, and his rapid-fire heart rate decreased until it was close to normal again.

Christ, but this was getting ridiculous. Every time he had the dream, it was taking him longer to calm himself down afterwards. Whoever said familiarity breeds contempt had clearly never been exposed to the midnight mind-movie that MacGowan was forced to watch at least once a month. The damn thing never got any less terrifying, never got any easier to bear. He had kicked the fags, cut down on the booze, just like the doctor ordered, but it was neither of those bad habits that was going to give him a coronary. The recurring nightmare – *that* was what was one day going to finish him off.

He sat up, the movement disturbing the woman who was lying beside him. She stirred and mumbled something. MacGowan absentmindedly laid a hand on her shoulder and patted her. She nuzzled up against his hand and sank back into slumber.

Her face, illuminated by the morning sunlight that framed the curtains, looked less like Sarah's than it had the previous evening, when, his perceptions admittedly dimmed by three pints of Guinness, MacGowan had crossed the drink-sodden, cigarette-burned carpet of the Pen and Sword to talk to her. It was the hair, really. Sarah had hair like that, messy ringlets that frizzed out at the sides like a lion's mane. She was a Leo, you see, Sarah was. Big into that astrology stuff. And in her book it was significant that her hair reflected her star-sign. In *his* book it was, at best, coincidence; at worst, meaningless. That had been one of the many differences between him and her. She saw signs and portents everywhere, in everything. He was of the opinion that it was all, frankly, bollocks. But then that was him – hard-nosed, sceptical. Typical bloody Capricorn.

He glanced down at his sleeping bed-companion again. Nope, nothing like Sarah. Except the hair.

Maybe it was just that he went for a certain physical type, that was all. Had a genetic predisposition to find a certain kind of woman attractive, nothing more to it than that. Certainly he was not pursuing an obsession with his ex-wife. Oh no, not at all.

What was her name, anyway? MacGowan racked his brains. Susan. Suzanne. Susie. Something along those lines. Or possibly Claire. Charlotte? Carrie?

He cursed himself under his breath. How low could

you sink? Shagging some pub pick-up, then forgetting her name the next morning. What kind of behaviour was that for a grown man?

Carrie, or Susie, or whatever she was called, had a bedside radio-alarm. The scarlet digits said it was 8.12 a.m. MacGowan eased himself out of bed and groped around the floor for his boxer shorts. His mouth was dry, his tongue rough. Coffee. Coffee would be good. His fingers encountered something clammy and jelly-like. Last night's condom, discarded. Wrinkling his nose, he continued to search the floor. Finding the boxer shorts, he tugged them on. Further probing failed to locate his shirt, so he took the woman's cotton dressing gown from a hook on the back of the bedroom door and wrapped that around his bulky frame. The dressing gown had puffed shoulders and was pink with red roses embroidered up the lapels. Nice. The sleeves were about twelve inches too short for his arms and there was barely enough left over of the sash, once it had encompassed his waist, to make a knot out of. He slipped quietly out of the bedroom and went downstairs.

It was a large, pleasant Islington semi. Well appointed. Claire-Charlotte-Suzanne had told him she was an interior designer, and every room looked like something out of a *Homes and Gardens* photo-spread. Even the magazines and books on the living-room coffee table looked like they had been carefully chosen and arranged for maximum aesthetic effect. Doubtful they had been read, or even opened.

The kitchen was all pine cupboards and marble slabs. Families of saucepans hung in rows, jars of lentils and pasta shapes were ranged along shelves, and the crockery set – thick earthenware painted in bold, primary colours – was displayed on a farmhouse dresser. A portable TV set sat on the counter. MacGowan switched it on and tuned it to BBC2. *Teletubbies*. His favourite. Nice, restful, uncomplicated viewing for the morning after a night out. Easy on the mind and the eyes.

The kettle was the old-fashioned dome-shaped kind

that you stuck on the gas hob and heated up until it whistled. Unfortunately the gas hob itself was the kind you needed to be a NASA scientist to operate, all touch-sensitive buttons and digital displays. Gingerly MacGowan started experimenting with the hob controls, praying he was not about to ignite a fireball. He had once known a bomb-disposal expert, Corporal Ashton, who had done exactly that. The man disarmed complicated and often booby-trapped antipersonnel devices for a living, and one day, while lighting an ordinary domestic gas cooker, he had not been concentrating and had managed to singe off his moustache. There was probably a moral in that somewhere. Like: *Only complete tits wear moustaches*.

MacGowan was still fumbling unsuccessfully with the hob controls when the woman came shuffling blearily in. She was wearing his shirt, and his pager was in her hand, beeping merrily away.

'It's for you,' she said, handing him the pager. She switched off the television and shunted him to one side. With two deft flicks of the hob controls, she lit a flame beneath the kettle. 'Looks good on you, by the way,' she added, with a nod at the dressing gown.

'Think so?' said MacGowan. 'I don't know if pink's my colour. I'm more of a lilac man, myself.'

He silenced the pager's beeping and glanced at the readout.

BRETHERTON
12.00 P.M.

Buggeration.

'Is it important?' she asked, watching his face.

'Nah,' he replied, flashing her a grin. 'Just an eager-beaver business colleague.'

'Not your wife, then. Wondering where you are.'

'I'm not married.'

Of all the looks he would have expected to see on her face upon learning this news, disappointment was not one of them.

'But your ring ...' She pointed to his left hand.

'This?' He thumb-twiddled the gold wedding band around the base of his fourth finger. 'I'm divorced. Just wear it for old times' sake.'

'Ah,' she said. 'I see.' She frowned for a moment, debating inwardly, then said, 'Look, this is going to sound absolutely dreadful, but I'm afraid I can't remember your name.'

'Bill,' he said, trying not to appear taken aback.

'Yes, of course. That's it. Bill. Look, Bill ...' She hesitated.

'Yes, Carla?' Carla. Typical that it should bloody come back to him *now*.

'This ... what we did last night.' She was avoiding his gaze, watching the kettle. 'It was just a ... you know, *thing*. Right? Between two consenting adults? A one-off. We both knew that from the outset, didn't we?'

'Erm, yeah. Sure.'

'Good.' Relieved, Carla suddenly became animated, fetching out some mugs, a cafetière, ground coffee. 'Good, that's good.'

Well, how do you like that? *That* was all she had been looking for – a quick fling with a married man. Married, so that there was no danger that he would want anything more from her than sex, no danger that anything more would come of it than a few seconds of mutual gratification.

Of all the ... !

MacGowan stopped himself there. It was no good being outraged. He had got what he wanted, she had got what she wanted. And he had not been intending to take it any further himself, had he? She might have let him down a bit more gently, perhaps, but all in all he could not really complain, could he?

'Coffee, then?' she said, as the kettle bubbled to the boil and began to emit a sibilant squeal.

'Yeah, that'd be great. And then I'd best be on my way.'

'Yes.'

As they drank their coffee in silence – she sitting at the table, he standing leaning against one of the worktops, each of them wearing an item of the other's clothing – MacGowan pondered why Rattray might have summoned him down to Lucretia's, and then decided not to think about it.

Let's face it: when Rattray got in contact with you, it was not to invite you to join him for a week's holiday at Disneyland Europe.

8

Wallowing on a slew of water-bed wobbles, Piers Pearson clambered over the recumbent Tara to reach the G-Plan bedside cabinet, where the phone – a rotary-dial model with an ornate ormolu base, a tall brass cradle and a receiver handset like a coffin handle – was trilling shrilly. Lady Grinning Soul, sprawled along the ottoman at the foot of the bed, raised her head and then her eyebrows. As he picked up the receiver Piers, in his Union Jack pyjamas, blew the beautiful Afghan hound a kiss. Tara, meanwhile, slithered across to join the third occupant of the bed, Emma. The two women snuggled happily together.

From the other end of the line a familiar dry, restrained monotone uttered his name, and immediately Piers's mental jukebox responded by offering up a short burst of theme music: seven timpani beats, spelling out the seven letters of each half of the name Captain Scarlet, which was how Piers liked to refer to the caller.

'Yes, this is Piers Pearson, Freelance Facilitator,' he said, and as he and Captain Scarlet continued to speak, he echoed and elaborated on each of Captain Scarlet's statements as though for the benefit of an audience who were privy only to his side of the conversation. 'What's that, old chap? You have need of my talents once again? I see. Another urgent crisis has arisen that requires me to drop everything and head down to Surrey. Do I have anything else on presently?' A sidelong smirk at Tara and

74

Emma, both wide awake, both feigning sleep. 'Well, I was attending to a couple of pieces of work last night, but I think I sorted them out to everyone's general satisfaction. Midday? I don't see that that should be a problem. You'll have the chilled Moët waiting for me, of course. Yes? Very well then.' Time for his catchphrase. 'All according to plan.'

He hung up the receiver and bounded to his feet, sending a heavy ripple undulating across the water-bed, which gave Tara and Emma an excuse to pretend to wake up. Both yawned, stretched, and sat up against the black silk pillows, drawing the matching top-sheet decorously up to their collarbones to preserve their modesty. Tara was brunette, and wore her hair short, in a pageboy cut. Emma was auburn, and wore her hair long and centre-parted.

'You aren't leaving us, are you, Piers?' said Emma, mimicking the plummy, proper diction of a former public schoolgirl.

'Afraid so,' said Piers, at the door to his dressing room.

'Right away?' said Tara. Her accent sounded more authentically South London.

'You can't spare us half an hour?' said Emma coquettishly.

Piers stroked one tip of his long moustache, pondering. 'Hmmm. Tempting though the offer is, my dears, I regret to say I'm going to have to turn it down.'

Emma and Tara groaned in disappointment.

'But perhaps later?' With a knowing twitch of his eyebrows, Piers turned and entered the dressing room.

No sooner had he slid the dressing-room door shut behind him than the two women burst into fits of snorting giggles. Each tried desperately to stifle her laughter, but all it took was an exchange of glances to set them both going again. In the end Tara (which was not her real name) had to thump Emma (which, by lucky happenstance, *was* her real name) on the arm several times in order to quieten her, and thus both of them. If Piers heard them laughing he might not employ them again, and it would be a shame to lose a good gig like this. All that was demanded of them, in return for being paid well, was that they sleep with him, play along with his timewarp fantasy of being a character out of a sixties TV adventure series, and keep a straight face at all times so as not to ruin the illusion. And 'sleep with him' meant precisely that. Piers, for all his innuendo-laden talk, showed no genuine interest in matters sexual, and that, for these two professionals, came as something of a relief.

In his dressing room Piers surveyed the various items of clothing on offer. With a sudden flurry of quick, decisive movements he selected a fawn velvet shirt with mushroom cuffs and delta-wing collars, a pair of mustard-yellow polyester bellbottoms, elastic-sided ankle boots and a purple waistcoat. He changed out of his pyjamas into this ensemble and examined himself in a full-length mirror. Not quite there. He added a pair of spectacles with turquoise-tinted hexagonal lenses and a white chiffon scarf, which he knotted at the side of his neck, then re-inspected his reflection. Perfect. Carnaby Street Man in all his flamboyant, tapered glory.

And the finishing touch, the *pièce de résistance* ...

From an ivory-inlaid box on top of the dresser Piers fished out an ovoid medallion composed of interlocking crystal segments and strung on a slender silver chain. The moment he touched the medallion it began to throb and pulse like a living thing, extruding and retracting parts of itself like a sea-anemone extruding and retracting its fronds. He gazed at it meditatively for a moment, smiling, then, with careful ceremony, hung it around his neck. As soon as it touched his skin, the medallion became inert again.

He packed a few items of spare clothing in a Gladstone bag, then passed through the door connecting the dressing room to the bathroom and packed a number of toiletry items as well. The bathroom's other door led him back to the bedroom.

The sight of Piers's outfit should have been enough to trigger another giggling fit, but Tara and Emma managed to remain impressively straight-faced. Lady Grinning Soul, spying the Gladstone bag, uttered a small whine. She climbed down off the ottoman and came trotting over to her master, her long blonde fur swaying silkily like a cornfield in the breeze. Piers stroked her muzzle and murmured soothingly to her. Then he addressed the two women in his bed.

'My dears,' he said, 'duty calls, England expects, and all that. I'll be gone a few days. Would you mind looking after Lady until I get back?'

Neither Tara nor Emma had any objection. Although Piers's taste in decor left something to be desired – the living room, for instance, was furnished with orange moulded-plastic bubble-chairs, brown carpeting and wood-effect laminate wall-covering – and his television for some reason showed only repeats of programmes that were at least twenty-five years old, when all was said and done there were far worse places to crash out for a while. Besides, it was fun taking Lady for walks along the King's Road. *And* Piers would be paying them at the full daily rate.

Lady's well-being assured, Piers set off down the spiral staircase to the hallway, timing his footsteps to tap out the rhythm of the closing Pearl & Dean theme on the iron risers: twenty notes, twenty steps.

His canary-yellow Caterham 7 was waiting in the garage, an Anthony Newley tape loaded into the eight-track. Captain Scarlet – or, if you must, John Rattray – had a job for him. The world needed saving yet again.

All was very much according to plan.

9

Bretherton Grange, the home of Lucretia Fisk, the noted sculptress, was located on the outskirts of the village of Bretherton, a few miles from Dorking, to the south-west of London.

Set in grounds covering approximately twenty acres, the main part of the Grange dated back to the middle of the eighteenth century, and was built by a certain Parson Herbert Woodbury.

Woodbury, the only son of a wealthy wool merchant, had disappointed his father greatly by choosing holy orders over the textile trade. His father frequently bemoaned the fact that his son had 'taken the wrong kind of cloth'. However, the senior Woodbury was not a man to hold a grudge, and did not, as many other fathers might have, cut the prodigal out of his will. Instead he chose to look upon his son's decision to enter the Church as a youthful whim, a passing fancy, and fully expected him to come to his senses in time, renounce his faith, and take up a position in the altogether more profitable world of mills and industry, where the only flocks he would have to care for were the baaing type.

The parish to which Woodbury was appointed was small and ailing, the church at which he ministered a humble, crumbling medieval edifice, damp, prone to draughts and animal infestations, and generally uninviting and uncomfortable. The role of parson itself was a modest one, requiring Woodbury to do nothing more than deliver one sermon a week (all other ecumenical duties were carried out by his curate). Woodbury none the less threw himself into it with vigour, and made each sermon as thought-provoking and entertaining as he could, but his services were poorly attended. Perhaps forgivably, most of his parishioners chose to seek their spiritual refreshment in the neighbouring parish, where a new house of worship had recently been erected, one that was larger, grander, and altogether warmer and more welcoming. Not only that, but it was the Age of Reason, that time when the light of science was banishing the darkness of superstition and turning religious orthodoxy on its head. Increasingly, Woodbury found himself preaching to empty pews.

This troubled the earnest young man. He took the parishioners' rejection of his parsonship personally, and was often to be found kneeling before the altar, praying for divine guidance. Sometimes, as he begged the Lord aloud to show him a way of coaxing members of his congregation back into the fold, he would have to raise his voice in order to make himself heard over the scuffles and rustlings of birds, bats and rats.

And it was as Woodbury was genuflecting in this manner late one winter's evening, a year and a half after he first assumed the mantle of priest, that he received a visitation.

Perceiving a sudden glow of light through his tight-shut eyelids, Woodbury's first thought was that, unbeknownst to him, a candle must have fallen over and set the altar cloth on fire. Upon opening his eyes, however, he discovered that the light was emanating not from any earthly conflagration but rather from a radiant, ethereal being that had manifested itself in the chancel and was floating a yard above the flagstone floor, gazing down on him.

The being's features were largely indistinguishable through the blaze of effulgence with which it was surrounded. Even squinting, all that Woodbury was able to make out was that it was at least eight feet tall, that it was naked but lacked any obvious primary or secondary sexual characteristics, and that it had a face of nigh-inhuman symmetry and beauty.

It was, quite clearly in his mind, an angel.

Trembling with awe and terror, the young priest listened as the angel, in a voice like cymbals and fire, addressed him by name and told him that it had an important message for him.

'From God?' stammered Woodbury.

Not from God, the angel said.

'Then,' said Woodbury, even more timorously, 'from the Devil?'

The angel assured him that the message was not from the Devil either.

'But you are, are you not, an angel?'

The being said that it was not.

Confused now, Woodbury covered his face and prayed for the manifestation to vanish and for all to be as it was before. He was coming to the conclusion that the creature must be a phantasm, a delusion, possibly a trick played by the Devil in order to test his faith at this already trying time. It had said it had not been sent by the Devil, but then an emissary of Satan would, naturally, lie rather than admit that fact, would it not?

The creature was still there when Woodbury finally took his hands away from his face, and this time he thought he detected a hint of a smile on its face.

'Please,' he groaned abjectly, 'what do you want with me?'

The creature said that it had a task for him, an important one. It told him that he was shortly to come into a great deal of money and that he should use some of that money to build a house according to certain specifications. When Woodbury enquired what those specifications were, the creature floated closer to him, reached down and touched his forehead with the tip of one index finger.

It was that touch that finally persuaded Woodbury of the reality of what he was seeing. Feeling the creature's finger upon his forehead, and realising that what he was seeing had form, flesh, warmth, substance, corporeality, he was convinced, one might even say converted.

The next instant, a silent, painless blue light sprang from the creature's fingertip, filling Woodbury's mind. There was a moment of pure, perfect oblivion, and then, as the blue light cleared, Woodbury understood things. Many things. Principally, he knew how the house which the creature wanted him to build was to look, from foundation to roof tile, down to the very last brick. But he knew, too, of a conflict which had been going on long before the Son of God was crucified and which continued to this day – a war waged in secret, fought by a chosen few. It seemed as if this knowledge had been present in his brain all along and the creature's touch had merely awakened what had hitherto lain dormant.

The creature told him not to worry and said that all would be well, then vanished, leaving Woodbury crouched, trembling, on the church flagstones, dizzy and nauseated with fear.

Upon returning to the vicarage Woodbury took to his bed, telling his curate, when he happened to call by, that he had developed a fever. Not surprisingly, given the amount of time he spent in the damp, chilly church, he *had* come down with a head-cold, but this merely provided him with a convenient set of symptoms on which he could blame his invalidity. His illness was more of the mind than of the body. The visitation in the chapel had forced him to reappraise his entire theological and philosophical world-view.

For three days and three long, sleepless nights Woodbury tossed and turned, grappling with the ramifications of everything the angelic creature had shown him. He would have stayed bedridden for longer, had a letter not arrived from his mother informing him that his father had, without warning, been struck down by a severe and inexplicable wasting disease.

Up until then Woodbury's father had enjoyed the rudest of health, but the disease brought him low, ravaging his body and defying the curative efforts of the best doctors money could buy. Within a matter of days, he had dwindled away to nothing and was dead.

About this time, the bishop in whose diocese the parish of Bretherton lay decided that the ailing parish should be incorporated into its neighbour and the old church building and grounds deconsecrated and sold off. He offered Woodbury a post in another parish. Woodbury, in response, penned a letter to the bishop informing him of his intention to resign from the Church and pursue a life of greater ease. Now that he had come into a sizeable inheritance, there really was no need for him to continue in the service of God.

The bishop was incensed, and in a bitterly worded reply to Woodbury's letter accused the young man of laziness, insufficient faith and misplaced priorities. If nothing else, rather than keeping the money he had inherited for himself, he should donate it all to the Church. After all, was not poverty the sincerest expression of spiritual purity?

Woodbury remained firm in his decision. He did, however, suggest a compromise that went some way towards placating the bishop. Having sold off the family business for a handsome sum and set his mother and his two sisters up in some comfort, Woodbury used the rest of the money to purchase the site of Bretherton Church from the Church of England.

He promptly razed the ancient building to the ground and, in its place, set about constructing a home for himself.

It was the source of some animosity among the local stonemasons and carpenters that no skilled (or for that matter manual) labourers from the immediate region were employed in the building's erection. Instead, the parson enlisted the aid of workmen drawn from various different corners of the country, small groups of whom toiled on a portion of the house for no more than a fortnight at a time before being sent back, well rewarded for their services, to whence they had come. Thus no one except the parson himself had any clear idea of the overall layout of the Grange.

Woodbury may have resigned from the priesthood, but it was not long before he took on a role that was the secular equivalent. For, not long after the building of the house was complete, the gatherings began. Odd types from all walks of life, and often from a number of different nations, would turn up at the Grange, would stay for a few hours, and then would disperse, singly or in groups, with a grim sense of purpose evident in their bearing and demeanour. Irregular in every sense, the gatherings aroused suspicion among the locals that the ex-parson was indulging in libertine activities of the kind good Christian minds, try though they might, could barely conceive. Nothing, however, was proved, and the rumours concerning the behaviour of the erstwhile minister remained just that: rumours.

Parson Woodbury had, in fact, become a Guardian, and the visitation by the angelic creature in the church had been the work of the Librans. It was Woodbury, incidentally, who first coined the terms Libran and Anarch. Before then Guardians had used a variety of obliquely mundane names to describe the entities they served – usually 'masters' or 'employers' – and had referred to the opposition simply as 'the enemy'. Drawing on his thorough grounding in the Classics, Woodbury codified and concretised what had up till then been nebulous and abstract.

The parson, though no longer obliged to as a cleric, none the less remained staunchly celibate throughout his life, producing no offspring to inherit the house after he died. In his will, he left the Grange to one of his associates, a Dutchman by the name of Anders van der Pool, who was a Guardian too, and a frequent attendee at the gatherings. Almost immediately after he moved in, van der Pool added a new wing to the building, this time sensibly engaging the services of the local workforce, and hence mollifying the inhabitants of Bretherton and its environs to such an extent that they were unable to find fault with anything about him, except perhaps his Dutchness. He also, in memory of his homeland, set a full-size working windmill atop a tor overlooking the Grange's ornamental lake. Guardian meetings continued to be held at the house, and when van der Pool died his role as co-ordinator of Guardian affairs (North Europe chapter) was taken over by his son, Willem. Willem added another new wing, and would doubtless have stuck another windmill somewhere in the grounds had his English wife Margery not perished in childbirth (the baby, which would have been their first, was stillborn). Stricken with grief, Willem drowned himself in the lake.

The Grange passed on, by dint of a provision in Willem's will, not to another member of the van der Pool family but to another Guardian. From then on, the pattern was set. Each subsequent occupant of the Grange contributed a new wing or a new architectural folly, sometimes both, and each, upon his or her demise, bequeathed the place to a fellow Guardian, if possible an immediate relative.

The net result, in architectural terms, was an unsightly mess. While the original Grange was still clearly visible as the epicentre around which all other parts of the house had accreted, its fine Augustan proportions were ruined by the profusion of outbuildings, annexes and excrescences that now surrounded it. The dome of an observatory, for instance, which had been appended during the late Victorian era, dominated the angled red rooftops like some huge copper-turquoise fungal growth, while the Arcadian landscaping of the grounds had been deprived of whatever pretensions to naturalness it might have had by the addition of clusters of miniature pyramids of differing sizes, arranged in patterns corresponding to the constellations, thus transforming the entire estate into a terrestrial map of the heavens.

The miniature pyramids were one of two outdoor features installed by the woman who owned the Grange during the first two decades of the twentieth century. She was Bridget St Swithin, a very minor poetess whose

84

career trajectory briefly and tangentially intersected with the Bloomsbury circle (in whose company she was not made to feel welcome, for although she was appropriately talentless, she was also rather too quick to draw attention to the talentlessness of others). The intelligent, mischievous and, frankly, barmy Bridget's other addition was a hedgerow maze, whose solution, she claimed, involved unlocking a riddle of the ancients. Taken at face value, this cryptic remark seemed to pertain to nothing more than the fact that, in order to find one's way from the entrance of the oval maze to its centre, one had to follow a course which roughly described the outline of a large, old-fashioned key, such as might be used to open a safe or a church door. If there were deeper levels of significance to her comment, they were not apparent to the naked eye.

During the Second World War, the British government, looking for somewhere to site a military intelligence headquarters specifically for the task of breaking Nazi transmission codes, decided to requisition Bretherton Grange for that purpose. Letters were sent to the then-current owner, Raymond Farquhar-Colquhoun, Bridget St Swithin's nephew. All were returned undelivered. A posse of civil servants went down to Surrey to deal with the matter in person, but they were unable to locate the house, or even the entrance to its driveway. Roads went past the Grange, around its perimeter as marked on the Ordnance Survey maps, but never actually *to* it. Moreover, while local residents agreed that a place answering to the name of Bretherton Grange did exist somewhere nearby, all of them experienced the same difficulty as the civil servants when it came to actually finding it. The civil servants returned to Whitehall utterly baffled. A plane was sent up to overfly the site, but even aerial reconnaissance failed to pin down the Grange's whereabouts. Where the building and grounds should have been visible from the air, there was only forest. It seemed, to all intents and purposes, that the Grange had disappeared, vanished from existence. However, because there was a war on, the matter was not investigated as thoroughly as it might otherwise have been, and another, less elusive location for the codebreaking headquarters, Bletchley Park, was chosen. Come VE-Day, Bretherton Grange was back as though it had never been away.

The sole architectural contribution of Farquhar-Colquhoun, who remained at the Grange through the post-war period up until the late 1960s, was perhaps its most austere and least lovely portion: a long, low, single-storey concrete block which, mercifully, was mostly shielded from view behind a cedar copse. Upon his death the house and the mantle of Guardian co-ordinator were passed on to a cousin of his, Ron Fisk, who was at that time the drummer with The Royals, a foundering Mod band who had, for a few months, caught a brief glimmer of the limelight but were now at the point in their career where the dwindling popularity of their musical style presented them with a choice between rethinking their approach or admitting defeat and calling it a day.

Ron ran the Grange and Guardian affairs as best he could, but as luck would have it The Royals, having decided to adopt a looser, more flamboyant look and sound, suddenly hit the big time. With massive chart success came, inevitably, the lure of massive hedonism, but while every other member of the band quickly and eagerly succumbed to the numerous temptations on offer, Ron, constrained by his obligation to the Libran cause, resisted, so earning himself the reputation as the band's 'Quiet One' and a bit of a prude. He had, in fact, been a poor choice of successor on Farquhar-Colquhoun's part, and it came as a relief to all when his older sister Lucretia, then in the struggling phase of her artistic career, recognised that her brother's reluctant self-denial was placing him under an intolerable strain and volunteered to assume his duties from him. Lucretia and Ron were close and had few secrets from each other, so Lucretia had a pretty clear idea what being a Guardian meant and knew the obligations and moral burdens she would be taking on. She weighed up the sacrifices she was going to have to make against the happiness of her little brother, and deemed it a fair trade.

Ron, freed from the yoke of responsibility, promptly went off the rails in spectacular fashion. Making up for lost time, he did in three months as much as the rest of the band had managed in three years. The outcome was as inevitable as it was tragic. To this day, ageing fans of The Royals' music commemorated the anniversary of Ron's death by tying ribbons around the tree into which Ron crashed his Aston Martin DB6 while doing ninety-five along the A24, simultaneously freebasing heroin and receiving oral gratification from a groupie (who was also killed in the accident). In order to leave his hands free for other things, Ron had been steering the car with his knees.

Lucretia refused to shoulder any of the blame for her brother's death. He had made his own choices, lived his life according to his own standards. She mourned him appropriately, then set about making her mark on the Grange. The first thing she did was erect an arching, palatial conservatory at the rear of the building, which she put to use as a studio. There she began turning out large-scale sculpture of the kind she had hitherto had the yearning but not the facilities to create. One of these spectacular, three-dimensional works could now be seen in front of the Grange, at the centre of the driveway turning circle, on the shallow grass mound that had previously supported a rather dull example of gambolling-satyr statuary.

Critics habitually used the adjectives 'industrial' and 'mechanistic' when referring to the sculptures of Lucretia Fisk, and, in attempting to convey the feelings aroused by her work, offered up phrases such as 'a potent synthesis of the scientific and the abstract' and 'both a cold statement on and an anguished cry of defiance against the dehumanisation of late-twentieth-century existence'. In truth, the effect of her work was hard to evoke in words (not that that prevented the critics, with column inches to fill and bills to pay, from trying). To stand before a Fisk and attempt to make practical, cerebral sense of it was nigh on impossible. There was beauty there, certainly, but it was difficult to know for sure how that beauty could be generated by such a concatenation of harsh shapes and angles.

In combining tortured, moulded metal with 'found' items of hardware, what Lucretia produced sometimes did and sometimes did not resemble an object you recognised, depending on the position from which you viewed the work, the setting, the light conditions, your mood, and even the time of day. There was always some element to each of her pieces that was instantly familiar even though you knew you had never seen it before. Each time you looked you experienced a *frisson* of intense aesthetic *déjà-vu*. But there was more to her work than that.

They moved, Lucretia's sculptures. Always some section of them was kinetic – beguilingly, mesmerisingly so – and a great deal of the delight to be derived from them came from trying to figure out how she had managed to get a particular part to whirl or spin or oscillate or flicker or hover. Where were the pulleys, the chains, the motors? How was the intricate system of balances and counter-weights hidden from view? Why did it seem that the laws of physics never applied to a Fisk?

Thus her sculptures offered a challenge to one's intellectual curiosity and at the same time fulfilled the criteria for that which, by consensus, the human race has come to consider visually pleasing. And thus original Fisks were extremely popular and extremely expensive.

The piece that greeted visitors to Bretherton Grange as they rounded the last turn of the driveway and the house itself hove into view stood some twenty feet from base to apex and was entitled *Da Vinci's Dreams Downcast*. More than anything it resembled aircraft wreckage piled high to form a rough inverted cone, with a sad, solitary propeller rotating mournfully near the bottom. If you looked closely, however, you would find, buried among the twists and tangles of steel, elements of the great

Leonardo's unrealised designs for a helicopter and a one-man flying machine, the former represented by a flat-plane spiral, the latter by a single, mangled batwing. The whole sculpture rested at an angle a few degrees from perpendicular, and seemed ever in danger of toppling over, like the Leaning Tower of Pisa, or like a child's top in the final throes of its spin just before it falls and goes skittering across the floor.

To a Guardian versed in the lore of past Guardian operations there was a deeper layer of significance to *Da Vinci's Dreams Downcast*, for it was thanks to Guardian intervention that the prototype vehicles depicted had remained nothing more than notebook sketches and scale models, the never realised fancies of a prolific genius. Had Leonardo been luckier in his choice of patrons, he might have been able to devote more energy into developing these inventions and making them workable and, more to the point, financially remunerative, but the behind-the-scenes machinations and string-pulling of the Renaissance era's pre-eminent Guardian, Niccolò Machiavelli, ensured that this never happened.

Rattray had seen the sculpture enough times now to be able to disregard anything but its weird elegance. He, like so many others, was an admirer of Lucretia's work and, although he harboured reservations about Lucretia's practice of inserting at least one item of Libran technology into each of her pieces, he believed her when she said that these contratemporal components were not only vital to the overall impact of her art but also that they were integrated so cunningly that no one would ever detect them, not even by dismantling a sculpture (unthinkable as that was!) and closely examining each of its parts.

Besides, on this particular occasion, Rattray had other things on his mind than contemplating art. He steered his Mercedes 600 SEC around *Da Vinci's Dreams Downcast* and pulled up before the flight of stone steps that led up to the Grange's front entrance, then switched off the CD of Rachmaninov piano concertos that was blaring out from the stereo and killed the engine. He sat for a moment, his hands resting on the steering wheel, his eyes unfocused. Then, with seemingly immense effort, he opened the door and stepped out of the car.

As he did so, one of the pair of half-glassed doors at the top of the steps opened and Lucretia's common-law husband Dennis Holman emerged, shading his eyes against the sunshine and offering Rattray a broad smile.

'John,' he said. 'How's tricks?'

The balding, bearded Holman was an affable, unassuming fellow, the perfect foil for a forthright, dynamic personality like Lucretia. His role in the household was to manage the buildings and grounds and oversee all the domestic affairs, leaving his wife free to pursue her muse. Just enough about the Guardians had been revealed to him for him to know that he was better off not prying into their business any more deeply.

Rattray closed the car door behind him, hearing it swing shut with a solid Teutonic thud. 'How's tricks?' he echoed, and then repeated the word 'tricks' softly to himself, as though savouring a private irony. Then he shook his head and offered Holman the closest thing to a smile he was going to manage for now.

Holman was used to the often melancholy temperament of this particular Guardian and did not discern anything out of the ordinary about his current air of distraction. As Rattray gained the top of the steps, Holman reached out to shake hands, then stepped back and ushered his guest into the house.

'Lu's beavering away,' he said, following Rattray indoors. 'She knows you're all coming, but she has a commission she's got to finish, and the deadline's looming. Something for a municipal shopping precinct.'

'That's fine,' said Rattray. 'I'm early, anyway.'

'Who else are we expecting?'

'Just Piers and Bill.'

'Ah, the full British contingent. Not Dieter? Not Carlo?'

'Both have expressed a preference only to be involved in Guardian actions that take place on the Continent.'

'Ah well. So much for the New Europe.'

The hallway was tall and spacious, its flagstone floor mostly covered by a large Persian kilim. Daytime illumination was provided by a skylight, while at night a chandelier with candle-shaped lightbulb fixtures took over the task. The house's main staircase ascended around the east and north walls to the upper storey, each turn in the balustrade marked by a newel-post whose crown had been carved in the shape of a geometrically grooved egg. The west wall was taken up entirely by a bas-relief Fisk. The surface of the sculpture, which was entitled *Daedalian*, was composed of jagged, interrupted ridges reminiscent of islands and archipelagos, over which objects glided to and fro in seemingly random trajectories. Some of the objects could have been designed to resemble winged men; others looked like nothing you could think of.

Both Rattray and Holman raised their heads as the sound of footsteps came echoing from the upstairs corridor. The footsteps were rapid and then, at the last moment, slowed, in an attempt to give the impression that their owner had not been hurrying after all.

Daisy Holman-Fisk appeared at the head of the staircase and leaned eagerly over the balustrade. The recently arrived visitor was not the person she had been hoping to see and her frown of disappointment was swiftly (though not quite swiftly enough) erased and replaced with a polite, friendly smile.

'Hi, Uncle John,' she said.

'Good morning, Daisy.'

You did not have to be a former detective inspector to be able to deduce that the elder of the two Holman-Fisk girls had spent the best part of the morning smartening herself up, doing her hair, gauging the amount of make-up she applied just right so that it accentuated her features to their best advantage without making her look tarty. Rattray wondered how many outfits she had tried on before settling on the Levi 501s, the strap-sandals and the figure-hugging crop-top T-shirt she now wore. None of which was for *his* benefit, of course. Though he and Daisy got on well enough, Rattray had known her since she had been born, and their relationship was steadfastly formal. He was, and always would be, senior, stern, aloof. 'Uncle' John.

Bill MacGowan, on the other hand ...

Holman gestured to the far end of the hallway, where the door to the dining room lay. 'You know the way,' he said. 'I'll get some refreshments together.'

Rattray thanked him, tendered Daisy a polite bow, and headed off to the dining room.

Next to turn up at Bretherton Grange was MacGowan in his slate-grey Saab 9000i.

For ordinary callers at the Grange there was a standard intercom system – a squat brick pillar to the right of the driveway entrance into which was set a panel with a push-button and a speaker grille. However, for MacGowan, as for other Guardians, this method of announcing your arrival was unnecessary. MacGowan's talisman of Guardianship, a puzzle-egg identical to Piers Pearson's crystal medallion but made of brass and disguised as a keyring, was detected by hidden instruments within the pillar, and the gates opened automatically.

MacGowan had it down to a fine art now, judging his speed precisely so that he could swerve off the road into the driveway entrance and, without decelerating, have the front of the Saab nudging between the gates when they were just far enough apart to permit the car through. By the time the wing mirrors were level with the gates there was an inch of clearance on either side, and by the time the gates had clanged fully open against their stops MacGowan was twenty yards beyond them.

It was, as ever, a smooth piece of driving. Eat your heart out, Jeremy Clarkson.

A minute or so later MacGowan was circumnavigating

Da Vinci's Dreams Downcast and drawing to a halt at the foot of the front steps to the Grange.

MacGowan was not much of a gambling man, but if he had been he would have laid good money on who was going to be at the door to greet him. And sure enough, just as he was applying the handbrake and turning off the engine, who should emerge from the house, nonchalantly, as though she were just popping out for a stroll, but Daisy.

The transition from girlish interest to an altogether more fixated form of attentiveness had occurred with such imperceptible slowness over the period during which MacGowan had been visiting the Grange as a Guardian that there was no way of knowing when was the exact point that Daisy had stopped thinking of him as a friend of her mother's and started regarding him as something more. The two of them had had a rapport from the start, that much was for certain, and he had always treated her as a grown-up, even though she had only been thirteen when they first met. She had always been pretty, too. It was her sister Alice, two years her junior, who had inherited their mother's pinched, toothy, slightly equine features. Daisy had big eyes and a nicely rounded face, and other parts of her body had likewise become big and nicely rounded in the time MacGowan had known her, but again, these changes had registered with him subliminally, if at all. It was only recently that it had dawned on him that Daisy was no longer simply a bright, lively, quick-witted child; that she had become, if not quite a woman, then a woman-in-waiting. Even then he had failed to recognise the signs that her interest in him might be a less than innocent one. He had noticed that she had taken to laughing rather too loudly at his jokes, that she liked to stand close to him whenever they were talking, and that, if she knew he was coming down to the Grange, she would make a point of being on hand to greet him when he got there, but to go from noticing these things to understanding what they signified required a deductive leap, one that he was neither mentally equipped nor prepared to make with any ease.

The penny had finally dropped when he had sent her a card for her nineteenth birthday (Sarah used to admit, grudgingly, that for all his faults he was pretty conscientious about remembering things like birthdays and anniversaries). Daisy had responded, not with a brief thank-you note but with a lengthy letter in which she described the parties she had been to recently, the albums she was currently listening to and the films and plays she had seen, the comical grottiness of college accommodation, the unpleasant personal habits of her tutors, and all the other ups and downs of life as a first-year English Literature undergraduate at Cambridge. Then, for a whole side of A4 paper, she had bemoaned the lack of decent *men* at university (and she had underlined 'men' several times, lest he miss her point), and at this stage the amusement with which MacGowan had begun reading the letter had curdled to an embarrassed kind of dread.

It was not his fault, he knew that. He could not help it if he was so damn sexy, could he? And it was not a case of him being like that Hubert Humble bloke, or whatever his name was, the one out of *Lolita*. Daisy, at least, was old enough to vote and drive a car and drink alcohol and … do the other thing, legally. Nor, perhaps more to the point, was it a case of him being like Woody Allen and fancying a girl he had watched grow up from a slip of a thing to full-blown maturity. Well, it *was* a bit like that, but at least Daisy was not his daughter. She was *Lucretia's* daughter, that was the real point. If she had not been Lucretia's daughter, MacGowan might well have done something about it. Capitalised on the interest she was showing in him. As it was, there was no way anything could happen between them. He did not even dare entertain the notion. Strictly *verboten*. If he embarked on an affair with Daisy and Lucretia found out … well, he doubted Lucretia would do anything as clean and final as simply kill him. Lucretia angry with him? He would rather have faced an IRA hit-squad, unarmed.

The worst of it was, like almost every other hetero-sexual male, MacGowan found it difficult to remain indifferent to the attentions of a member of the opposite sex, especially if the member of the opposite sex was young and good-looking. It was flattering, too, to the ego of a man in his late thirties that he could still be attractive to the kind of woman he had been attractive to twenty years ago.

And so it was with an uneasy mixture of pleasure and resignation that MacGowan stepped out of the Saab, pocketed his keys, and waited for Daisy to pretend to notice he was there. And when she did, saying, 'Oh! Bill!' and managing to sound ever so surprised as she said it, his answering grin was forced, but not wholly so.

'I forgot Mummy said you were coming,' said Daisy.

'How appalling that you could forget a thing like that,' MacGowan replied, and no sooner had the words left his mouth than he thought, For God's sake, what do you think you're doing, making a flirty remark like that? The last thing you want is to *encourage* her.

'It *is* appalling,' Daisy said brightly, watching him with a keen eye as he jogged smartly up the steps. 'I'll have to make sure it never happens again.'

'You do that,' said MacGowan. 'I see the old fart's already here.' He jerked a thumb in the direction of Rattray's Mercedes.

Daisy peered up at him. She stood a little over five and a half feet tall. At six feet seven MacGowan towered over her. He liked it that she had to crane her neck to look up to him. He could tell she liked it, too. 'The old fart?' she said. 'Oh, you mean Uncle John. Yes. He's in the dining room.'

'And how's your sister?'

'Actually, I'm looking for her right now. I promised her a game of croquet.' Then, as though the thought had just occurred to her, Daisy asked, 'I don't suppose you'd like to join us? After all, croquet's much more fun with three players than two.'

'I dunno. I'm pretty crap at it.'

'That doesn't matter. Alice and I would beat you hollow no matter how good you were.'

'That sounds like a challenge.'

'And you're the kind of guy who doesn't back away from a challenge, Bill.'

'How right you are,' said MacGowan. 'OK then. You're on.' Well, he thought, what the hell. Given the moderate bruising his ego had received earlier that morning, perhaps a soothing balm of uncomplicated teenage adoration was just what the doctor ordered. He consulted his watch. 'Meeting's not till twelve, which gives us a little over half an hour. I'll pop in and say hello, then come and find you.'

'We'll be out on the lawn. You know where it is, don't you?'

'I do.'

Daisy managed to contain herself until MacGowan had entered the house and closed the front door behind him before she let out a hissed 'Yes!' of triumph and jabbed the air with a clenched fist.

As for MacGowan, he shook his head while crossing the hallway and chided himself – Bill, Bill, Bill – all the way to the dining room.

Last to arrive at the Grange was Piers. This was because he had chosen a route to Bretherton that avoided motorways and dual carriageways. Call him old-fashioned (many people did) but there was nothing, really nothing, to compare with the joy of tooling along B-roads and sideroads at fifty m.p.h. in an open-topped car with the wind in your hair, listening to the throaty chortle of the Caterham's engine and the Cockney stylings of Anthony Newley, and gazing out at the passing world through turquoise-tinted spectacles. Indeed, what better pastime was there than driving a top-notch English roadster on a splendid English spring day through the English countryside to the accompaniment of sublime English pop?

Down lanes lined with blurred verges and hedgerows

Piers propelled the Caterham, past fields and forests, village cricket greens and arcanely named pubs, randomly selecting which way to turn at junctions, ignoring the destinations named on the finger-shaped signposts, losing his way and then finding it again, shuttling aimlessly through Surrey's rural loom. It was almost more by accident than design that he wound up at the gates to the Grange, and as he braked to a halt in front of them while they slowly opened he experienced a more-than-mild twinge of regret. He could happily have spent the entire day joyriding around the area.

Ah well. No one said the life of the international playboy adventurer was without its sacrifices.

Holman entered the conservatory, shielding his eyes against the retina-roasting flare of Lucretia's welding torch. The air was pungent with the smells of melting metal and ozone, and spark-chased shadows darted this way and that as Lucretia, bent-backed, face hidden behind a protective mask, ministered to her nascent creation.

The sculpture had no title as yet, and so far resembled nothing so much as the body of a whale lying on its side, flensed of its flesh, its skeleton composed of blackened, bent scaffolding, its innards old dishwashers, refrigerators and ovens. Lucretia had scoured the county for every discarded item of white goods she could find, and currently the studio was filled with so much of the stuff, haphazardly and hazardously stacked, that it looked as though a scrap-metal merchant had set up shop there.

Holman picked his way carefully to a position where he knew he would be within the limited field of vision afforded Lucretia by the mask's smoked-glass visor. He halted and waited for her to finish welding. Finally she twisted a dial on the torch, reducing its flame to a pale blue cone, and stepped back to view her work-in-progress. Noticing her husband, she raised the mask. Her eyes shone ferociously from a face covered in smoke smudges.

'All here then?' she asked.

'All present and correct,' said Holman. 'John and Piers are in the dining room. Bill's out playing croquet with the girls.'

Lucretia spun the valve on top of the gas cylinder behind her, extinguishing the flame completely, then removed the mask and divested herself of her heavy work-gloves. 'I need to go and clean up,' she said. 'Tell them I'll be with them in quarter of an hour.'

'Fine.'

'And go and rescue Bill.'

'I was just on my way.'

'Poor man.' Lucretia shook her head in mock-pity. 'Those girls'll have him for breakfast.'

'I know,' said Holman. 'Years of SAS training never prepared him for Daisy and Alice.'

10

Bretherton Grange croquet differed in many respects from the standard game, not least because Bridget St Swithin's terrestrial representation of Orion intruded into one corner of the croquet lawn. Rather than move the lawn to another location, Bridget had elected to leave it where it was and had instead rearranged the layout of the hoops to accommodate the constellation. This added a crazy-golf dimension to the proceedings. To reach the third hoop, for example, one first had to negotiate a path through the cluster of small pyramids that depicted the faint star-swarm θ Orionis, and to finish a round one had to drive one's ball, not at a striped hoop, but at the somewhat broader target of Betelgeuse, one of the four stars that made up the constellation's principal quadrant.

Moreover, a variety of complicated house rules applied, some of which Daisy and Alice outlined to MacGowan before they started, others of which they neglected to mention until the need arose during play. It was not long before MacGowan began to suspect that the Holman-Fisk girls were making up many of these rules as they went along, but he raised no objections and gamely allowed them to bash his ball around the lawn with ferocious abandon as and when they liked.

'So how do you think you'll be distributing cash today?' Alice asked, after she and Daisy had trounced MacGowan for two games running and were on course to do so a third time.

As far as the girls were aware, their mother, Rattray, MacGowan and Piers Pierson were members of a government-sponsored committee who met irregularly to decide how best to distribute Arts Council grants in the Surrey area. The cover story had been instituted at Lucretia's request. She wanted her daughters to be innocent of all things Guardian-related until they were old enough and mature enough to deal with the full implications of what their mother and her associates were involved in. MacGowan, for his part, felt that both Daisy and Alice had achieved the level of precocious sophistication where they could deal with just about anything, but Lucretia insisted that the truth was not to be revealed to them until their twenty-first birthdays, whereupon they would be entrusted with a whole lot more than just the proverbial key of the door.

'Oh, I don't know,' he said. 'We'll probably pay some kids to graffiti trains, or something.'

Alice was preparing to knock MacGowan's ball yet again to kingdom come. She was taking her time over it. MacGowan had seen gunnery officers calibrating L-16 mortars less painstakingly.

'You know, Bill,' said Daisy, 'you're the last person I'd have thought of as – what's a good way of putting this? – artistically orientated.'

'I have hidden depths,' said MacGowan, and then watched resignedly as Alice swung her mallet and sent his ball zooming across the lawn to strike the base of Rigel, which, according to house rules, meant he had to miss a turn and then start again a mallet's length from the last hoop he had gone through. 'Beneath my rough, tough exterior lurks the soul of a poet,' he added, as he trooped off after his ball.

Alice, hearing this, sniggered, but Daisy took the remark seriously. 'A lot of famous poets have been soldiers. Owen, Brooke, Sassoon ...'

'What, the shampoo bloke?'

'Not him. They wrote while they were serving in the trenches during the First World War. The proximity of death seemed to sharpen their sensitivity. Owen was killed just one week before the Armistice, you know. It was awfully tragic. And Sassoon spent time in a lunatic asylum.'

'Probably used too much of his own shampoo.'

'It's not the same Sassoon!' Daisy exclaimed indignantly, and Alice sniggered again, this time at her sister, who appeared unable to tell when she was being wound up.

MacGowan bent to retrieve his ball. 'My go, right?'

'I've got a shot in hand,' said Alice, and took aim once again. MacGowan did not think she was allowed to croquet him twice in the same turn, but said nothing. The point of the particular version of the game they were playing was not, it seemed, to win but to inflict the maximum possible humiliation on William Patrick MacGowan.

'You've been in battle, Bill,' said Daisy, ambling towards him, idly swinging her mallet, not-so-idly swinging her hips. 'Hasn't it made you more appreciative of life? More eager to grasp whatever opportunities life throws at you?'

'Nope,' he replied. His considered opinion. 'Nope, all it's done is given me a strong sense of self-preservation and a healthy dislike of looking down the barrel of an enemy's gun.' Not to mention nightmares. Nightmares from having witnessed, at first hand, the results of science untempered by any moral responsibility; from having seen the very worst that humans will do to each other in the name of Progress.

Alice's ball came trundling towards his, missed by a whisker and rolled to a standstill about a yard beyond.

'Aha!' said MacGowan. 'Now I shall have my revenge!'

'You can't,' said Alice matter-of-factly. 'You can't do me until after you've been through that hoop.'

And then Daisy, softly so that only MacGowan could hear (and even then he had to replay the sentence twice through his mind to be sure that his ears had not deceived him), said: 'You can do *me* any time.'

MacGowan fluffed his next shot completely, Alice crowed, Daisy smirked to herself, and the game dragged on, excruciatingly, for another three minutes, until Holman appeared from the house to let MacGowan know that everyone was here and the meeting was due to begin.

MacGowan thrust his mallet at Holman, saying, 'You take over, mate,' and departed from the croquet lawn with what can only be described as unseemly haste.

11

'All right,' said Rattray. 'This is what we know.'

In the drawing room next door, a grandfather clock chimed twelve. Piers set his champagne flute down on the dining table, sliding it out of easy reach so that he would not be able to take another sip, even if he were tempted to, until the meeting was over. MacGowan helped himself to one last ginger nut from the tray of refreshments provided by Holman, gobbling the biscuit swiftly down. Lucretia, face fresh-scrubbed and alert, leaned forwards, resting her elbows on the tabletop and clasping together her hands, which were as callused and coarse as any workman's. She had changed out of her overalls into a navy-blue fisherman's smock and black leggings, and her auburn hair was tied back in a thick, ropy plait. Around her right middle finger she wore a silver ring wrought in the same segmented puzzle-egg shape as Piers's medallion and MacGowan's keyring.

'At the end of the nineteenth century,' Rattray continued, 'a Russian physicist by the name of Anton Krilov, born in Moscow in 1867 and educated at the Imperial Academy of Sciences in St Petersburg, began conducting research into the nature of gravity and how gravity might be resisted or rescinded. Basically what he was trying to achieve was a means of levitating heavy objects. Wanting to take things one step further in the field of aviation after the successes of the Wright brothers and the Graf von Zeppelin, his ultimate goal was a method of propelling passenger-carrying and cargo-carrying vehicles through the air regardless of aerodynamics or weight or cubic capacity, and by a non-mechanical means.'

'In short,' said Piers, 'antigravity flight.'

'Exactly. Krilov claimed to have received his initial inspiration from a picture in a book in his father's library, an engraving of the Montgolfier brothers rising above the Paris crowds in their hot-air balloon.'

'But actually … ?' said Lucretia.

'We'll come to that in a moment,' said Rattray. 'The name Krilov, by the way, is Russian for "winged one". One hopes that this is just a coincidence, but one suspects otherwise.'

There was a smattering of mirthless laughter around the table, which Rattray acknowledged with a twitch of the corners of his mouth that fell well short of being a smile.

'Fifty years before Krilov began his experiments,' he said, 'the Scots mathematician James Clerk Maxwell had proved, mathematically, that electricity and magnetism were linked. Extrapolating from Maxwell's theories, Krilov hypothesised that there had to be a way of harnessing the force of an electromagnetic field and using it to negate the magnetic field that surrounds the earth, thus enabling a vehicle to ride the currents of terrestrial magnetism like a surfboard skimming the waves. His early attempts at achieving this met with failure, the only tangible result of his efforts being that they brought him to the attention of an outfit known as the Moscow Engineering Foundation, which decided to endorse his work and endow him with a handsome, no-strings-attached grant.'

'The Moscow Engineering Foundation being an Anarch "front",' said Lucretia.

Rattray nodded. 'This was in' – he glanced at the hard-copy of Kim's e-mail – 'early 1903. Financially backed, Krilov was able to resign from his position as a lecturer at the Academy, return to Moscow with his family, and devote himself full-time to his researches. Two years later he made his breakthrough, and set about transforming his theoretical principles into a practical, functioning reality – building an antigravity vehicle. At which point the Librans brought him to the attention of the Guardians' Russian chapter.'

'An idea out of its time,' said Lucretia. 'But where's the evidence for this?'

'Up until 1905, everything is a matter of public record, including Krilov's patent application for his design. What happened next, between 1905 and mid-1908, Kim has inferred from circumstantial evidence, and the facts bear her inferences out. History remembers Krilov, if it remembers him at all, as a crackpot, one of science's great lost causes, like Tesla, or Wilhelm Reich. However ...'

'However, between 1905 and mid-1908 Krilov did succeed in building his antigravity craft,' said Lucretia. 'Am I right?'

'He did,' Rattray confirmed.

'Tunguska,' said Piers.

'Bless you,' said MacGowan.

Piers ignored the flippancy. 'The dates tally,' he explained. 'Clearly something must have gone wrong.'

'Something did,' said Rattray, glancing briefly at the hard-copy again. 'Krilov's working prototype flew, but then crashed into the Siberian forest and was blown to smithereens.'

'Resulting in a lot of free toothpicks,' said Piers. 'But forgive me, old chap. I don't quite see how a vehicle of the kind you've described could trigger the release of huge amounts of energy simply by crashing.'

'It's not absolutely clear, but it seems that Krilov may well have discovered, inadvertently, another physical principle well ahead of its time, namely zero-point theory.'

'Refresh my memory,' said MacGowan, scratching his head in a parody of puzzlement. 'How does that one go?'

'Simply put,' said Rattray, 'zero-point theory posits the existence of huge amounts of energy latent within space at a quantum level – energy which is created by subatomic particles blinking in and out of existence, and which is immune to the laws of entropy and momentum. It's possible that, through a combination of heat, acceleration and negative mass, Krilov's craft inadvertently tapped into this sea of free energy, and an explosion of A-bomb proportions was the result.'

'Whoa, sorry, hold on there,' said MacGowan. 'A-bomb proportions? I'd assumed we were talking about a few trees getting flattened. You're telling me that a bloody great big chunk of Russia got wiped off the map, and nobody stopped to ask what the hell happened?'

'Tunguska is a remote region of Siberia, Bill, sparsely inhabited even today. News of the explosion spread slowly, and from the evidence the general assumption was that it must have been a meteor strike. To give credence to that assumption, a number of eyewitnesses – fur trappers, Tungus natives – reported seeing a fireball streak across the sky shortly before the explosion occurred. The "fireball" effect may have been the glow of air ionising around the hull of Krilov's vehicle. A meteor strike, at any rate, remains the accepted explanation for the blast.'

'Thanks, no doubt, to the efforts of Guardian misinformation specialists,' said Lucretia.

'Oh yes,' said Rattray, 'I think it would be fair to say that pretty much everyone was kept in the dark.'

Neither MacGowan nor Piers detected the slight catch in Rattray's voice as he spoke these words. Lucretia did, but had no idea what it might signify.

'All right,' said MacGowan, who had been thinking. 'Fair enough. So Krilov got incinerated and his anti-gravity knowhow died with him.'

'No,' said Rattray.

MacGowan sighed. 'How come I knew you were going to say that?'

'No,' Rattray repeated. 'Krilov had a family. A wife and a son. They emigrated to the United States in 1915, a couple of years before the Revolution. Among the possessions they took with them were Krilov's papers, including his research notes and design sketches. These are currently in the care of the Smithsonian Institution in Washington.'

'So anyone could have access to them and reproduce the results he achieved?'

'Yes and no, Lucretia. What the Smithsonian received in 1947, after the death of his son, was an edited selection of Krilov's papers. Certain documents had been removed.'

'Roswell,' said Piers.

MacGowan turned to him, frowning. 'Look, are you coming down with a cold or something? 'Cause if you are, I really don't want to catch it.'

'Bill,' said Lucretia, 'I know you like to give the impression that you're just a thick ex-squaddie, just as Piers likes to give the impression that everything's just a game to him ...'

'But it is,' Piers insisted.

'... but even you've heard of the Roswell crash.'

MacGowan shrugged and grinned. 'Yeah, but hey, I have to think about my image. I mean, without my naïve, brutish charm, where would I be?'

'Piers is correct,' said Rattray. '1947. Roswell. But let's backtrack for a moment. Professor Krilov's son, also called Anton, demonstrated an aptitude for science from an early age. In 1920, aged nineteen, he won a scholarship to Berkeley. He graduated *summa cum laude*, stayed on to complete his doctorate, then went to work for the US military. Weapons research and development. Highly classified stuff. In 1940, somewhat late in life, he married, and in 1944 his wife bore him a child. A son. The boy, with startling originality, was christened Anton. By now Dr Krilov was helping out with the Manhattan Project, albeit in an advisory capacity. Oppenheimer was known to refer to him as 'the oracle', and would phone him at all hours of the day or night to chew over problems. Krilov's energies, though, were mostly devoted to a project of his own, which was –'

'Let me guess,' interrupted MacGowan. 'Antigravity?'

'Indeed. The jet engine was just coming into production, but already the Pentagon was interested in developing the next generation of aircraft propulsion. Krilov was able to propose an antigravity drive. This time Anarch backing wasn't necessary. The US military were more than happy to offer him all the finance and facilities he could possibly want.'

'Were the Anarchs involved at all this time round?' Lucretia enquired.

'There must have been some Anarch stooges in the US Defense Department,' said Piers. 'There certainly are now.'

'Equally,' said MacGowan, 'the top brass of any military wouldn't be doing their job properly if they didn't investigate every possible new defence technology.'

'Like the Strategic Defense Initiative, you mean?' said Lucretia. 'Several billion dollars of American taxpayers' money wasted on a scheme a ten-year-old child could have told them was unworkable.'

'*Worthwhile* new defence technology,' amended MacGowan. 'Anyway, the "Star Wars" thing was just Reagan's excuse for not making cuts in the defence budget.'

'Reagan thought it would work,' said Lucretia. 'He believed he could make America invulnerable, a Superman among nations.'

'Reagan believed a lot of daft things,' said MacGowan. 'Hey, maybe the Anarchs messed with his brain. That would explain a lot. No, scratch that. Not even the Anarchs have microscopes powerful enough to find Ronald Reagan's brain.'

'I feel,' said Rattray, with immaculate self-restraint, 'that we are straying somewhat from the point.' Some levity at Guardian meetings was acceptable, but only some.

'Permit me to guess what comes next,' said Piers. 'The second Krilov got his antigravity drive up and running, but Guardian intervention brought the craft down on its test flight.'

'On the Foster Ranch near Corona, New Mexico, on July the second, 1947,' said Rattray. 'An event which has entered the realm of folklore, and thus sideways the annals of history, as the Roswell Incident, or, to the cognoscenti, simply Roswell.'

'You involved, John?' MacGowan asked.

'Cecil asked me the same question yesterday, as a matter of fact. No, I wasn't. I was aware that an action-to-suppress was taking place and that there was to be an associated invalidation, but the North America chapter dealt with it. Garrett and his Men in Black. It was, by all accounts, a textbook operation. There was no extraneous loss of life apart from the test pilot, all the vital functioning components were removed from the craft before the US Air Force reached the crash site, and those pages of Krilov senior's notes pertaining to the antigravity drive were retrieved and destroyed. Krilov junior's notes, also. In addition, certain materials were planted with the downed craft which were intended to give rise to discrediting rumours.'

'The "alien" corpses, you mean?' said Lucretia.

'Dead chimpanzees whose bodies had been shaved and mutilated so that they weren't immediately recognisable for what they were,' said Rattray. 'Also, some fragments of "futuristic" metal alloy provided by the Librans, and some pieces of balsa wood marked with "alien" inscriptions, a combination of Egyptian and Mayan hieroglyphs and Sanskrit symbols which, knowing Garrett, probably translated into something extremely uncomplimentary about Mamie Eisenhower. All of which were seen by the owner of the ranch, William Brazel, and by a number of others who arrived at the crash site before the military did. As for Krilov himself, he, of course, was quietly abducted and invalidated.'

' "Quietly abducted and invalidated",' echoed Lucretia, with a subdued, despairing shudder. 'Sometimes it's easy to forget that part of what we do is murder people.'

'It's not easy to forget,' said Rattray. 'It's convenient to.'

'It's *better* to,' added MacGowan. 'Otherwise you begin to start asking yourself questions you can't find any good answers to.'

Piers nodded, and Rattray nodded, too, but more slowly, and with a middle-distance stare.

There was silence around the table, broken by Lucretia, who urged Rattray to continue with the briefing.

Rattray consulted Kim's e-mail once again. 'The Roswell wreckage was transported by B-29 to Carswell Air Force Base at Fort Worth, Texas, and on from there to Wright-Patterson Field in Dayton, Ohio, where it was stored in the now infamous Hangar 18,' he said. 'Attempts were made to reverse-engineer the propulsion system, but without the relevant components and, more importantly, without Krilov or his notes, met with failure. The antigravity project was closed down in '48. It was after the Roswell Incident, of course, that stories began to circulate that the US military had captured a downed UFO and were examining it, trying to ascertain how its alien technology worked.'

'The stuff Garrett planted helped, of course,' said MacGowan.

'That and the fact that the military kept denying any such craft existed. It was claimed that the wreckage belonged to a Rawin atmospheric research balloon, and anyone who had seen the bodies and the various "alien" artefacts was intimidated into silence. In short, a classic cover-up. Meanwhile, Guardian misinformation specialists kept the rumour mill turning, playing up the "alien" angle in order to downplay the antigravity-technology angle. The concept of extraterrestrial entities whizzing around the world in flying saucers seeded itself in the public consciousness, and all of a sudden people were seeing UFOs everywhere. By virtue of the fact that Dr Krilov's craft was silver and lenticular, a Jungian archetype was born.'

' "From tiny acorns ..." ' said Lucretia.

'It's now become a common cover-story for Guardian actions,' said Rattray. 'For instance, that time in the early eighties when we suppressed an exotic-matter propulsion system at a NATO base in Suffolk.'

'RAF Bentwaters,' said Lucretia, remembering.

'Aliens,' said MacGowan. 'It's just so absurd, it couldn't possibly be true.'

'Only, of course, it almost *is* the truth,' said Lucretia. 'Hiding in plain sight.'

'I wonder, John,' said Piers to Rattray, 'is this ability to engineer an antigravity drive a hereditary thing, or is it simply that the second Krilov was able to manage it because he had his father's notes to go on?'

'That's something we have to establish,' said Rattray. 'It would certainly appear that the notes were a factor, because Anton Krilov junior's son did not grow up to follow in his father's and grandfather's footsteps and become a scientist. Instead, he turned to painting as a career, and became quite successful at it. This was in the sixties, when, as I'm sure Lucretia will confirm, almost everyone was becoming an artist of one kind or another.'

'What can I say? We were victims of the *Zeitgeist*.' Lucretia frowned. 'Though I'm not sure I've heard of a painter by the name of Krilov.'

'That's because he changed his name, or rather his mother did, during the fifties. More victims of the *Zeitgeist*. At the height of the Cold War, with the HUAC sessions taking place and McCarthyism rampant, anything Russian-sounding didn't go down too well in America. Hence Anton Krilov became Antony Creel.'

'Oh, him,' said Lucretia, with a hand-flap of recognition. 'I met him once. The Tate mounted an exhibition of his work. Him and a few of his contemporaries. Somebody hoping to be credited with identifying a brand-new art movement dubbed them the New Wave of American Surrealists, but it didn't catch on. 1974, I think this was. I remember Creel as a tall, thin, broad-shouldered man. Long hair, long beard, wearing a lot of denim. Quite handsome, after a fashion, but completely impossible to have a conversation with. It was all "man" this and "man" that. Everything was "beautiful" and "a trip". He turned out some quite good stuff, though. Dali-esque desertscapes. Cactus plants writhing like soldiers on barbed wire. Mescaline skies. Very much of its period.'

'Sounds modern enough to me,' remarked Piers.

'Piers,' said MacGowan, 'to you, punk rock is modern.'

Piers looked over his spectacles at MacGowan. 'What on earth is punk rock?'

MacGowan sighed. He did not think he was ever going to fathom Piers Pearson.

'Creel's name still crops up occasionally in the pages of magazines like the New York *Review of Art*,' said Lucretia. 'Usually prefaced by "reminiscent of the style of …". I can't remember when I last read about an actual exhibition of his work. I'd have to look it up. It would have to be at least three years ago.'

'Creel has since become something of a recluse,' said Rattray. 'The only current mailing address Kim has been able to unearth for him is a gallery in Santa Fe, which he owns.'

'If this Creel bloke's been a bit quiet on the painting front for a while,' said MacGowan, 'then he could secretly be working on an antigravity drive, too.'

'He could, or he could simply have bucked the family trend,' said Rattray. 'That is also something we'll have to establish. Now, next: has anyone here heard of Nowhere?'

Piers and Lucretia shrugged. MacGowan gave a comical frown. The question sounded absurd.

Rattray handed each Guardian a sheet of paper on which was printed a grainy image of a small desert town, photographed from the air. Small houses clustered around two streets that joined in a T-junction. The town was surrounded by wilderness.

'Kim pulled this image from the files at INSCOM, the US Army's Intelligence and Security Command base at Fort Meade, Maryland,' Rattray said. 'It's of Nowhere, a tiny, no-account town way out in the Nevada desert, home to just over a hundred men and women, all of them in their sixties and seventies, all of them subsisting on state pensions. That is, if you believe Nevada State Department records. If, however, you believe rumours that have persisted since Nowhere's incorporation in the late eighties, beneath the town lies a high-level-clearance subterranean research facility whose existence is unknown to the Senate, the House of Congress and the House of Representatives, in fact to everyone except a few people in the uppermost echelons of the Pentagon and the National Security Council.'

'And Kim believes that antigravity experiments are being carried out there?' asked Lucretia.

'She doesn't know. But it's possible Nowhere may have some connection with this man.'

He held up another screen-grabbed black and white image, this one of a young man with a sheepish grin, a floppy-fringed early-eighties haircut and a chin slung in a hammock of fat.

'This is the driver's-licence photograph of someone by the name of Tony Byrne.'

'Who he?' said MacGowan.

'Byrne was born in 1964 to a single mother called Mary, who died in 1988 of multiple sclerosis. He was a science prodigy at school, and won a scholarship at the age of eighteen to read theoretical physics at Cal Tech, from where he graduated with top honours. He then, in 1985, went to work at the Stanford Research Institute at Menlo Park, which receives approximately seventy million dollars in funding per year in the form of government contracts, many of them for highly classified projects. Along with an engineering colleague, Robyn Hansen, Byrne left SRI a couple of years ago. Both are believed to have been headhunted by a major aerospace corporation, but there's no record of their names on the payroll of any such company. At SRI the two of them had teamed up to carry out research into anti-mass fields, or AMF. Which is another way of saying antigravity.'

'Ah,' said Piers softly.

'A visual clue in Cecil's vision would appear to be directing our attention to Byrne and indicating some kind of connection between him and both Krilovs and Creel. Some kind of genetic link.'

'How do you get that?' said MacGowan.

'A pair of lines, neatly plaited around each other and coloured crimson.' Rattray held up his notebook, open at the sketch he had made from Cecil's ketchup illustration. 'Remind anyone of anything?'

'A DNA helix,' said Lucretia instantly.

'And the colour crimson,' said Piers, 'is highly suggestive of blood.'

'And therefore blood-relation,' said Rattray, lowering the notebook.

'In other words,' said Lucretia, 'this affinity for, and aptitude in, the field of antigravity is an hereditary characteristic.'

'To be precise,' said Rattray, 'engrammatic programming. The insertion of latent and inheritable knowledge into the human brain. We know that the Anarchs are capable of it, and we can make an educated guess as to how they achieved it with the first Anton Krilov.'

'The book you mentioned earlier,' said Lucretia. 'The one with the engraving of the Montgolfier balloon.'

Rattray gave a confirming nod. 'Kim was able to access a translation of Krilov's notes, and in them he mentions the engraving several times. He says how, as a small boy, he was given the book as a gift from a friend of his father. His father, incidentally, was an architect, one of the few professions that demand a balanced synthesis of artistic and scientific abilities. The name of this friend of his father isn't mentioned, but I think we can safely assume he was an Anarch agent. Krilov says that from the first moment he laid eyes on the Montgolfier picture, he was enraptured. The engraving is something of a repeated refrain in the notes. It's as though he can't shift the image from his head no matter how hard he tries.'

'And the engram was contained in the page itself,' said

114

Lucretia. 'The paper had been impregnated with a nanotechnological transmission medium.'

'He literally absorbed the knowledge,' said Piers. 'Either through his fingertips or by inhalation.'

'Sorry to come over like a doubting Thomas, but do we know this for sure?' said MacGowan. 'I mean, yes, the Anarchs *and* the Librans are capable of pretty much anything. You yourself, John, are living proof of that. But knowledge you can inhale?' He shook his head. 'I dunno.'

'Whether our suppositions are correct or not, Bill,' said Rattray, 'it would seem on the strength of the available evidence that Krilov came by his design for an antigravity drive by an artificial method.'

'How the engram came to be inserted into the first Krilov's brain isn't really relevant, anyway,' said Lucretia. 'What's important is that the packet of contra-temporal knowledge has since been passed on to Krilov's descendants via his DNA.'

'Quite,' said Rattray. 'It was assumed by Garrett that the second Anton Krilov was successful because he had his father's notes to go on, and that assumption was reinforced when *his* son, Creel, pursued an altogether different profession. But what if the notes were a red herring? What if the second Anton Krilov hadn't needed them? What if he hadn't even been able to *use* them? They were written in Russian, don't forget, and Krilov junior left Russia with his mother when he was ten years old. He would have been able to read and write the language with reasonable facility, but English would have become his first language not long after he reached the States. Not only that, but the notes would have contained a great deal of jargon and complex terminology which a ten-year-old's knowledge of Russian would be inadequate to cope with. After a few years in America, he would probably have forgotten half the Russian he ever knew, anyway.'

'In Creel's case, then,' said Piers, 'the antigravity trait, as it were, is recessive.'

'That, as I said, remains to be established,' replied Rattray.

'All right,' said MacGowan. He was growing impatient now, and eager to be getting on with things, to formulate a plan of action. 'So our mission parameters would seem to be pretty clear. Some of us are to go and investigate Creel, see if he's up to any antigravity naughtiness. The rest should find out what they can about Nowhere and, if this Byrne fellow's up to no good there, initiate an action-to-suppress.'

'That would appear to be what the Librans want,' said Rattray.

'Since I've met Creel before and we're both in the same line of work,' said Lucretia, 'it would seem sensible if I was the one to approach him.'

'You have a deadline, though, don't you?' said Rattray.

'They'll give me an extension. If they want their Fisk badly enough, they'll be prepared to wait for it.' With a hint of self-mockery, Lucretia added, 'You can't rush genius.'

'Very well,' said Rattray. 'Then I propose that you and Piers travel to New Mexico and sound out Creel.'

'Meanwhile you and I head for Nevada,' said Mac-Gowan.

Rattray nodded. 'Any questions?'

Silence around the table.

'Then,' said Rattray, 'each of us knows what he or she should be doing. I suggest we get started.'

12

Originally, the entrance to the complex of cellars beneath Bretherton Grange had been of the common-or-garden false-bookcase variety, accessible by tweaking a certain volume of Gibbon's *Decline and Fall of the Roman Empire*. Lucretia had refashioned it to her own taste.

Now, standing in the hallway in front of *Daedalian*, she turned to Rattray beside her. 'Shall you do the honours or shall I?'

'If you don't mind,' replied Rattray, with an inviting gesture. 'I'd prefer not to have to bleed again so soon.'

Lucretia extended her right hand towards the bas-relief, clenching it into a fist so that the egg portion of her ring was prominent. She inserted the egg into a small, roughly cog-shaped hollow. Segments of the egg shot outwards, slotting snugly into the openings. A perfect fit. The moving parts of the frieze froze, and a ker-chink of unlocking was followed by a pneumatic exhalation of unsealing, as the rough outline of a door appeared amid the sculpture's contours. The door sank inwards, then swung to one side, exposing an aperture like the mouth of a cave, large enough to admit one person at a time. Beyond the doorway automatic lights came on, revealing a set of smooth-worn stone steps that descended into darkness.

Lucretia passed through the doorway, and Rattray followed, carrying the whip and the electric-flame knife, still bundled up in his torn, blood-stained overcoat. After the meeting had adjourned, he had gone to his car to fetch the two weapons, while Piers had repaired to the Grange's library in order to cogitate, fulminate and ruminate (and also to polish off the remainder of the bottle of champagne) and MacGowan had headed off to Holman's study, where he was currently on the telephone, booking flights and making contact with a representative of the Guardians' North America chapter.

Daedalian indeed, the cellars beneath the Grange mazed for miles underground, chamber leading to chamber like an Egyptian tomb. Lucretia had explored them extensively, but there were still far-off corners where she had yet to venture, sub-levels she knew must exist but had so far had no cause to investigate. Sometimes it seemed to her that no matter how diligently she mapped out the cellars and their contents, there would always, somewhere, be a fresh zone of *terra incognita*, more treasures to be discovered. She likened the cellars to an inquisitive mind, constantly growing and expanding to absorb new knowledge.

And knowledge *was* what they contained, in a sense. In every chamber, on shelves and in alcoves, specimens of contratemporal technology were stockpiled. Devices that past Guardians had suppressed. Inventions deemed by the Librans to be inappropriate to their time. Things that were not meant to have been or had yet to come. Weaponry such as muskets that fired with an accuracy unheard of, plastic explosive that antedated dynamite by several decades, and swords and daggers whose blades were composed of 'intelligent' metal. Gadgets such as pre-Edisonian recording instruments, headsets that gave a person batlike powers of sonar echolocation in the dark, and stealth boots that employed an inverse-feedback system pressure-triggered by a footfall so as to enable the wearer to walk in perfect silence. All manner of paraphernalia could be found down here, packed, racked and stacked. A hardware history of the past two and a half centuries, stowed away in subterranean secrecy.

And just like the labyrinth that Daedalus devised for King Minos of Crete, this one, too, had its Minotaur.

The two Guardians had not gone far down the stone steps when a loud yowling reached their ears, echoing through the cellars' vaulted spaces. The yowls were drawn out and guttural, each lasting several seconds and starting as a low, bassy wail that rose in a throbbing, shrieking crescendo and tailed away again, with the next yowl following on almost immediately. The sound resembled a cross between a horny tomcat and a foghorn.

'The Domestic's restless,' Rattray observed.

'She gets like this after a feed,' replied Lucretia. 'Greedy for more.' She raised her voice. 'Go to sleep!'

The Domestic issued a whine of protest, and then it could be heard huffing and snuffling grumpily off into the depths of the cellars.

Rattray and Lucretia continued their journey. Lights came on ahead of them; lights switched off behind. Soon they reached the chamber where Lucretia stored close-combat weaponry. Lucretia took the whip and knife off Rattray, found places for them on the shelves, and made a note of their location in a digital personal organiser.

They walked on for another minute in silence, until Rattray finally said, 'Go on then, Lucretia. I know you're dying to ask me something. Get it off your chest.'

'I rather think it's *you* who has something to get off his chest.'

'What makes you say that?'

'Well, for one thing, you seemed a little ... distracted during the meeting just now.'

'Did I? I suppose I'm not up to one hundred per cent peak operating efficiency after being attacked yesterday. I was injured quite badly.'

'If that's all it is ...'

'That's all, Lucretia.'

'You know that if something was bothering you, you could talk to me about it?'

'I know.'

'I'm not prying, John. You've got that harassed,

defensive look on your face, like I *am* prying, but I'm not. All I am is concerned. You've been at this longer than any of us. You, of all of us, are the one who must have faith.'

'Faith?'

'Well, that's what it's about, isn't it? Being a Guardian? Faith. Believing that the Librans are right. Believing that they know what's best for mankind. We just have to trust that it's all for the greater good, don't we? We just have to hope that we've nailed our colours to the right mast.'

'Whom are you trying to convince, Lucretia?' said Rattray. His tone was bitter but not unkind. 'Me? You?'

'I'm not trying to convince anyone, John. I'm just saying that what we do as Guardians isn't easy to justify all the time, and if you think about it too hard, you may find yourself starting to have doubts, starting to ask yourself the kind of questions to which there are no good answers. Just as Gayle Kantowsky did.'

The defection of Gayle Kantowsky to the Anarch cause two years ago had resulted in a catastrophic episode in Oregon, a betrayal and massacre from which the Guardians' North America chapter had yet to recover fully. It was not a pleasant topic of discussion among Guardians, and therefore there was a forgivable edge of testiness in Rattray's voice as he said, 'Gayle always had inner demons, Lucretia. She was an unsuitable candidate for recruitment from the start.'

'All right. Yes. I shouldn't have mentioned her. The subject is officially dropped. But John ...' Lucretia laid a hand on Rattray's arm. 'Something's going on inside that wonderful, wise, complicated brain of yours, and I don't know what it is, but whatever it is, don't let it prey on you. Rise above it, rationalise it into insignificance, do whatever you have to, but don't give in. We need you. We need your conviction.'

Rattray frowned for a moment – a long moment – then said, 'Thank you for your concern.'

Lucretia realised that she had got out of him all she

was going to. Had they been anything less than firm friends, she might have pressed him further.

As it was, just then they arrived at the chamber where the covert equipment was kept – gadgets disguised to look like ordinary toiletry items, impervious to detection by the X-ray machines at airport customs – and both of them immediately settled down to the business of selecting what might be needed for the mission ahead, discussing and evaluating the merits and usefulness of various devices with impassive, professional detachment. Two people with a job to do. The previous conversation terminated, but not forgotten.

13

It was a château, but it was no longer grand. It perched on the top of a high sandstone cliff overlooking a broad, placid reach of the Loire, and from all its windows, in all directions, there were views of undulating fairytale forest – views that had enchanted guests in the past but did so no more, for guests seldom came to stay at the château now. Instead the château housed, amid its crumbling turrets, its deserted bedrooms, its flaking giltwork and its patches of exposed lath and plaster, just one man. A single, solitary, driven man. Gérard de Sade.

He claimed direct descendancy from the infamous marquis who had borne the same surname, and it was not a claim many people would have disputed. Equally, it was not a claim many people would have made themselves. The true facts of the marquis's life notwithstanding, the name de Sade was, and forever would be, inextricably associated with debauchery and depravity, and nothing *this* de Sade could say or do would alter that. He could, of course, have adopted another identity, but obstinacy and a perverse pride prevented him.

He lived alone, surrounded by splendid decay and decaying splendour, because he chose to. Contact with the outside world was limited to phone, fax and computer, and to brief conversations with Madame Laforgue, his housekeeper, who drove up to the château twice a week in her sputtering 2CV, its back seat laden with groceries, and restocked her employer's larder and did her best to keep clean the few rooms he frequented. She also brought him up to date on news he could not get from the television, the Internet or Minitel – local politics mainly, local events, local scandals – and avoided him whenever he was in one of his dark moods. She had learned to divine his frame of mind from his response to the cheery '*Bonjour*' she sang out as she let herself in through the huge oak front door. A moderately informal '*Ça va, Madame Laforgue?*' meant he was prepared to be communicative. Anything else – a grunt, say, or simply silence – meant she was to work around him as if he were not there. And though he did not reward her amazingly well for her services, as part of her salary she was allowed, once a month, to choose for herself and Monsieur Laforgue a bottle of wine from the château's plentifully stocked cellars, and the wine was invariably of an excellent provenance and vintage.

Other than Madame Laforgue, de Sade had no company but his cats. Of these he had at least a hundred, probably closer to a hundred and fifty, for they were breeding prolifically. The cats roamed the château as though they, not de Sade, owned it and he were merely a sitting tenant whom they could not dislodge. A few of them were in the habit of following him around, not as a display of affection but simply so that they could keep an eye on what he was up to. The majority ignored him altogether and went about their business as if he was not there. There were very few rats or mice in de Sade's château, but there was a distinct background odour of feline urine which, for all Madame Laforgue's efforts with bleach and scrubbing brush, could not be lifted. The smell got into the housekeeper's clothing and lingered there, prompting Monsieur Laforgue to joke to friends that his wife came home twice a week from the 'chât-eau' reeking of *eau de chat*.

The cats were judgemental, contrary and malodorous, yet de Sade kept them around because they were almost all of them descendants of Mimi and Édouard, the pair given him over a decade ago by his soulmate, Jean-

Claude. (Those that were not of this lineage were strays that had found their way to the château, no doubt by following their noses, and had been assimilated into the cat community.) The cats' presence was Jean-Claude's legacy, a growing memorial to the love of de Sade's life, now lost. De Sade's romantic dream for his own death was for his corpse, after a sudden, painless demise, to lie undiscovered for at least a week, during which time the cats would gnaw away his flesh and clean every scrap of edible organic matter from his bones. What gorgeous symbolism there would be in that! For his mortal remains to be dispersed by an army of feline scavengers, the gift of his former lover – what poetry!

De Sade was a tall, stooped man with lugubrious eyes and a nose which looked as though a large blob of pink putty had attached itself to his face seemingly by accident. He cut his charcoal-coloured hair short, and his cheeks and chin were more often than not covered in a ragged growth of stubble. Most of the time he went around in slippers and a quilted burgundy-red dressing gown with velvet lapels, its tails and the tassels of its untied gold-braid cord swishing behind him as he strode along corridors hung with gloomy portraits and land-scapes. For at least an hour each day, however, he was to be found in a tracksuit and trainers, jogging around his home to stay in trim. He followed routes through room after room, up and down winding staircases, and around and around the perimeter of the floor of the great ballroom where Marie Antoinette herself was said to have once danced and where, legend had it, her hoop-skirted, extravagantly wigged ghost could be glimpsed waltzing in the moonlight every 15 October, the eve of the anniversary of her execution. All over the castle de Sade would go, his trainers kicking up puffs of dust and his panting breaths and the squeak of his rubber-soled footfalls echoing through the cobwebbed, neglected spaces and high up among the rough-hewn rafters; and everywhere he went cats would scatter out of his way, escaping to high ground – shelves, the backs of chairs, windowsills – and crouching there, glaring resentfully at him. Sometimes he would venture outside on to the terrace that ran along the clifftop overlooking the river, and sometimes he would trot down the driveway to the main gates and back up again, but he seldom left the château for long, as though scared that, bereft of any human occupant, the building might finally succumb to a sense of futility and collapse.

He kept a telephone in every room, and carried a cordless handset on his person at all times, its base located in the dining hall where resided also the other pieces of communications equipment that put him in touch with the rest of the world. He was, at this moment, jogging, and had just completed a twentieth lap of the ballroom, when the handset, which was tucked into the waistband of his tracksuit bottoms, let out a shrill bleat. A split-second later every other telephone in the château followed suit, filling the tottering, aged edifice with a stunningly loud hallelujah-chorus of beeps and rings and chirps and chimes.

De Sade came to a halt and pulled out the handset. It bleated again, and again the other phones responded with a massed chorus of sound that made the château throb like an old man in the grip of a seizure.

De Sade silenced the cacophony with the stab of a button.

'*Allô?*'

'Gérard, it's me – Xavier.'

Xavier was using a payphone at a street café. De Sade heard traffic noise in the background, and the chatter of conversation and the clink of cutlery and crockery. Someone was ordering moules marinières. Was it lunch-time already? In his solitude, de Sade often lost track of the passing hours.

'Tell me you got it.'

'I got ... some of it.'

'How much is "some"?'

'Bits and pieces. Fragments. I have decrypted it and put everything together in, I think, the correct order.'

'And you are about to send it over to me?'

'Perhaps. First, we must discuss my fee.'

De Sade ran a thumb along the line of his eyebrows and flicked away the accumulated sweat from its tip. Money. Always with these people it was money. Not the cause. Not the mission. Cash. 'Yes. Your fee.'

'Plus expenses, of course. The cost of logging-on time at the library, where I have been all morning, deciphering the data. And a new computer.'

'A new computer?'

'She destroyed my hard drive.'

'Wiped it, you mean.'

'No, destroyed.'

'That is not possible.'

'For her it is.'

De Sade knew that Xavier was lying. The kid fancied an upgrade, that was all, and thought de Sade was the man to provide it. 'Twenty thousand francs. That is all I can lay my hands on at this moment.'

'Thirty.'

De Sade wanted to haggle, but he was too excited, and though he was trying hard to disguise the fact, it must have been obvious to Xavier. 'Twenty is the best I can do for now. I will get you the other ten as soon as I can.'

'Maybe there are others who would pay more for this information,' said Xavier.

De Sade mentally cursed the hacker: *salaud*! 'It's worth nothing to anyone else,' he said.

'But how do I know that?'

'You know because I am telling you. And if what you have obtained is what I am looking for, then of course there will be more work for you.'

'Work for which I will not be fairly paid.'

Naturally, because he lived in a castle, it was assumed – by those who had not seen the condition of the building – that de Sade was richer than he really was. Even more naturally, it was assumed that he was ripe for fleecing. But in spite of the home, the heirlooms and the modest share portfolio he had inherited from his parents, de Sade had little in the way of income. The wine in the cellars was his principal (and literal) liquid asset, and in order to meet Xavier's fee he would have to sell off some bottles. A half-crate of the '61 Latour, probably. It pained him to do so, but what alternative did he have?

He succeeded in keeping the irritation out of his voice as he said, 'You will be paid everything you are owed.'

There was nothing but the sounds of street and café while Xavier weighed up the pros and cons: should he push de Sade further, or should he accept what he was being offered? De Sade knew that Xavier, who came from a poor background and lived in one of those godforsaken housing developments on the Parisian outskirts, was enjoying making the rich man squirm. The supposedly rich man.

'*D'accord*,' said Xavier, finally. 'Twenty is acceptable. As a downpayment. But I will not transmit the data until after the funds have been transferred to my account.'

These damned hackers – a bunch of mummy's boys who acted as though they were Hollywood tough guys. De Sade reined in his irritation. 'I will do that immediately. Check with you bank in an hour.'

'Good. Gérard, I must go. No more units on my *télécarte*.'

'Xavier? Before you hang up.'

'Yes?'

'Is it what I want? Is it going to be useful?' How he hated to ask these questions. How he hated to have to abase himself before this employee, this boy, this nobody.

'I think it is what you have been seeking.'

'A first move, then. An opening gambit.'

'Yes,' said Xavier.

'Very good. *Vive la Société Pour la Vérité*, then.'

Xavier repeated the slogan in an embarrassed mumble – '*Vive la Société Pour la Vérité*' – and then the line was disconnected.

De Sade lowered the handset from his ear and clasped it to his chest.

So. Ten years of preparation were at an end. That was

how long it had been since the walking holiday in the Balkans, the walking holiday that had cost him Jean-Claude and gained him a mission, a sense of purpose that had until then been lacking in his life. A decade of planning and establishing and researching and groundwork-laying was at last about to see its fruition.

De Sade smiled.

It was a gloomy smile, but it was the best he could manage, and the fact that he was smiling at all was, in itself, cause for celebration. Savagely joyful celebration.

It had begun.

PART 2

14

A tentative knock at the door. 'Byrne?'

Though Hansen and Byrne had been working closely together for over a decade, it was still surnames-only between them. Hansen preferred it that way.

'Come on in. The door's not locked.' Returning his attention to the small mirror above the basin, Byrne brought up the disposable razor to cut another swath through the shaving foam that covered the lower half of his face.

Hansen entered nervously. Seeing Byrne standing at the basin, clad only in jockey shorts, with his ginger-furred belly bulging out over the waistband, she searched the cramped, windowless sleeping quarters urgently for something else to look at. The stack of unread paperbacks. The portable TV set. The framed photograph of Byrne's wife and son. The pictures his son had drawn for him, stuck up on the rough concrete walls (even if Byrne had not been in the habit of bragging about Ant's artistic ability, Hansen could tell the pictures were incredibly sophisticated for a nine-year-old). Finally she elected the rumpled, unmade bed as a suitable object for scrutiny, and stood there, staring at it and wringing her hands into pretzels.

'Sleep OK?' said Byrne.

'Yes. Thanks.'

He glanced at her. 'That surprises me. From the look of you, I'd have guessed you napped at your desk for a couple of hours and worked the rest of the night through.'

'I'm not completely happy about the cabin shielding.'

'You built it, it's going to work fine,' he reassured her. 'But that's not why you came to see me.'

'Um, no, it's not. Colonel Clayton's here. He wants a word with you.'

'Damn!'

Hansen flinched. 'I'm sorry,' she said. 'I didn't want to disturb you before breakfast, but he just turned up out of the blue, and he was very insistent, said he wanted to see you right away.'

'No, no, it's not that,' Byrne said calmly, raising his chin to the mirror. A drop of blood was welling up where he had just shaved beneath his lower lip. 'Isn't it annoying how you always nick yourself just before an important meeting?'

As Byrne entered Lab 1, he found Colonel Willard T. Clayton bending over Hansen's terminal, peering intently at the screen, his hands clasped behind his back and his bushy eyebrows furrowed. He was puzzling over the geometric configuration that was bouncing gracefully around the confines of the screen, shifting, furling, tangling, changing colour. Turning to Byrne, the colonel jerked his head in the direction of the computer. 'Looks impressive, Tony. What the heck's it for?'

Byrne was sorely tempted to give a bogus answer, something along the lines of: *Well, Colonel, it's a two-dimensional representation of an electromagnetic tensor field wave dynamic*. Then he could have the pleasure of watching Clayton squirm in his scientific ignorance. Instead, he settled for the truth: 'It's a screen-saver, sir.'

It was no less satisfying to see Colonel Clayton struggle to hide his embarrassment.

'Ah,' the colonel said, coughing and straightening up. 'Well, mine's a military brain. Not really geared for this computer stuff. Not like you boffins.'

In order to enter Nowhere incognito the colonel was

out of uniform, but plaid golf slacks and a Ralph Lauren polo shirt did not make him appear any more approachable. Rather, because casual clothes sat so uncomfortably on so martial and muscular a man, they made him look unpredictable, even dangerous.

Byrne decided that the best defence was offence. 'So, to what do we owe the pleasure of this unexpected visit?'

'I think that should be obvious, Tony.'

'Not necessarily, sir. Not to a boffin.'

'You're behind schedule,' said the colonel, oblivious to the sour emphasis Byrne had laid on the word 'boffin'. 'Way behind.'

'Sir,' Byrne replied, 'as I believe I explained the last time we discussed this, you can't rush this kind of a project. We're dealing with a branch of physics that's, at best, unproven. Apart from Searle's experiments with scalar electrostatic potential and Townsend Brown's research into high-capacitance dielectrics, almost no one –'

'Please.' Colonel Clayton held up a hand. 'No long words. They give me a headache.'

'All I'm saying, sir, is that the majority of defence contract R and D work has the advantage of being an offshoot of an already extant, well-investigated body of knowledge. Standing on the shoulders of giants, as the saying goes. We don't have that advantage. Everyone who's worked in this particular field, from Krilov onwards, has been a maverick, a dabbler. Their results have been inconsistent, inconclusive and often contradictory. The waters we're sailing in are not exactly uncharted, it's just that you can't trust the maps.'

'Excuses,' snapped the colonel. 'Damned feeble ones at that.'

Byrne found his gaze drawn to the marvellous flatness of the colonel's regulation Marine buzz-cut. The top of the man's hair was trimmed as square as any brush, and Byrne imagined the colonel's barber wielding a spirit level alongside a pair of scissors.

'We've pumped hundreds of millions of taxpayers'

dollars into this facility, Tony,' the colonel went on. 'Keeping that level of funding hidden from Congress is hard enough.'

'Yeah, I know, it's a hell of a lot of fifty-cent paper-clips.'

'Harder still is justifying the expenditure to ourselves when so far all we've had from you in return are vague promises and precious few results. My superiors are losing patience with me, and I'm losing patience with *you.* I'm this close' – Clayton held up a thumb and forefinger half an inch apart – 'to shutting Nowhere down. *This* close.'

Byrne adopted a suitably contrite air. 'I understand, sir, and I appreciate your continuing faith in the project.'

'Good. I hope you also appreciate that I've been putting my ass on the line for you, Tony. General Winter, in particular, is keen to see results. You've never met General Winter.'

'I've heard of him. He has a ... fearsome reputation.'

'Take it from me, the reality is ten times worse. I've had General Winter breathing down my neck for nearly a month now. I had him on the phone last night. He tore me a new hole.' Clayton's expression became pained, almost pitiful to behold. 'I *have* to have something to show him, Tony.'

'Your faith in me will be rewarded soon, sir.'

'But how soon, Tony? How soon?'

Byrne felt he had jerked the colonel's chain enough. 'How about this weekend, sir?'

Colonel Clayton blinked slowly. 'She's ready?'

'As good as.'

'Don't B.S. me, Tony,' said the colonel in a low voice. 'Either she's ready or she isn't.'

'She's ready.'

'Swear to God?'

As a lapsed Catholic, Byrne had no difficulty with the oath. 'Swear to God.'

'When?' The colonel was trying his best not to appear excited.

'Saturday, she'll be given her test-flight,' said Byrne. 'Sunday, you bring along the top brass and we'll put on a display.'

'Excellent news, Tony, excellent news!' Clayton rubbed his hands together and clapped Byrne on the back.

But if you want to know the truth, Colonel, thought Byrne, by Sunday the top brass won't need to see a display. By Sunday they'll already know what she can do. *Everything* she can do.

15

Six hours after this conversation took place, and approximately three thousand miles east of Nowhere, an American Airlines jumbo touched down at JFK Airport, New York. Among the passengers disembarking were a middle-aged woman and a young man just too old to be her son. They had travelled up at the front of the plane in club class, and the young man had spent the entire journey coaxing the cabin staff into keeping him plied with complimentary champagne. Although he had insisted on addressing them, in a louche, effete drawl, as 'my dear' and 'ducks', the flight attendants – male and female alike – had none the less found him oddly charming, not least because he was so oddly dressed: purple suit, silk shirt with frilly collar and cuffs, winklepicker boots, spectacles with hexagonal, turquoise-tinted lenses. You could not really dislike someone who looked and obviously felt as though he belonged to a bygone era. They had, therefore, good-naturedly kept his glass topped up.

As for the middle-aged woman, who had occupied the seat next to this man, she had opened an Anita Brookner while the plane was taxiing towards take-off, had read the book straight through, had begun a Margaret Atwood while over the Arctic Circle, and, finishing that, had straight away embarked on an Anne Tyler, which she had got halfway through by the time the plane was making its final approach and descent to JFK. Serially

136

devouring literature was the only cure she knew of for an almost pathological fear of flying.

She polished off the Anne Tyler during the two-hour connecting flight from New York to Albuquerque, while the young man polished off a further, individual-serving bottle of champagne.

Having retrieved their luggage from the carousel at Albuquerque, the woman and the young man approached the desk of a car-rental agency, where they were served by a clerk whose zeal for his job was as tireless as that of a Labrador for fetching sticks. The clerk was palpably distressed that he could not accommodate the young man's request for a 1974 Ford Torino in chilli pepper red with a white flash along each side. Would a one-year-old Ford *Taurus* do instead? He perked up when the woman, having cast a mildly exasperated glance at her companion, replied that a Ford Taurus would be fine, and by the time the paperwork had been filled out and the keys handed over, the clerk was firing on all enthusiasm cylinders once again. He wished the two tourists a wonderful vacation and many, many hours of happy motoring.

The young man and the woman found the car out on the rental agency's parking lot. The New Mexico heat was fierce, a scorching exhalation direct from the lungs of the sun. As he climbed into the passenger seat, the young man exchanged his hexagonal spectacles for a pair of mirror-shades with small, round lenses. The woman followed suit with a pair of fly's-eye sunglasses, and took her position behind the wheel.

'Audrey Hepburn,' said the young man to his companion, approvingly. 'Or Jackie Kennedy.'

'God bless you, Piers, I think that's the most flattering thing anyone's ever said to me,' said Lucretia. 'Just don't, whatever you do, add Grace Kelly to that list.'

'As a matter of fact I was just about to. What's wrong with likening a woman in sunglasses at the wheel of a car to Grace Kelly?'

'If you don't know, Piers,' said Lucretia, firing up the Ford's engine, '*I'm* not going to tell you.'

Forty-five minutes later, two Englishmen stepped off a plane at McCarran International airport, Las Vegas.

On their boarding cards, when asked to state the purpose of their visit, both had ticked the box marked PLEASURE, for what other reason was there to travel to the gambling capital of the world? They passed unhindered through customs and entered the arrivals lounge as part of a jabbering influx of brightly dressed tourists and holidaymakers, people who had been drawn to the city in the hope of at least winning back the price of the trip and accommodation, but who really, secretly, were dreaming of the Big Score. Quitting Money. Easy Street.

The Englishmen were met by a handsome black Chicagoan.

'John,' said the Chicagoan to Rattray, shaking him by the hand and clapping him on the shoulder. 'And Bill.' He did the same with MacGowan.

MacGowan grinned. 'Arnold X. It's been a while.'

The Chicagoan had gone by many names during his lifetime, but Arnold X, the *nom de guerre* he had adopted upon joining the Guardians, was the only one by which Rattray and MacGowan knew him. The X did not stand for anything, not even a show of spiritual solidarity with the civil rights leader who had also used the letter as a surname. Rather, it represented anonymity, a disconnection from the man Arnold used to be, a symbolic crossing-out of deeds he had done under other aliases – deeds of which he was none too proud.

He was short and lithe, with a sprinkling of coffee-ground pockmarks across his cheeks and a smattering of grey in his close-cropped hair. He dressed expensively and, apart from a predilection for ostentatious gold jewellery, tastefully. A cornflower-blue Van Heusen shirt, opened to the third button to allow a modest escape of chest hair, was complemented by tasselled loafers and a pair of fawn chinos whose legs were sharply creased and whose seat strained taut over his steatopygous backside. His voice, for so small a man, was surprisingly deep. His accent was pure southside Chicago: throaty and syllable-stabbing.

'Is that all you brought?' he asked, indicating the medium-sized leather holdalls Rattray and MacGowan were carrying.

'Yeah, well,' said MacGowan, 'the Armalites wouldn't fit in the overhead compartments so we had to leave them at Heathrow.'

Arnold chuckled at that, but Rattray seemed in no mood for pleasantries. 'You've booked us into a hotel?'

'Sure. Nothing fancy, but there's a pool and air-conditioning. I know you Brits think that sorta thing's a luxury, but over here it pretty much comes as standard.'

MacGowan was not about to stand back and allow a crack like that to pass unchallenged. 'And I suppose over here a cocky attitude comes as standard, too.'

'Least in this country we got something to be cocky about,' replied Arnold, 'unlike in some pissant nations I could mention that used to have an empire but don't even got that any more.'

MacGowan was all set to deliver a suitably patronising anti-colonial retort, but Rattray interrupted. 'Let's save the banter for later, shall we?' He started off in the direction of the exit.

Arnold and MacGowan shrugged at one another and trudged off after him, unconsciously falling into step.

'So tell me,' Arnold asked MacGowan, 'how is your shit?'

'My shit,' said MacGowan, 'is the same colour and consistency it's always been, but that's not what you wanted to know.'

'It isn't, and I'm sorry I asked now.'

'How about you? How's the recruiting going?'

'Slow,' came the grave reply. 'Real damn slow. There's a shortage of decent material, you know what I'm saying? I don't think we're going to have the chapter fully

139

back online for another six months at least. That Judas bitch screwed us pretty bad.'

'That Judas bitch' was a reference to none other than Gayle Kantowsky. Arnold had been part of the team of American Guardians that had responded to Kantowsky's summons and travelled to Oregon to carry out a raid on the mountain-ranch headquarters of the Children of Oblivion, a doomsday sect which Kantowsky claimed had got hold of a laser-powered seismic weapon and were planning to use it on the San Andreas fault in order to trigger an apocalyptic earthquake that would dunk the whole of the Western Seaboard into the Pacific. The Children of Oblivion turned out not to have any such device in their possession, but they did have guns – plenty of them – and, furthermore, they had been tipped off to expect an assault on their headquarters. In the ensuing firefight the seven-strong Guardian team, taken by surprise, and with a low quotient of combat-grade members, was annihilated. Four were killed outright, another two were taken captive and summarily executed, and one was wounded in the shoulder and thigh but escaped. That one was Arnold, and as soon as he had recuperated from his injuries he set off after Kantowsky, hell-bent on vengeance. He found her in Quebec, doing a deal with some francophone terrorists to supply them with handheld plasma weapons. She had made hardly any effort to cover her tracks. She had wanted to be caught and punished.

Her final words, however, were neither a confession nor an apology but a question. 'Do it, Arnold,' she had said, in the tone of someone for whom death was going to come as a relief and a release. 'Kill me. And, as you pull the trigger, ask yourself this: what greater deception could there be than the illusion of free will?'

Arnold had thought about this for a moment, then replied, 'How the fuck should I know?' and capped off a silenced .22 round into Kantowsky's skull, right between her defeated yet still defiant eyes.

Her question haunted him to this day, but only because it was such a damn-fool thing to say and made no sense.

'Yeah,' said MacGowan, 'John reckons that's why we've been called in to sort out a problem on your territory. Because you're not back up to speed yet.'

'Kind of a novelty, huh?' said Arnold. 'Brits coming in to help out Yanks. Normally it's the other way around.'

'Oh, ha ha.'

On arriving in Las Vegas earlier that day, Arnold had bought a used car from a local dealership, a boxy old Dodge sedan. It was hardly the kind of vehicle he wanted to be seen behind the wheel of (back in Chicago he had a Mustang convertible), but covert was covert.

The Guardians drove the mile from the airport to the city, Las Vegas's fantasy skyline looming ahead. The casinos, the hotels and the ersatz palaces and pyramids seemed subdued in the daylight, as though dozing, waiting for night-time and the chance to shine again with neon exuberance. For now the mountains on the horizon were the spectacle, rising higher than the high-rises, their sides lilac through the desert haze, their peaks capped with a lacy filigree of snow.

The hotel Arnold had chosen was one of the lesser ones, not attached to its own casino and located near the corner of Main Street and Fremont Street, the so-called Glitter Gulch area of Las Vegas, a poor cousin of the more famous and more prosperous Strip. The hotel consisted of four three-storey blocks laid out in a rectangle around the swimming pool Arnold had mentioned, which was kidney-shaped and fringed with sun-loungers and parasol-shaded tables. The rooms were spacious, filled with coolness and the breezy rumble of the air-conditioning.

It was agreed that Rattray and MacGowan should take a few minutes to get settled in, then the three Guardians would reconvene in the lobby and go for a meal.

Rattray spent the time unpacking the few items of clothing he had brought and placing them, neatly folded, on the shelves of the room's fitted wardrobes. He laid out his shaving and tooth-cleaning implements on the glass shelf below the bathroom mirror, leaving the other, bogus toiletry items in the holdall. He placed the laptop computer he had brought over with him from England on the bedside table, connected it up to a wall-mounted powerpoint using a multiple-adapter plug, and via the hotel phone-line logged on with a local service provider, downloading the requisite software and paying by credit card.

MacGowan, meanwhile, busied himself humanising his room – tearing back the tight-as-a-drumskin bed-covers, switching on the television, emptying his bladder and leaving the toilet unflushed, rumpling the stack of towels beside the basin and partly drawing the curtains. He cracked open one of the cans of Coca-Cola from the mini-bar 'fridge, gulped half of it straight down, emitted a huge belch, then left the half-drunk can on the bedside table.

In the event the three Guardians decided to eat supper at the hotel restaurant – bland food, huge helpings. By the time the dessert course came around MacGowan had begun to feel thirsty and dull with the onset of jetlag, but when Arnold proposed an evening on the town, he readily went along with the idea. Arnold generously included Rattray in the invitation, but, Rattray being no one's idea of a wild party-animal, both Arnold and MacGowan were relieved when he declined.

Rattray expressed a reservation about any of them going out for a night on the town. It would not do to draw attention to themselves, he said. To which Arnold replied that they were in Las Vegas – it would draw more attention to themselves if they did *not* go out and play the tables. This argument appeared to convince Rattray, but he advised MacGowan and Arnold to maintain a low profile and, more importantly, to return to the hotel in good time and in no one's company but their own. MacGowan and Arnold groaned like exasperated school-boys, but they saw the sense in what Rattray had said and agreed to his conditions.

'Is it just me,' said Arnold as he and MacGowan exited the hotel lobby, 'or does John have a bigger-than-usual bug up his ass at the moment? I mean, I hardly know the guy, certainly not as well as you do, but ...' The sentence lapsed into a shrug.

'It's been four years since John recruited me,' said MacGowan. 'No, Christ, more like five now. Five years! And he and I have been on fourteen actions-to-suppress together, as well as a couple of other missions that don't strictly fall into that category, and d'you know what? Despite that, I still feel like I hardly know him at all.'

As soldiers serving in their countries' élite forces, the 22 SAS Regiment and the Green Berets respectively, MacGowan and Arnold had learned the art of seizing pleasure when and where it could be found. Tomorrow was not only another day; it might well be your last. As Guardians, the philosophy was no less relevant. That night, as the temperature dropped and the streets surrendered their borrowed heat, the two men took advantage of almost everything that Las Vegas had to offer. Tacky cabaret shows. Roulette, blackjack, craps and slot machines. Bars and beer. The attentions of tipsy, over-excited women at the gaming tables, rather too free with their hands, despite their husbands being nearby. The attentions of lonely single women, too, who made it obvious that they were looking for company for the night.

Midnight, however, found the two men wending their way back to the hotel alone, in accordance with Rattray's orders. Arnold was drunk but lucid, MacGowan just plain drunk.

Neither felt like going straight to bed, so they stretched themselves out on two of the poolside sun-loungers. There was no one else about. The dark water of the unlit pool lapped beside their feet. Cicadas stridulated relentlessly in the background.

'So many,' said MacGowan, gazing up at the heavens. He was slurring his words. 'So many of them. It's like a great big black velvet blanket covered in ... in ...'

'Stars?' suggested Arnold.

'Stars, exactly. A great big black velvet blanket covered in stars. Last time I saw so many stars was when I was in ...' MacGowan's voice trailed away. He had been about to say 'the Gulf', but then remembered that he did not talk about that. Not because he did not want to. Because there were not the words.

'They aren't from there, though, are they,' said Arnold. 'That's what I can never quite get my head around.'

MacGowan was about to ask him *who* was not from the Gulf, then realised what his companion was referring to.

'Paraterrestrials,' he said. It took him several attempts to get the word out properly. 'Or so the old fart calls them.' He waved a hand in what he thought was the direction of Rattray's room. 'They're not from any *place* at all. Any geographical location. They're from here but not here. An intersecting reality.'

'Funny how it doesn't seem so fuckin' loonytunes when you've had a few beers,' said Arnold. 'Doesn't seem like some lame concept from a low-rent TV sci-fi series. Seems to make sense, almost.'

'I know what you mean.'

'I thought she was crazy when she first told me about them. Librans. Anarchs. A struggle that's been going on since Atlantis sank. I thought, "You want me on your side, you gotta come up with a better story than this *E.T.* shit." '

'She?'

'Gayle,' said Arnold, and added, a touch belatedly, 'The Judas bitch.'

'She recruited you? I didn't know that.'

'Uh-huh. It was the money that won me over, of course. Once a mercenary, always a mercenary, I guess. That and the chance to get to play with some serious toys. The rest – well, I figured so long as we steered clear of the subject, everything'd be fine. But after a while, things I saw, I got to realising that what we're doing, it's the right thing to do. Maybe I'm wrong, but I *feel* like I'm

144

on the side of good. Like my momma used to say to me: "If it feels good, child, do it." '

'My mother used to say the exact opposite, but then that's a good Irish girl for you.'

'Oh yeah, you're Irish, aren't you?'

'Technically. Born and raised in Hounslow. First time I set foot on the Auld Sod was my first tour of duty in Belfast. 1978.'

'And how did that feel?'

'In what respect?'

'Going to Ireland. Fighting your own countrymen.'

'Well, for one thing, I don't consider myself Irish. Never have done, never will. And for another thing, the IRA aren't freedom fighters, whatever Noraid and a million bloody Irish-American "patriots" would have you believe. They're a mafia, they're the O'Corleone family, they're murdering, hypocritical scum trading under a Republican flag of convenience, and I feel about as much kinship with them as I do with Hannibal bloody Lecter. You were in Angola, right?'

'I might have been.'

'When you were training Unita rebels to take on the MPLA, did you feel like you were betraying your own people?'

'No.'

'There you are. Same thing. I don't have many principles. Can't afford them in our line of work, can we? But I do have a pretty strong sense of what's right and what's wrong. I like to think that if someone's my enemy, they're not my enemy just because I've been told they are. I like to think they're the enemy of … I don't know, of a standard of moral decency. Of humanity. Of what *I* consider to be good.'

'That's a subjective quality, though.'

'Of course it is. Of course it is. And I'm sure there have been times when I've been on the wrong side without really realising it. I know there have. In fact, I quit the damn army because of' – MacGowan paused – 'of something that happened that I believed was wrong.'

'That incident in the Gulf?'

'I've mentioned that before?'

'Only in passing. You never told me what actually happened.'

MacGowan frowned for a moment, debating whether he could bring himself to relate the events of that terrible January day in 1991, the day that had shattered every belief he had ever held and had, in the end, cost him his marriage and very nearly his sanity. 'Nah,' he said, eventually. 'Sorry. Too close to the bone, you know what I mean?'

'I understand. Another time, maybe.'

'That, at any rate, was what led, in a roundabout way, to me joining our little global gang. Although, like you said, the money didn't hurt either.'

Arnold uttered a deep, rich laugh. 'Yup, money's a moral improver all right. Great for consciences. Colours everything a nice shade of rose-pink.'

'But money notwithstanding ...' 'Notwithstanding', like 'paraterrestrials', MacGowan articulated correctly only after several abortive attempts. 'If I didn't think our friends the Librarians –'

'Librans.'

'Yeah, them. If I didn't think they were steering us straight, I'd jump ship. Just like that.' He snapped his fingers. 'Tomorrow. Gone. Without a moment's hesitation.'

'And the money?'

'Well, there's always publishing, isn't there? Books by ex-members of the Regiment are selling by the shedload in Britain at the moment. I know of at least two blokes who've made a mint, and almost everyone else I served with is either working on a memoir or has a literary agent negotiating for them. But I think, as matters stand, it's unlikely I'm going to quit until I'm too old and decrepit to be of any use to anyone. In fact, not only do I think I'm on the side of the angels right now, I also believe this is the most important war I've ever taken part in. We aren't fighting just to recapture a couple of islands or make sure the oil supplies keep flowing. We're fighting for the future of the whole human race. And unless or until someone can prove to me, beyond a shadow of a doubt, that the Librarians haven't got the right idea, then I'm going to stick with them.'

'You called them Librarians again.'

'Did I? That's usually a pretty good sign that I'm drunk. That and banging on about a subject till I bore everyone senseless.' MacGowan yawned and stretched. 'Any idea what time it is?'

'Getting on for 00.30 hours. Past my bedtime.' Arnold got unsteadily to his feet. 'How 'bout you?'

'I think I'll stay right where I am,' said MacGowan, making himself comfortable on the sun-lounger. 'Nice place to kip down.'

'OK. If you're sure.'

'I'm sure.'

'Only you're gonna wake up pretty damn cold.'

'I don't mind that.'

Arnold wavered for a moment, then decided Mac-Gowan wasn't his responsibility. If the fool wanted to give himself pneumonia, that was *his* lookout.

'G'night then,' he said.

'Yeah. See you in the morning,' MacGowan mumbled, already drifting off to sleep.

Arnold headed up to his room.

16

With contemptuous ease Kawai Kim entered the mainframe at the US Air Force base at Ballard, Nevada, slicing
through layers of passwords, entry protocols and access
codes as though they barely existed. Once inside, she
explored as casually as a tourist roaming around a
museum, examining the communications set-up, the
personnel files, the radar system and the security arrangements, and never once betraying her presence.

For Kim, digitally trespassing on forbidden territory
had long since ceased to be a novelty. Indeed, hacking in
general offered little excitement for her any more. Now
and then, usually in an off-guard moment while she was
pounding away at her keyboard, she would find herself
remembering how it used to feel back in the old days, the
early days; she would catch a fleeting memory-glimpse of
the era when she had been one of a select few, one of an
élite cadre of cutting-edge dissidents bent on wresting
control of information technology back from the powers-
that-be. Nostalgia, at her age! But back then, in her early
twenties, life *had* been exciting. She had been finding out
that she did have a role in the world after all. She had
been discovering her niche, and gradually developing the
avatar-persona that would eventually become Otaku
Queen.

Part of the problem for her now, of course, was that
she had climbed her way to the top of the hacking tree
and had become the best there was at what she did. No

question. And it was hard not to be complacent when you considered no one your peer, or even your close rival. Although there was no lack of individuals who thought they *were*. The 'Net teemed with pretenders to the Otaku Queen's crown. But they seemed to spend more time bragging about their programming abilities and flaming one another than actually honing and exhibiting the talents of which they spoke so highly.

Of all of them, perhaps the most boastful was a fellow countryman of Kim's who went by the codename Emperor Dragon. For some time now he had been touting himself around, claiming that he could easily out-hack the great Otaku Queen and that one day soon he was going to prove it. So far, however, Kim had seen precious little evidence of his self-vaunted skills, and she had come to the conclusion that all Emperor Dragon had going for him was that he was a bigger loudmouth than the rest.

So routine and unchallenging had hacking become for Kim that, a few years ago, she had nearly given it up altogether. Like an athlete, it was best to retire while you were young, in your prime and at the top of your game. After all, when the thrill has gone, what remains but a long, slow slide into boredom, disappointment and bitterness?

It was fortunate, then, that a member of the Guardians' Pacific Rim chapter had approached her when he had, and offered her the chance to use her abilities for a new purpose, to place her talents in the service of a higher, nobler ideal. Otherwise she would probably be a schoolteacher by now, or a data-crunching drone for some vast multinational conglomerate, or even – shudder – a supermarket-shopping, child-rearing, obedient little housewife. An ordinary, dull citizen living an ordinary, dull life. It had, in retrospect, been a narrow escape.

Part of the reason why Kim had willingly and unhesitatingly accepted the offer to join the Guardians was that the Guardian cause was very similar to that which her parents had espoused. Her parents had been vehemently and sometimes, when necessary, violently opposed to the environmental degradation that was being accelerated by mankind's increasing demand for natural resources and the rapidly improving technological capability which helped supply that demand. They had devoted their lives to fighting that battle, and had, in the end, died for their beliefs. They would have approved of what she was doing now. Her beloved grandmother, Kim was sure, would have approved, too, although all three of them – mother, father and grandmother – might have raised an eyebrow at the fact that Kim, a confirmed technophile, was a member of a group whose sole aim was the limiting and control of technology. It was an irony Kim herself appreciated.

At last, deep within the system at Ballard, Kim found what she was looking for: a schematic of the Nowhere facility, showing living quarters, laboratories, entrance and exit points, and the locations of the alarms. The alarm system was wired straight in to Ballard, but in the unlikely event that the infiltrating Guardians did trigger it at any stage, Kim would have no trouble ensuring that none of the klaxons within the facility sounded and that the Nowhere security-status indicators at Ballard stayed at green.

After exploring the Ballard mainframe further and finding nothing else of interest, Kim withdrew. On the way out she paused to install a trapdoor that would allow her, and her alone, easy readmittance.

It was late, getting on for two in the morning, when Kim emerged from that state of transfixed, hypnotic screen-stare known as deep hack, utter oneness with one's computer. She had been at her desk since breakfast. Her body was racked by a yawn so powerful it was almost a convulsion.

Bidding Haiiro No goodnight, she shut down her system and went to her bedroom. There, setting her spectacles on the bedside table, she crawled under the covers and fell straight asleep.

17

At dawn that morning Xavier Barraud was awoken by the wail of police sirens, a regrettably familiar sound in the *banlieue* where he lived. He went to his bedroom window, peeled back the curtain and peered out. The *flics* were raiding one of the estate's drug dens. Someone, clearly, had forgotten to pay his kickback this month.

There were scuffles in the street. Running battles. Batons rose and fell.

And Xavier was reminded – as if he needed reminding – how much he hated this place where he had been born and had lived all of his life, and how much he was looking forward to the day when he could afford to move out. He had nearly saved up enough money for the deposit on a small apartment in the centre of Paris. A few more jobs like the one he had just done for de Sade, and he would be there.

Thinking of de Sade, Xavier remembered that his new Apple Mac was waiting for him. He had bought it yesterday using the money that de Sade had wired him (and he had talked the computer dealer into giving him a discount, which pleased him greatly). The Mac was sitting in the living room, its component parts still bundled neatly up in crisp, taped cartons. The old, previous-model Mac was lying out in the hallway. Xavier could not be bothered to cart it down to the dustbins. Sooner rather than later, someone would save him the trouble by stealing it.

Xavier dressed, made coffee, and settled down to unpacking the new computer.

He passed an enjoyable morning connecting up the Mac and its peripherals, loading the hard drive up with software, customising the computer's features, turning it from blank-slate factory-product into something tailored to his own needs, as unique to him as his fingerprints.

Around midday, he was interrupted by a knock at the door.

Xavier undid the door's several bolts and locks and opened it on its security chain. He peered through the gap to find an unhappy-looking man in a courier's uniform standing in the corridor outside. The courier had a package addressed to 'M. Xavier Barraud': a small, slim cardboard envelope.

'Any return address?' Xavier asked, puzzled, because he had not been expecting any such delivery.

The courier said no, and passed a clipboard through the gap between the door and jamb, telling Xavier to sign the receipt. Xavier did so, passed the clipboard back, and mischievously wished the courier good luck getting back to his van. The courier rolled his eyes, shook his head, and set off reluctantly and warily towards the concrete staircase that led down to the ground floor.

The cardboard envelope was lined with anti-static metallic film, and contained an ordinary-looking $3\frac{1}{2}$-inch diskette. The label on the diskette said, in plain, hand-written capitals, LOAD ME.

Xavier was not in the habit of just sticking any old diskette into his computer, and particularly not into a brand-new, virgin Mac. God knows what the diskette might contain. It could, for all he knew, be seething with viruses.

But then that message: LOAD ME. What was that about?

Curiosity, eventually, got the better of him. He sat down at his computer and inserted the diskette.

And within seconds he was elsewhere.

It happened so quickly that it took him several

moments to figure out where he had been taken. He had been patched through into someone else's mainframe, that much was clear. But whose? And how had he got there, when he had not even punched a single key?

He recognised some of the programming. Sophisticated stuff. There was something very familiar about this system. Its design, its layout ...

Eventually it dawned on him.

The *Japonaise*.

Holy Christ and all the Saints, he was inside Kawai Kim's mainframe! And not just anywhere inside, either, but close to the central core.

For a while Xavier was too stunned to do anything. He was also too scared to move, in case he triggered one of the tripwire intruder-alarms with which Kawai Kim had doubtless rigged her system and ended up having his new computer's freshly loaded hard drive erased.

At last he dared to bring his fingers to the keyboard and attempt to explore. After all, who was he to pass up an opportunity like this? A chance to roam around the palace of the Otaku Queen? It would have been rude to turn it down.

He passed by several regions of thick encryption, code so complex you would have needed several Crays to penetrate it. Sensitive material was stored there, clearly. He carefully skirted the sector. Shortly, he came across a trail: a sequence of telephone numbers that stretched from Tokyo, across the Pacific, to somewhere in America, bouncing from terminal to terminal. Kim had travelled this route recently.

Curiosity had led Xavier this far. He let it take him further, and followed the trail to its end.

Very interesting ...

Some time later Xavier, blinking, resurfaced into Real Life.

It was late afternoon, and things had settled down in the *banlieue*. Here and there could be heard an echoing yell from a balcony. Near and far, stereos pumped out dance beats.

Reaching for the bottle of eyewash he kept on his desk, Xavier bathed and soothed his dry, gritty-feeling eyeballs, then stood up and went to fix himself a snack in his narrow galley-kitchen. He had not eaten all day, and he was starving hungry.

As he munched on a stale brioche and a hunk of Gruyère, Xavier pondered on the identity of his anonymous benefactor, the person who had sent him the diskette. How had he or she been able to get Xavier inside Kawai Kim's system, inside that mainframe fortress whose lofty, well-defended ramparts so many others had tried and failed to scale before?

He pondered, too, on the morsel of information he had turned up while inside the *Japonaise*'s system. What he had found was definitely something Gérard de Sade would want to know about.

And de Sade, of course, still owed him 10,000 francs.

18

The mahogany table in the dining hall of Gérard de Sade's château was large enough to seat twenty people comfortably, with elbow-room to spare, but de Sade did not host dinner parties, and so, instead of plates, candelabra and cutlery, the table's veneered surface was laid with items of communications hardware that sat amid spaghetti-spirals of leads and connective cables. Vents expelling circuitry-heated air filled the room with the whisper and warmth of a sirocco.

De Sade was sitting at the head of a table in one of the brocade-upholstered dining chairs. He had just finished a supper of *entrecôte* and salad, the steak cooked *bleu* and bloody – just the way he liked it, just the way Jean-Claude used to insist was *not* good for him – and he was presently sipping his way through a bottle of that understated and underrated wine, the '47 Clos René (the choice of vintage had been deliberate), while, for the umpteenth time, he applied his mind to the transcript of the e-mail Xavier Barraud had intercepted, decrypted and transmitted to him two days ago. A cat, a plump female tortoiseshell, was sprawled heavily on his lap, well nested in the folds of his dressing gown, and he was absent-mindedly stroking her, tickling behind her ears and under her chin. If he paused from these ministrations for more than a few seconds, the cat would raise her head and butt his neglectful hand, demanding that he resume his duties immediately. More cats, a score of them, were perched around the dining hall on chairs, sideboards and serving tables, either asleep or washing themselves in preparation for going to sleep, the busy chorus of wet tongues serenely lulling. The only illumination in the room was provided by a standard lamp that stood at de Sade's shoulder. Every now and then, a pair of eyes in a darkened corner would catch the lamp's light and flash greenly, like two courting fireflies.

Since Xavier had sent him the e-mail transcript, de Sade had puzzled long and hard over its content but had so far made little headway with it. What Xavier had managed to salvage, after he had edited out the garbled portions and eliminated the strings of nonsense characters, had amounted to a little less than two pages of text, and it was fragmentary and incoherent stuff – partial sentences, most of which made little grammatical sense, and here and there a solitary word stranded on its own. The transcript read like the poetry of a madman. And for this de Sade had paid 20,000 francs and was expected to cough up another 10,000 – the nerve of it!

Still, de Sade had persevered, scouring the text for some hint as to where and when *les Gardiens* might strike next.

One of the few proper nouns that had survived intact through the theft and the decryption process was 'Brazel', and upon first spotting this word de Sade had become quite excited. Perhaps a misspelling of 'Brazil'? Could the Guardians be up to something in South America? Upon further examination, however, he had decided that the context did not suit such an interpretation, and had then recalled that Brazel was the name of the ranch-owner who discovered the alleged crashed UFO at Roswell. With that, the upsurge of hope that had momentarily lifted his heart had receded.

Now, after two days spent poring over the transcript like a classics scholar with a hitherto undiscovered fragment of Ovid or Herodotus; after two days of going over and over its every line in minute detail until the nonsensical rhythms and cadences of its whole and partial sentences were ingrained so deeply in his mind that he could recite the text, in its entirety, from start to finish, by heart; after two full days in which he had looked up countless references over the Internet and in books in his library and had followed up every tiny, frail lead he could think of; after two long days of concerted but ultimately fruitless brain-racking, de Sade was finally prepared to admit defeat.

His investigations over the past few years had led him inescapably to the conclusion that Kawai Kim was closely involved with the Guardians' operations, but he was beginning to wonder, now, whether that conclusion might not be incorrect after all. Perhaps Kim was no more than she appeared to be – a strange-phenomena fanatic who ran a homepage haven for other individuals who shared her interests. Certainly nothing in the e-mail contradicted that impression. Indeed, the Roswell reference served only to confirm it.

The thought of 30,000 francs going to waste aggrieved and depressed him. How much money had he so far hurled, with increasingly desperate abandon, into the gaping, bottomless pit of his obsession? He did not care to calculate the total. And how much more could he expect to hurl in the future? He did not like to think. Nor did he like to think what would happen if one day he ran out of capital, the racks in his cellars lay empty, and the Guardians had still not been exposed and brought to answer for their crimes before the European Court of Human Rights. What would he do then? Suicide seemed the likeliest option. He did not think he could bear to live with the burden of such failure on his shoulders.

There is always hope.

That was what Jean-Claude used to say, one of those cheery, essentially meaningless maxims that would trip off his tongue so easily, so without irony.

There is always hope.

And that was what de Sade had loved most about Jean-Claude: his breezy optimism, so wonderfully out of synch with his own gloomy outlook on life, so much the sunlight to his full moon.

The massed, multiple peals of an incoming phone call awoke the sleeping cats and caused the washing ones to pause from their ablutions and look up, some with their tongues sticking out mid-lick. De Sade picked up the cordless handset and pressed the RECEIVE button.

'Gérard,' said Xavier Barraud, 'tell me I am the most brilliant and talented hacking genius you have ever known.'

'You are the most brilliant and talented hacking genius I have ever known.' De Sade had not met any other hackers, so it was not precisely a lie. 'Why, what have you done?'

'Well, having bought myself a new computer – thanks for the money, by the way – I decided I would put it through its paces. So I penetrated the *Japonaise*'s system.'

It was an edited and embellished version of the truth, but de Sade could not have known that. 'And?' he said.

'I penetrated her *system*, Gérard.'

'Congratulations. Thank you for informing me. If that's all ... ?'

'Aren't you impressed?' Xavier sounded hurt.

'I'm impressed,' said de Sade dutifully, and rolled his eyes at the tortoiseshell, who was looking up at him wondering why he was wasting valuable cat-petting time talking on the telephone.

Xavier cheered up. 'Then this should impress you more. She has recently been doing some system-penetrating herself, and I was able to retrace her route.'

'And where has she been?' Now de Sade was paying attention. Please, he prayed, please let this be a lead.

'If I tell you, do I get the final ten thousand francs you still owe me?'

'You will have it, I swear.'

'An air force base in America. I recognised the address-codes.'

'Which air force base? Can you be any more exact?'

'In the Nevada desert. A place called Ballard.' He spelled out the name for de Sade.

'Xavier, that's an excellent piece of work.'

'Thank you, Gérard. And my money?'

'Will be in your personal account by midday tomorrow.'

No sooner had Xavier hung up than de Sade was booting up his computer.

A swift search through the 'Net turned up as much as he needed to know about Ballard, but while he was perusing a map of the region of Nevada in which the air force base was sited, he spotted something else: a word which also cropped up twice in the transcript, a perfectly ordinary and innocuous English term which, even though it was capitalised both times it appeared in the text, had not struck him as significant before.

Nowhere.

De Sade knew that Americans had a penchant for peculiar town-names. There was, for instance, a place called Intercourse in Arizona, and another place called Truth Or Consequences in New Mexico (a mayor, apparently, had renamed the town after his favourite TV gameshow). Usually such names were chosen to draw attention to conurbations of little other significance; to put them, in more ways than one, on the map.

And now here, on the screen in front of him, was Nowhere.

He trawled for more information on Nowhere (Town, Nevada), and turned up one hit, on a homepage entitled 'Out From Under A Rock'. Like most homepages, this one existed for no other reason than to provide its author with a soapbox from which to rant about anything and everything that obsessed him. For such people the use of technology somehow conferred legitimacy on their opinions, and in this respect the Internet fulfilled a useful social function. Without it, there would be many more shambling, badly dressed lunatics wandering the streets, haranguing passers-by.

The reference to Nowhere turned up in the course of a rambling disquisition on Area 51 and other classified military sites in the United States. The author of the homepage mentioned a rumour he had heard about the town, claiming that a friend of a friend – translation: 'unsubstantiated hearsay' – had once met a construction worker in a bar who had spoken about a job he had done out in the Nevada desert, helping to build a town called Nowhere. According to the construction worker, parts of the town were already finished when he and his crew arrived at the site. The crew, scenting non-union work, complained to the foreman, who complained to the contractor, who told him that if he and his men knew what was good for them they would shut up, do the job and not ask any more questions.

'Now,' the author of the homepage wrote, 'I'm not saying this is definitive proof that there's something hinky about Nowhere. But think about it. If you were the Pentagon and you were building a top-secret military research installation and you wanted people to believe it was just an ordinary little town way out in the boonies, you'd get in a bunch of army engineers to construct all the classified stuff first and then bring in a civilian contractor to do the rest – the houses, the roads, the "uncovert" bits. Wouldn't you?'

That was all de Sade could find about the town, other than its date of incorporation.

But it was enough.

A possible US military research installation at a town called Nowhere in Nevada. It was just the kind of place the Guardians would hit. And Kawai Kim, who was in league with that paramilitary terrorist organisation, had just hacked into an air force base not fifty miles from the town. Coincidence? A hardened paranoiac like de Sade knew that there was no such thing.

Nowhere had to be the Guardians' target. And, from what de Sade knew of their patterns of behaviour, if they had not attacked it by now, they were going to very soon.

There were preparations to be made, plans to be laid. And there was no time to waste. It might even be too late already.

De Sade drained his wineglass and set to work.

19

Lucretia and Piers spent the night at a Holiday Inn on the outskirts of Albuquerque, and, after breakfast, hit the road, travelling north out of the city on I-25. Lucretia again drove, and Piers, affecting boredom, picked up the copy of an American arts magazine that Lucretia had dug out from her files before leaving England. He leafed through until he reached the article that she had ear-marked with a yellow Post-it note.

The magazine was four years old, and the article, a short critique in the 'Exhibitions in Review' section at the rear of the magazine, concerned the last-recorded public showing of work by Antony Creel.

It read:

Over the course of a twenty-five-year career Antony Creel's subject-matter has remained consistent and unvarying, the landscape of California and the South-West providing him – as it did Blumenschein and, of course, O'Keeffe – with both inspiration and an echoing emptiness on to which to back-project his emotional innerscape.

Creel is a former member of that school of artists that nobody now remembers as the New Wave of American Surrealists, and the only one of that media-generated agglomeration of disparate individuals still producing work of any note. His paintings are gravid with secrets like sentences that have not quite been uttered, words that are not yet in the human language. Within the desert scenery that he depicts, behind the stormy, roiling cloud-cover, among the rocks and shrubs, are to be found all manner of ominous shapes and concepts as-yet-undreamed-of, ready to emerge at ...

Piers let out a huge, stultified yawn and allowed the magazine to slip from his fingers and fall, flapping, on to the floor-mat.

'Interesting?' asked Lucretia.

'Utterly.'

After an hour's journey, Lucretia turned off the Interstate on to the Cerillos Road, a long sprawl of motels and fast-food restaurants that led into the heart of Santa Fe.

During the late eighties the ailing New Mexican capital had undergone something of a renaissance. Hardware stores and grocery stores had closed down, and in their place art galleries had appeared. Now this city of 65,000 souls was a Mecca for over half a million culture-hungry tourists a year.

Lucretia parked the Ford Taurus near the central plaza. All the buildings within sight of the plaza had been designed or redecorated to suit the city-mandated Spanish Revival mode, with mud-coloured plaster walls and thick pine roof beams. These days Santa Fe was more Spanish-looking than it had been a hundred years ago.

With the aid of a tourist map, the two Guardians found the gallery they were looking for. It was situated amid the web of narrow streets that surrounded the plaza, and it was called One From The Art.

Currently on display was an exhibition of paintings by local artists, which ranged in quality from not bad to wince-inducing. Lucretia was glad to see that most of the not-bads sported orange dots on their frames while none of the wince-inducers had yet found a buyer. It was reassuring to know that her sense of what was good was shared by others.

Lucretia, leaving Piers idly examining the paintings, approached the table where a man was sitting, leafing through this month's *Art in America*. Fixed in the corner of the ceiling above him, a closed-circuit security camera discreetly eyed the premises.

The man was not Creel. He was a short, fat, cheery-looking Hispanic who, twenty years, fifty pounds and a head of hair ago, would have been quite a Romeo. His eyes, although their whites had yellowed, were still alluringly expressive, with limpid, topaz irises. Lucretia could tell that, purely on account of the fact that she was a woman, his smile was an inch or so broader than his standard, greeting-a-customer smile. *Her* smile broadened, too, when his eyes bulged and his face fell.

He had recognised her.

'*Ay caramba*,' he said. 'Oh, please tell me you are who I think you are. Please speak to me in a British accent.'

'Good morning,' said Lucretia, as Britishly as possible.

'*¡Increíble!* In my own gallery! *The* Lucretia Fisk! How in the world – ?' The Hispanic stood up and stepped out from behind the table. 'No. No, I mustn't question. Please, Señora Fisk. May I shake you by the hand?'

Lucretia graciously offered her hand. It was enclosed in a pair of moist, pudgy paws and squeezed hard.

'I have been a *huge* admirer of your work for many years. Your last exhibition at the MOMA – I made a special trip all the way to New York to see it. The lines of some of the pieces. The shapes.' The man had not let go of her hand yet. 'There is much darkness in what you do. A sense that, no matter hard we try, the human race is doomed to failure. And yet there is compassion there, too. An understanding that error and frailty are as much a part of the human condition as hope. I'm thinking especially of *Progress Considered as a Downhill Skiing Race*, although *Prometheus Pressurised* as well. With all the fire extinguishers – you know the one?'

'I know the one.' Lucretia politely tried to extricate her hand.

'Were I a John Paul Getty or a Bill Gates, I would own

a dozen of your sculptures. A hundred! But I am just Ramón Ramos, modest manager of a modest gallery, and the closest I will ever come to possessing a Fisk is having a book of your work.'

'And which book do you have?' Again Lucretia tried to tug her hand out of Ramos's grasp, but he was too awed to notice.

He named one of the coffee-table compendiums of her work, annotated by a pre-eminent member of the Royal Academy.

'Ah,' she said. 'Lovely photographs. Shame about the text.'

'I couldn't agree more. But it isn't for the text that I bought the book.'

'Señor Ramos,' said Lucretia. She forcibly unpicked his fingers from her hand. 'I have a small favour to ask of you.'

'Of me? Lucretia Fisk has a small favour to ask of *me*?' Ramos seemed not at all fazed by having had the physical contact between them unilaterally terminated. 'But of course. Name it. Anything.'

'This gallery is, is it not, owned by Antony Creel?'

'It is indeed.'

'I was wondering. He and I are old acquaintances, but we've been out of touch for a while, and I happen to be on a driving tour of the South-West with my friend here …'

Ramos peered over her shoulder at Piers and frowned slightly. Not only did Lucretia's 'friend' look somewhat young for her, but Ramos remembered reading that she was happily married to a man her own age, Dennis someone-or-other, and had two daughters. Ah well. He shrugged. Artists.

'I thought I would pay Antony a visit,' said Lucretia. 'As I'm in the area. It'd be a nice surprise for him.'

'A very nice surprise.'

'And I was hoping you'd be able to tell me where he lives.'

'I regret,' said Ramos, 'that I have no address for

Antony. He comes in once a week to pick up his mail and discuss business affairs, but that is all I ever see of him. I know that he lives in Los Vientos, which is a small, artist-colony town up in the Sangre de Cristo mountains, about seventy miles north of here. Beyond that ...' His shoulders rose up to his ears. 'I cannot help you.'

'How about a phone number for him?'

'Antony has no phone. He cherishes his solitude very much.' Ramos wrestled with his conscience for a moment, but thanks to his admiration for Lucretia Fisk, it was a one-sided fight. 'Were it anyone but you, I would not do this, Ms Fisk, but ... There is a bar in Los Vientos where I can leave messages for Antony in an emergency. The Thirsty Cactus, it's called. I cannot remember the phone number off the top of my head, but I have it on the Rolodex in the back room. I will go and look for you.'

'Señor Ramos, I'd be extremely grateful.'

'Señora Fisk, please, I am the one who has to be grateful to *you*. For the pleasure your work has brought to my eyes and to my soul. One moment. I will return.'

Ramos disappeared through a door behind him into a back room.

Lucretia turned to find Piers standing beside her.

'That could have gone worse,' he said.

'A fan.' Lucretia was always touched to meet an admirer of her work, and never anything less than respectful of their admiration. 'Who'd have thought it? A genuine aFiskionado.'

'He wasn't lying, either.' Piers tapped midway down his sternum, where his crystal puzzle-egg rested beneath his shirt-collar frill. 'Not a twitch.'

'Why *would* he lie about liking my work?'

'Oh, he was telling the truth about that, too.'

Lucretia shot Piers a dirty look.

'There's only one problem, of course,' Piers said, oblivious. 'He's going to remember us now.'

'He was going to anyway,' Lucretia replied, nodding at her companion's attire.

'I'd better go and have a word with him, then.'

Reaching behind his neck, Piers undid his puzzle-egg's silver chain and drew out the egg from his shirt collar. Skirting the table, he entered the back room.

Lucretia waited a couple of minutes, then followed.

The room was small and stuffy, its single window barred and fitted with panes of frosted glass. Rolls of corrugated cardboard and bubble-wrap were stacked against one wall. On a steel desk sat an electric typewriter, a telephone and the Rolodex that Ramos had mentioned. On a high shelf sat a softly whirring VCR and beside it a small black and white monitor showing a warped, fish-eye view of the gallery. On a plastic chair sat Ramos, staring cross-eyed at the crystal puzzle-egg, which Piers was dangling three inches away from the bridge of his nose. Piers was talking softly, soothingly, to the manager of One From The Art. Lucretia could not make out what her fellow Guardian was saying, but his tone was measured and serious, his voice hardly recognisable as a product of the same larynx that generated the wry, insinuating coo he usually affected.

Piers was keeping his hand perfectly still so that the medallion did not swing on its chain. The crystal puzzle-egg, however, was not inert. Seemingly of their own accord, its component parts were moving, the tiny asymmetrical polyhedra sliding slowly and smoothly in and out, rubbing against one another in a manner that was oddly organic and strangely sensuous. Again and again, by means of some undetectable mechanism, the egg's segments fanned and flourished, rippling into new configurations, patterns that stayed still for barely a second before shifting into other patterns, metamorphosing in time to an unheard beat, lulling and polyrhythmic. Pinpoints of light, reflected from the sixty-watt bulb that illuminated the room, glittered off the puzzle-egg's shifting multiplicity of corners, edges and planes, twinkling like a kaleidoscope of stars.

Knowing she ought not to look at it, Lucretia did so all the same, and in looking became a magpie. She wanted to keep staring at the puzzle-egg, to drink in the beauty of its restless stellar dazzle with her eyes, to possess it and, in turn, be possessed by it.

With an effort, she tore her gaze away.

The Rolodex gaped open at the 'C' section. Lucretia fingered through the cards and found 'Creel, Antony' and, beneath, the address of the Thirsty Cactus.

She copied the address down on a sheet of the gallery's headed notepaper, then went over to examine the VCR. She quickly identified the system. The tape was a half-hour loop, constantly recording over itself.

Opening her shoulder bag, she delved in, rummaged around and produced what appeared to be a mirror compact. Opening this, she inserted a fingernail beneath the edge of the shallow tray of blusher and levered it up, to reveal a small liquid-crystal numerical display nestling amid a delicate fretwork of wires and circuitry. Using a tiny button just beneath the display, she set the numerals to 09.00, then closed the compact.

'Ready when you are,' she told Piers in a soft voice.

Piers gently touched the egg with the tip of his index finger, and immediately it folded in on itself, its segments retracting, and became a solid, crystalline ovoid once more.

'Ramón?' said Piers.

Ramos mumbled, '¿Si?'

'In a moment I'm going to ask you to count down from five hundred slowly. When you reach zero, you'll wake up relaxed and refreshed from that lovely dream we discussed. OK?'

Ramos nodded dully.

'Good. Off you go, then.'

'Quinientos,' said Ramos, in sleepy, slurred tones. 'Cuatrocientos noventa nueve. Cuatrocientos noventa ocho. . .'

Lucretia touched the compact to the side of the VCR and was rewarded with the squeak of rewinding tape as the machine set about erasing the previous nine minutes of footage. Both Ramos and the VCR were going to experience a period of blankness. Missing time. Wherever

167

they went, Guardians left few traces behind. They were truly ghosts in the global machine.

As they were driving out of Santa Fe towards Los Vientos, Lucretia asked Piers what was the 'lovely dream' he had been talking about with Ramos.

Piers cleared his throat and began tapping his fingers against his lips.

'*Piers*,' she said, mock-menacingly.

'I'm not sure I should tell you, old girl.'

'Did it, by any chance, involve me?'

'Let's just say that Señor Ramos dreamed he received a visit from his favourite sculptress and got to express his admiration for her in the fullest way possible.'

'Piers! Honestly!' She wanted to be angry, but she could not, not really. 'The poor man's going to wake up hopelessly confused.'

'Hopelessly confused,' said Piers, 'but, with any luck, happy.'

20

Arnold was at the wheel of the Dodge sedan, MacGowan was sprawled asleep in the back, snoring, and Rattray occupied the passenger seat and was sitting with his elbow jammed against the side-window and his cheek on his fist, staring out at the desert. It was noon, and the sun, at its zenith, had sent creatures and shadows into hiding. Distant mountain ranges moved beneath the pure blue sky with the stateliness of gigantic ocean liners. The rhythmic rise and fall of roadside wires, travelling from telegraph pole to telegraph pole in shallow parabolas, was mesmerising.

Arnold maintained a steady fifty-five m.p.h., accelerating only to overtake the occasional slow-moving recreational vehicle or thundering eighteen-wheeler. Gas stations passed. Truck stops passed. Concession stands selling authentic Indian and Mexican handicrafts passed. Battered billboards warned of upcoming attractions: 2 Miles To The Prairie Dog Museum. 1 Mile To The Prairie Dog Museum. Prairie Dog Museum Next Exit. Even the most insignificant flyspeck of a town offered gambling in one form or another, and always with the promise of the best odds and biggest jackpots available anywhere.

The Guardians were following US 95 on its long, slow curve north-west through the Amargosa Desert. The highway, like a river, had grown a crust of civilisation at its edges. Beyond lay only desolate, forbidding emptiness.

Conversation among the three men, desultory since leaving Las Vegas, had dwindled away to nothing an hour ago. Arnold had attempted to fill the void with music, but the AM reception on the car radio was weak and the only FM stations he had been able to pick up were either Country and Western or evangelical Christian, neither of which could be listened to for long. Silence was preferable, and in that silence each man had sunk into his own thoughts, and MacGowan, not long after, into slumber.

Now, with a single soft word, Arnold interrupted Rattray's sombre reverie.

'There,' he said, raising a finger from the steering wheel to point ahead.

A narrow strip of blacktop forked off to the right, the turning unmarked by anything other than a no-through-road sign.

Rattray checked the Rand McNally map that lay folded open on his thighs. 'That's it,' he said. 'The road to Nowhere.'

Arnold made the turn. The change in the hum of the tyres, as they went from tarmac to bitumen, woke MacGowan. He stirred, snuffling and groaning.

'Sleeping Ugly's back in the land of the living,' Arnold announced, glancing in the rearview mirror.

'Oh, Christ,' sighed MacGowan, rubbing his eyes. 'I was having this nightmare about being trapped in a car with a loudmouthed American, and it turns out it was true.'

'Ah, you just can't handle the fact that I'm so much smarter and prettier than you.'

'You've really got to do something about this low self-esteem of yours, Arnie old mate. You'll never make anything of yourself if you keep running yourself down this way.'

About a mile down the road they passed a large, solitary knob of rock that thrust up from the earth at a forty-five-degree angle, like the clenched fist of some buried, petrified giant. Arnold slowed to a halt.

'This looks as good a place as any for you-all to bale out,' he said.

It had been agreed beforehand that Arnold would perform a preliminary 'eyeball' reconnaissance of Nowhere alone. An American on his own would not arouse suspicion. An American in the company of two Britons might.

Rattray and MacGowan stepped out on to the shingly roadside. MacGowan, clutching a large bottle of mineral water, made for the tiny pool of shade beneath the rock outcrop's northern edge. He checked the ground and the clefts in the rock for crawling or slithering creatures that bit or stung, and, satisfied that there were none, settled down on his backside. It was only marginally cooler in the rock's shadow, but the main thing was to be out of the sun. His time in the Gulf had taught him to fear and respect the sun.

Rattray squatted down by the driver's-side window. 'It's just a quiet nose-around,' he said to Arnold. 'Don't take any unnecessary risks.'

Arnold could have told Rattray that everything was under control, this was Arnold X he was talking to, remember? Instead he chose simply to say, 'Ay-firmative.'

As he was pulling away, MacGowan called out, 'And bring back something to eat, will you?'

Arnold gave a salute – two fingers from the forehead – then wound up the window to preserve the car's inner capsule of air-conditioned refrigeration.

Rattray, shading his eyes, watched the Dodge drive away. When, about two miles further on, it reached a slight rise in the road and disappeared over the other side, he turned and crossed over to join MacGowan, hunkering down beside him. MacGowan uncapped the water, took a swig and held out the bottle to Rattray.

Rattray shook his head. 'Save it for yourself. I don't need it.'

Despite the fact that MacGowan had been breathing through his nose in order to retard the pace of dehydration, a layer of perspiration had already begun to form on his forehead and his armpits had begun to dampen. Rattray, on the other hand, was dry and cucumber-cool, and would remain so no matter how high the temperature went.

MacGowan would have been envious of Rattray's superhuman abilities if there had not been something a little *in*human about the man as well. It was as though you could not have the one without the other, super-humanity without inhumanity; as though you could not possess mastery of your own physiological processes without, at the same time, losing touch with what it meant to be a *Homo sapiens*. The price of freedom from harm and pain and decay was, it seemed, nothing less than a portion of your soul.

It puzzled MacGowan that the Librans had apparently decided not to make the same modifications to anyone else that they had to Rattray. The only explanation he could come up with was that Rattray was a continuing experiment, a Mark One prototype still undergoing tests. It had occurred to him – and though he had dismissed it immediately, the thought had a kind of slimy tenacity which prevented it from being shaken completely loose – that maybe the Librans had chosen not to repeat the process because they considered Rattray a failure.

'I suppose you aren't hungry, either,' he said.

'I don't get hungry, but I do need to eat.'

'Well, that's good to hear. Me, I'm bloody Hank Marvin. Hope Arnold doesn't take too long.'

Arnold was into Nowhere and out the other side almost before he realised it. Where the houses stopped, the main street stopped too, the road ending in a knobbly line like the edge of an unfinished jigsaw, and beyond only rocks and scrub and desert. A blink-and-you-missed-it kind of a burg.

He executed a three-point turn and headed back the way he had come, more slowly this time, casting a watchful eye over the slumped, dilapidated buildings, the peeling paintwork, the lazy well-windmills, the dusty solar panels. There was nobody out on the streets, but then only a madman would be outdoors in the middle of the day in this heat. Besides, Arnold had glimpsed people in the diner at the main intersection on his first pass through the town. Nowhere was not deserted. The condition of most of the cars he had seen, the relatively new yard furniture, the chained dogs panting in the shade (it was too hot for them to bark at him, but he could tell by their eyes they wanted to), the plants growing in pots on window ledges and in tended lots, all were evidence of inhabitation. Even if the diner had been empty it would have been clear that this was no ghost town.

At the intersection he glanced into the diner window again. Faces were peering out at him now – frowning faces, inhospitable faces. He saw one old man mutter a comment to another old man. He flipped up the turn-signal stalk and went right, past the locked-up, disused chapel. This street, after an even shorter distance, petered out also, and as before he brought the car around and retraced his tracks.

The diner was clearly Nowhere's social focus, and it was there that he would be able to get a better sense of the general vibe of the place. He would also be able, there, to fulfil MacGowan's demand for something to eat.

He pulled into the parking lot and selected the next parking space but one to a compact black Mazda which, to judge by the even coating of dust on its glass and bodywork, had been sitting in that spot for at least three days. He gave its licence plate a brief glance as he stepped out of the Dodge.

Several people were now looking out of the window. Eyes peered at him intently as he sauntered from his car to the diner's door.

Upon entering, he was confronted by a tableau of stares, silence and stillness. Nothing, not so much as a coffee spoon, stirred.

He crossed over to the serving counter, leaned on it with both forearms and said hi to the waitress. She ignored him, examining her cuticles. Arnold cast a look around at the other patrons, eyebrows raised, as if to say, What do you make of that, then? Some service, huh? Grim faces glared back at him.

It was then that he became aware that everyone in the diner was either bald or sported a head of white, grey or greying hair (with the exception of the waitress, and her great pompadour of a hairdo was so black it could only have been dyed). Not only that, but there was not one face that was not seamed with the crags and creases of seniority. The average age of the clientele was mid-to-late-sixties. Arnold was the youngest person there by at least a decade.

Which was odd in itself, but odder still was the fact that all the men there held themselves with a particular bearing – an erectness of spine, a certain set of the jaw – that was extremely familiar to him. Most of them were in good physical condition, and those that were not clearly *had* been in shape at one time in their lives. The few bulging pot-bellies he spotted were slack muscle mass, not fat. As for the women present, they, too, conformed to a type that Arnold knew well. Small, tough, competent, compliant on the surface but hard as nails underneath.

Keeping his eyebrows raised and his expression goofily quizzical, in order to hide the fact that he had recognised everyone in the diner for what they were, or rather used to be, he turned his attention to the menu on the wall.

'I guess I'd like something to eat,' he said to the waitress. 'If that wouldn't be too much trouble.'

'To go?'

The question was framed in a tone of voice that did not anticipate the answer no.

'Yeah, to go. What are the specials?'

'We don't got no specials. Only what you see on the board.'

'Well, it all just looks so tempting. What would you recommend?'

She said the club sandwich was good, and the apple pie.

'Then I'll have a club sandwich and a slice of apple pie, please. And coffee. And may I use your men's room?'

'The john ain't working,' she said.

'That's fine. I just want to freshen up a bit before I get back on the road. Passing through, you know.'

He had not been in the men's room more than ten seconds when one of the other customers entered, a thickset man in a short-sleeved Hawaiian shirt that featured a garish sunset-behind-palm-trees design across the front and back. A moment later the Hawaiian-shirt man was followed in by another man, the only other black man Arnold had seen on the premises, whose clean-shaven cranium was as gnarled and furrowed as a walnut. He watched in the mirror as the two men assumed the position side by side at the two urinals. He splashed cold water on his face, then lathered his hands with liquid soap from the dispenser. The two men continued to stand at the urinals. Arnold did not hear the sort of noises you would have expected to hear. He rinsed his hands and dried them on a paper towel. Still not a sound from the men at the urinals, not so much as a trickle. Then, in the mirror, Arnold saw Hawaiian Shirt raise his left arm to scratch the back of his neck. The gesture lifted his shirtsleeve and revealed part of a tattoo on the man's biceps. Arnold did not need to see the whole of the tattoo to recognise the eagle, globe and anchor of the US Marine Corps.

Semper Fi. Forever loyal. Even in retirement.

Hawaiian Shirt spoke. 'Kinda dumb thing to do, huh?'

'What's that?' said Walnut Head.

'Drive down a road marked no exit.'

Walnut Head nodded slowly. 'Yep, that's pretty dumb all right. Kinda thing only a fool'd do.'

And that was it. A few casual sentences of conversation, not addressed to Arnold but intended for his benefit none the less, and the menace implied in them as clear as day.

He grinned to himself. You don't scare me, you old coots.

Finished in the men's room, he returned to the diner, where he found his food waiting for him on the counter in a brown paper bag, along with a Styrofoam cup of coffee.

'Boy, that was fast.'

'Four dollars fifty,' said the waitress.

He handed her a five and told her to keep the change.

Nice town, he thought as he drove out of Nowhere. Think I'll move here when *I* get old and decrepit.

'All of them?' said Rattray, as the three Guardians headed back towards the main highway in the sedan.

'Takes one to know one, you know what I'm sayin'?' Arnold replied. 'You spend most of your adult life in the armed forces, it moulds you a certain way, assuming you ain't that way already to start with. And there's only a certain kinda woman can stick out the life of an army wife.'

MacGowan, through a mouthful of club sandwich, mumbled an agreement. Sarah had not been that kind of woman. She had not been able to cope with the fact that, much though he loved her, he loved the Regiment more. As close as he and she were, nothing they had could ever equal the bond that had been forged between him and his comrades by the battle experiences they had shared, the sights they had seen, the places they had been, the secrets they knew.

'The Marine tattoo clinched it,' Arnold continued. 'Nowhere is a goddamn retirement community for old soldiers.'

'And Byrne's car?'

'... was there in the parking lot outside the diner. Black Mazda Protégé. Correct licence plate. Looked like it hadn't moved in a while. Three, four days at least.'

'Good, good,' said Rattray.

'So what's the deal, John? We gonna infiltrate or what?'

'I think further reconnaissance would be advisable.'

'Yeah, definitely,' said MacGowan. The old military adage, the Seven Ps, had served him well in the past: Proper Planning and Preparation Prevents Piss-Poor Performance.

'What we need to do first,' Rattray went on, 'is find somewhere to stay.'

'There was a town, 'bout fifteen, twenty miles back the way we came,' said Arnold. 'Though when I say "town", it wasn't really much more'n a mom-and-pop general store, coupla houses and a motel.'

'I remember the one.'

'Motel looked like roaches were its best customers,' said Arnold, hoping to discourage Rattray from suggesting that they stay there.

'It'll do us fine.'

Arnold sighed. 'Boy, this job is all glitz and glamour, ain't it?'

21

The mom-and-pop store was a bogus pioneer-era building with a front porch that was home to a painted wooden Indian whose sun-faded eyes gazed with long-suffering solemnity at the passing traffic. Yellow cellophane lined the inside of the store's windows. A handwritten cardboard notice taped inside the glass front door touted One-Armed Bandits On The Premises – Best-Ever Payouts!

The motel, on the opposite side of the highway, was a single-storey cinderblock building with about two dozen rooms all in a row, each with a parking space out front. It, too, had slot machines, a line of them in its lobby, whistling and flashing.

The proprietor was an old-timer whose teeth were too gleamingly white to be anything other than dentures and whose scalp was as blotchy and as sparsely haired as a dog's underbelly. In the patches where luxuriant locks had once grown, there was now a proliferation of dark brown moles that were a few UV-doses short of developing into full-blown melanomas. The proprietor subjected Rattray's and MacGowan's passports and Arnold's driver's licence to a close-up, squinting scrutiny, not because anything about the documents could have given him cause to believe that they were forged and that the names and identities on them were bogus (although this was the case), but simply because his eyesight was extremely poor, beyond the ability of his windowpane-thick bifocals to remedy.

The first thing Rattray did, after keys were handed over and the three of them had found their rooms, was obtain an outside line on the telephone by his bedside and dial Kim's number.

'Hello?'

'Good evening, Kim. *Konnichi-wa*?'

'I'm doing fine, thank you very much, John.'

'What's the news?'

'Good.' Kim told him about the Nowhere facility schematic she had found at Ballard. 'I can use it to guide you once you're in and to disable any alarms if you trigger them. Access is through the diner. The restrooms double as elevators, believe it or not.'

'Fine. Keep me up to date if you find out anything else.' He gave Kim the number of the motel. 'Lucretia will probably ring you at some point, wanting to know where I am.'

'That's me. Guardian telephone directory. Yellow Pages!' Kim laughed. 'That was a joke by the way, John.'

'I know. Oh, and Kim? I haven't had a chance to congratulate you on the job you did interpreting Cecil's vision. Thorough stuff.'

'High praise, John, coming from you,' said Kim, and she sounded genuinely flattered.

Rattray said goodbye, replaced the handset and settled back on the bed, folding his arms behind his head on the pillow. He gazed up at a column of black ants that was traversing the cracked terrain of the ceiling and scaling one corner of the wall.

Kim had, indeed, been thorough. More so than even she could have realised. In the course of putting flesh on the bare bones of the hints provided by the Librans, she had inadvertently turned up a piece of information which had supplied the answer to the vague intimation – the foreshadowing of a certainty – that Rattray had felt at the fast-food restaurant with Cecil. She had given Rattray the link he had needed to make a crucial connection; the final piece of a jigsaw puzzle that he had not even known needed to be assembled; the solution to a mystery that he had not even known existed.

He had not divulged the information to his fellow Guardians because it was not directly relevant to the task at hand and, more to the point, because it did not immediately concern them. In keeping it to himself, however, he had provided a mind already inclined to morbid speculation with fresh material upon which to meditate darkly. The information had lodged in his thoughts like a fish-bone in a throat, becoming an obstruction that no amount of swallowing would make go down. Worse, the harder he tried *not* to think about it, the more aware he was of its awkwardness, its thorny, irreconcilable shape.

And as he brooded on it now – unable to help himself doing so – his brow furrowed, and his eyes, fixed on the two-way flow of the ants, were thrown into deeper-than-usual shadow.

22

Los Vientos straggled higgledy-piggledy over a series of dry, sun-bleached foothills, with the Sangre de Cristo Mountains, tall and pine-forested, rising majestically behind.

Lucretia had heard much about the famous 'light' in this region, which had enraptured not only O'Keeffe – who had spent the best part of her life in the area, painting her sensual desert abstracts – but numerous lesser-known artists as well. The 'light' was so famous, in fact, that like almost every other regional feature in the States it had become a tourist cliché. Clichés, though, by their very nature, have a habit of being broadly, universally true, and this one was no exception. As she and Piers drove along the ridgetop road that led into the town, Lucretia was able to see for herself how the sun picked out every detail of the landscape – every rock, ripple and rill – with startling clarity, and lent every surface a gemlike gleam, and drew out the richness of the natural colours.

But even without the 'light' it was easy to understand why artists congregated here and in nearby Taos. When it came to working conditions, what more could an artist ask for than clear skies and a constant source of illumination? Since Los Vientos was at an altitude of some 400 metres above sea-level, the climate was kind, too, the air cooler and sweeter than down in the desert cauldrons.

It was not a large town, and having obtained directions from a passing pedestrian the two Guardians had no trouble finding the main square, where the Thirsty Cactus was located. On all four sides of the square there were jewellery shops, art galleries, curio shops and restaurants. In one corner a busker was strumming out Eagles tunes on a twelve-string acoustic guitar. His playing and singing, more enthusiastic than skilful, competed with the rumpus of the birds which filled the trees that thronged the centre of the square, and came off worst.

They parked the car in a space almost directly outside the Thirsty Cactus. The bar was sandwiched between two retail outlets, one a boutique selling hand-tooled leather goods, Navajo blankets, and authentic pre-Columbian Hopi and Zuñi pottery, the other a New Age healing centre that advertised courses in drum therapy, vibrasound relaxation, harmony massage, crystal-assisted allergy-diagnosis, chakra massage, cranial therapy, and various other forms of non-orthodox medical remedy. According to a sign in the window, psychic readings were also available, courtesy of an INTERNATIONALLY RENOWNED CLAIRVOYANT AND CHANNELER. The notice added, APPOINTMENTS NOT NECESSARY, which could be considered a ringing endorsement of the clairvoyant's psychic abilities.

The exterior of the Thirsty Cactus, like that of every other building in the square, and indeed in the town, was bedecked with mud-coloured plaster. The bar had louvred swing-doors like a saloon in a Western movie, and neon logos for Dos Equis and Red Wolf beer in its windows.

Before they entered, Piers paused to query the wisdom of Lucretia going in with him. There was a risk that she might be recognised again.

She replied that Ramos had been an exception. 'A few people here may have heard of me but they're unlikely to know my face.'

'Just thought I'd make the point, dear girl.'

'And it's a valid one. Perhaps I am a little too high-profile for fieldwork, but I'd much rather be doing this than sitting back home twiddling my thumbs.'

'Quite. Why miss out on all the fun?'

Tejano music was playing at a discreet volume inside the bar. Ceiling fans whirled hummingly. Two men were seated at the counter; a young couple were sharing quiet confidences at a small, round table. No one gave Piers or Lucretia anything more than a quick, incurious glance.

'No chance of a drop of champagne, I suppose,' Piers said, eyeing the racks of inverted bottles on the wall behind the counter mournfully.

The bartender, a young Hispanic in a crisp white shirt, came up and asked his two new customers what they would like. Lucretia ordered two beers, ignoring Piers's wrinkled nose. As she paid for the drinks she asked the bartender if he knew, or knew of, Antony Creel.

'Sure, ma'am, I know Antony. Everybody knows Antony. You a friend of his?'

'An old friend. We haven't seen each other in quite a while, and he's a tough one to get hold of. No phone, no home address. I was told he sometimes comes in to pick up phone messages from here.'

'He does,' said the bartender. 'You hang around here long enough, he's bound to drop by.'

'I was rather hoping you might be able to tell me actually where he lives. I'd love to pay him a call.'

Piers was sniffing at the rim of the open beer-bottle, as though wary of what it might contain. Raising it to his lips (little finger crooked, in the manner of a refined person lifting a cup of tea), he took a very tentative sip and swilled the liquid around his tongue before plucking up the courage to swallow it. He cocked his head. Not what you might call pleasant, but tolerable.

The bartender shrugged regretfully. 'I only see him here, ma'am. I think he's got a place somewhere out on Copperhead.'

'Yup,' said one of the customers sitting at the counter. ''Bout two miles north outta town on Copperhead Road, past the pueblo, up into the mountains – that's where Antony Creel lives. You guys English?'

Lucretia nodded.

'My grand-daddy came from England. Birmingham.' He pronounced it as they did in Birmingham, Alabama, making the 'h' audible and laying the stress on the final syllable rather than, as in England, the first.

'Nice place,' lied Lucretia.

'Lovely,' echoed Piers, feeling his puzzle-egg writhe against his chest.

The man laughed. 'That ain't what my grand-daddy said.' He turned to the bartender. 'Hey, Paco. You got a pen there, *muchacho*?'

The bartender rummaged beneath the counter and produced a click-action ballpoint.

The man slid a paper napkin from the countertop dispenser in front of him and took the pen from the bartender.

'I'll just draw our nice friends from England here a map ...'

Copperhead Road headed north out of Los Vientos. After about a mile Lucretia and Piers passed the parking lot outside the entrance to Los Vientos Pueblo, the separate Indian village that was open to tourists, for a steep admission fee. In the midst of the pueblo's rounded brown dwellings a pink and white adobe mission-church arose, its high, buttressed sides dwarfing the humbler buildings around it. With its pink and white paintwork the church resembled some vast, fantasy ice-cream cake. Pressured and proselytised by Catholic missionaries throughout the nineteenth century, the Pueblo Indians of the South-West had eventually (anything for a quiet life) incorporated Christianity into their traditional system of beliefs. The resulting synthesis of the best aspects of both religions was an appealing one, but also epitomised the bemused willingness to appease the white man that had come dangerously close to wiping out Native American culture for good.

Past the pueblo, Copperhead Road curved east and began a long, steady climb up the mountainside, becoming as sinuous and winding as its serpentine namesake. For a while there were houses on either side, but as the road steepened and entered pine forest, the houses became few and far between. Lucretia had to downshift the Taurus's automatic gearbox into second, and then soon after that into first, to maintain a reasonable speed of ten m.p.h. She fed the car carefully around each corner, frowning in concentration.

At last, a slow two miles later, the apex of a cedar-shake shingle roof came into sight above the camber of the road. Beneath was visible a triangular segment of a pine-log outer wall. The rest of the house was hidden from view.

'That'll be the place,' said Piers. The man at the Thirsty Cactus had told them that Creel had had the log home built in the early eighties, and had designed its floorplan himself.

Lucretia nosed the car down the sloping driveway to the house, tyres crunching on cracked white gravel. She halted in a terraced parking bay next to a battered Toyota pickup.

The house nestled amid the trees, looking as if it belonged there, a natural rather than a manmade artefact. Its exterior bore a pale green tinge, courtesy of a woodworm-resistant stain treatment. Windows fitted with close-mesh flyscreens were sited all over the building at irregular intervals. A spacious deck jutted out on cantilevered struts, westward-facing for sunset views, the handrail of its enclosing balustrade level with the tips of the pines. A flight of crazy-paved steps led down from the parking bay to the front door.

Lucretia pressed the doorbell button twice, but no one came to answer it. She was about to go for third time lucky when she and Piers both became aware of a faint sound of scraping coming from further downhill, beyond a screen of trees. By silent, mutual consent the two Guardians ventured down in the direction of the sound.

Through the trees they came to the edge of a small formal garden of succulents – cacti, saguaro, yucca – and there found a man bent double, raking up weeds with a hand-trowel. He had his back to them and was so absorbed in his labours that he had not heard the car pulling up or the doorbell chiming within the house.

Lucretia and Piers watched him for nearly a minute, each waiting for the other to announce their presence. Then the man, as though sixth-sensing their scrutiny, stopped weeding and straightened up stiffly. Pressing a hand into the small of his back and kneading away an ache, he turned.

He was wearing a broad-brimmed straw sunhat that cast his face into shadow, so that Lucretia could not tell at first whether he was Creel or not. Still staring at them, he removed the hat in order to swipe sweat from his forehead with one sleeve of his denim workshirt. She recognised him then as the same man she had met at the Tate back in the seventies.

A quarter of a century on, Antony Creel's hair had gone from chestnut to magnesium-grey, and where it had once, in the fashion of the times, hung either side of his face in a thick, frizzy curtain, it was now slicked down and lashed back in a ponytail. His formerly bushy and unruly beard had been pared back to a moustache and goatee, and there were crow's feet radiating from the corners of his eyes and vertical lines scoring his cheeks that were not so much wrinkles as deep-etched grooves.

These age-related changes were of the kind Lucretia had been expecting to see. What she had not been prepared for was for Creel to have lost so much weight. Rangy back then, he was positively gaunt now. His cheeks were hollow, his eyes seemed too large for his face, and in spite of his suntan there was a greyish tinge to his complexion that was distinctly unhealthy. The denim workshirt hung loosely off his frame, as though borrowed from someone two sizes larger.

'Yes?' Creel said, warily, but also wearily, as if talking was an effort.

'Antony Creel?' said Lucretia.

'That's me.'

'Perhaps you don't remember ...'

But she had barely finished the sentence before Creel was wagging a finger at her, head canted to one side, squinting.

'I know you, don't I?'

'We met once. A long time ago.'

'London.'

'That's right.'

'You're the sculptress lady, aren't you? Fish? Fist?'

'Fisk. Lucretia Fisk. And this is a colleague of mine, Piers Pearson.'

'How do you do, old chap?' said Piers.

'Not so good,' replied Creel matter-of-factly. 'But then how many people ask that question actually expecting to learn about the state of your health?' He looked at Lucretia again and gave a crooked half-smile. 'This is a hell of a long way for somebody to come just to renew old acquaintance.'

'It is, Mr Creel.'

'But that's not the purpose of your visit.'

'No. We need to talk to you, Mr Creel.'

'To talk, huh?'

'That's all.'

Creel's gaze travelled from Lucretia to Piers and back again. 'Well, I'm not in the habit of laying out the welcome mat to just anyone who turns up at my door, but you two look like the kind of people a guy can trust.' He glanced down at the dry, raked-over soil and the pile of uprooted weeds at his feet. 'And I reckon I've pretty much done all the gardening I can manage for one day. What say we head inside?'

The interior of the house was open-plan, its various sections on different levels cordoned off from one another by waist-high balustrades. A short staircase led down from the entrance hall to the living area, which was airy and spacious, its thirty-foot-high vaulted ceiling traversed by a huge, smooth beam made of an entire pine trunk stripped of its bark. A row of vista windows gave on to the deck, affording a view of diminishing ripples of orange-tawny hills that grew paler the further they receded into the distance. The huddled brown buildings of the pueblo were visible below, to the south.

Creel ushered his guests ahead of him and followed after them with slow, shuffling steps. Inviting them to sit on a pair of sofas that were positioned at right angles around two sides of a low, square wickerwork table, he asked if they were hungry.

'I could rustle us up some lunch,' he said. 'Vegetarian tortillas. Nothing fancy.'

'Sounds delicious,' said Lucretia. 'But only if it's not too much trouble.'

'Hey, it'll be a treat to cook for someone besides myself,' said Creel, hobbling off to the kitchen.

Arthritis? Lucretia wondered, observing the artist's unsteady, uncomfortable progress. Was that why he had stopped painting? Because holding a brush had become too painful?

Piers, with a discreet gesture, drew her attention to a large canvas that dominated one wall of the living area. Lucretia had registered the painting as she came in, immediately recognising the style as Creel's. Now she gave it a closer look, and almost straight away realised why Piers had thought it deserving of her attention.

Taller than it was wide – its dimensions those of a doorway, albeit a large one – the painting depicted a desert landscape complete with the tormented vegetation and multi-hued maelstrom sky that were common elements in Creel's work. Dominating the scene was a vast, numinous figure, more mist than substance. It was possible to make out a pair of eyes, but otherwise its features were blurry and indistinct. It was as though the figure was in the process of dissolving or materialising – either way, not wholly in or of this world. Its arms were outstretched, a pose that, owing to the lack of physical detail, could be interpreted as either welcome or crucifixion. At its feet, dwarfed by its hugeness, stood a long-haired, naked man. He was gazing, not up at the immense apparition looming over him, but down at an object that floated a few inches above the ground in front of him. An egg. Ostrich-sized, but metallic rather than organic, and made up of tightly interlocking segments. The man was on the verge of bending down to pick the egg up. His hands were held out, fingers splayed. Tension was visible in the muscles of his back. Hesitation? Fear?

'Its title is *The Pandora Possibility*,' said Creel, standing at the kitchen balustrade. He was holding a small, serrated knife in one hand, a red capsicum pepper in the other. 'I put a man there because I don't think it's cool that women should get the blame for unleashing troubles on the world. That's the message of the Pandora myth, it seems to me, but it's usually men who cause all the trouble, don't you agree?'

'How could I possibly *dis*agree?' said Lucretia with a light little laugh. 'The egg is a gift, isn't it?'

'Got it in one.'

'From the ... angel, is it?'

'Good guess, but not quite.'

'A god, then.'

'Again, sort of yes, sort of no. It's not easy to explain. That picture's kind of personal. So personal, in fact, sometimes I'm not sure even *I* know what the damn thing's about.'

'If you *could* tell me, I'd be very interested,' said Lucretia.

'I'll try,' said Creel. 'And in return, perhaps *you* could tell *me* why you happen to be wearing a ring that's an exact replica of the egg in that picture.'

Lucretia glanced guiltily at her right hand. 'When did you notice?'

'As we were walking to the house.'

'And I don't suppose "sheer coincidence" will do as an explanation?'

Creel shook his head. 'But I'll tell you what,' he said.

'Let's put all this on hold until I've finished getting lunch together and we've eaten. I'm the kind of guy who starts getting irritable if he doesn't put food inside his belly at the proper time.'

'Perhaps there's something I might do to assist.'

'Can you grate cheese, Ms Fisk?'

'I think that's within the scope of my culinary expertise. And please, call me Lucretia.'

'OK then, Lucretia. Grater's on the worktop over there, cheese is in the 'fridge. Knock yourself out.'

They ate out on the deck at a wooden trestle table, to the accompaniment of the gentle sift of the wind in the treetops and the plaintive screeches of a far-off ferruginous buzzard circling on thermal updraughts. With its rust-coloured plumage the bird looked like a flake of rock that had been dislodged from the hills below and lent avian form and flight.

The tortilla pancakes, which Creel had made himself, were just the right consistency, not too thick, not too floury, and he laid on a tasty selection of ingredients to be wrapped inside them: refried beans, green salad, chopped tomatoes, sliced peppers, salsa, yoghurt, cubes of grilled tofu, and of course grated cheese. A pitcher of iced tea washed it all down nicely. Piers, dabbing at his mouth with a square of kitchen paper, pronounced himself replete, and Lucretia, who had munched her way through a fourth tortilla even though she knew, for her figure's sake, she ought to have stopped at three, groaned and patted her belly and said it was going to be watercress soup for her for the next week.

The presence of guests seemed to enliven Creel. He became animated over the course of the meal as he and Lucretia talked about their contemporaries and also about the current generation of artists, praising this one's work, dissecting another's. Creel's opinions were well informed, and unlike many in the field he was not inclined to bitchiness. If he did not like what someone was doing he gave a considered reason for it, although in the case of one young turk currently making a name for himself with crudely rendered images of necrophilia, he had to go along with Lucretia's assessment that the fellow did not know his gouache from his elbow.

When Creel returned from clearing away the dishes, he was keen to continue the discussion. It was nice, he said, to be able to have a conversation about art with a successful professional. The art community at Los Vientos was made up of pleasant, enthusiastic and occasionally even talented people, but the majority of them survived by other means than their creativity, through day jobs, trust funds or pensions. In other words, amateurs. Dabblers. Toe-dippers. Wannabes who had neither the guts nor the heart to immerse themselves fully in their vocation the way he and Lucretia did. Or rather, Lucretia did and he *had*. All that was behind him now.

'You've given up for good, then?' Lucretia asked.

'It's all to do with that picture back there, the one you're so intrigued by,' replied Creel, inclining his head in the direction of the house. 'That's the last work I ever produced. After that, nothing seemed worth the effort any more, so I called it a day, sold off my brushes and equipment, and used the money I'd saved up over the years to buy myself a gallery. I haven't once regretted my decision.'

'And why was that particular painting such a watershed?'

'Watershed's too weak a word. I'd use "epiphany" myself.' Creel bent towards Lucretia conspiratorially. 'Let me ask you, Lucretia. Did you always know, even from an early age, that what you were going to do, what you always wanted to do, was be an artist? That that was the role for which nature intended you?'

Lucretia answered without hesitation. 'I did.'

'Thought so,' said Creel, sitting back. 'Me, too. At grade school there was only one subject I was any good at and enjoyed, and that was art. Nothing else really interested me. And your parents? Did they approve when you told them that what you wanted to do with your life was make sculptures?'

'Initially my parents, in typical middle-class fashion, despaired of both me *and* my brother, who wanted to be a musician. They couldn't understand where they'd gone wrong with us. But when each of us started doing well at our chosen professions, they couldn't have been happier. It gave them something to boast about to their friends.' She omitted to add that, after her brother Ron wrapped his Aston Martin around that tree, killing himself and the obliging Royals groupie, her grief-stricken parents had refused to allow his name ever again to be mentioned in their presence. It was, it seemed, possible to do *too* well at your chosen profession.

'For me it was a bit different,' said Creel. '*My* mom actively encouraged me to be an artist. My father, you see, was a scientist – a physicist – and he was killed by some experiment he was working on. The circumstances surrounding his death are murky, because he was employed by the government and the government don't like us to know what they're up to, do they? Because if we knew even half of what they were up to, there'd be bloody revolution in the streets tomorrow. Anyhow, I was two when my dad died, so I hardly remember him at all, and my mom would never talk about what happened to him, but I know she was pretty cut up by it, and that was why she was keen for me to do something that was almost the complete opposite of what *he* had done. She didn't just stick my potato-prints up on the 'fridge door. Any mom would do that. She bought me materials, paints and stuff, books on famous artists. Took me to galleries and museums, cheered me on all the way.'

'You were lucky.'

'Yep, I guess in many respects I was. I got a scholarship to the first art college I applied to, in San Francisco, and I made my first professional sale at my degree show. After that, I never had much of a problem getting exhibitions and selling work. But I never got complacent. That was perhaps the most valuable lesson my mom taught me.

Even if you have a talent for something, she said, you've always got to keep pushing yourself, you can't ever rest on your laurels.'

'You said San Francisco,' said Piers. 'Would I be correct in thinking that this was during the late sixties?'

'I moved there in the late sixties, left to come here in the late seventies,' Creel confirmed. 'Guess you must have heard about life in San Francisco back then. Well, it's all true. It was a great place to be and a great time to be there. I pretty much went all the way with the scene that was going down. I did the Haight-Ashbury thing, the radical, counter-culture, Vietnam-protester thing, the communal living thing. I'm not ashamed of any of it, either. It was a fine time to be young and alive.'

Piers was nodding avidly.

'Drugs, Free Love,' Creel went on, 'and a feeling in the air like a taste, an electric current. We *were* going to change everything. Perhaps, in a little way, we even did. And, of course, I was bombed out of my gourd quite a lot of the time. Everyone was. Drugs played an enormous part in what I painted.'

'One would never have suspected,' said Lucretia, with a wry twist of her mouth.

'Yeah, well, hey, if the doors of perception won't budge open of their own accord, you've got to kick those suckers down. I started out on dope, naturally, and quickly graduated to acid, but then I learned that the LSD compound had been developed by the CIA as part of their MK-ULTRA mind-control programme. After that it was nothing but natural, organic psychoactives for me, thank you very much. Peyote, yage, 'shrooms – if you could grow it, I'd ingest it. I didn't look on it as frying my brain, I looked on it as letting the synapses simmer, you know? Cook 'em for a while and see what comes out. As a result, my memory's got more holes in it now than Swiss cheese, but I don't think I've lost anything worth remembering. By the way, I am getting round to explaining that painting, I'm just taking the scenic route.'

'That's fine by us,' said Lucretia.

'And that's very polite of you to say so. I'm not one of life's great conversational ramblers. I guess I've forgotten how much I miss having company around.'

'Then carry on.'

'I will. But first, I think, some tequila. Either of you care to join me?'

Piers shook his head. International playboy adventurers rarely let any drink other than champagne pass their lips, and he had already tried one alcoholic beverage today that was not his preferred tipple. Lucretia also declined, excusing herself on account of the fact that she was going to have to drive later.

Creel went into the house and returned with a bottle of Cuervo Gold and a shot-glass. He knocked back two measures in quick succession, paused for a moment to collect his thoughts, then went on with his reminiscence.

'Last time I swallowed anything non-prescription was four years back. Bought a handful of peyote buttons off an Indian down in the pueblo and went up on to one of the mesas in a canyon about twenty miles east of here. That isn't a particularly wise thing to do, by the way – "trip" on top of a mesa. You could start wandering around not looking where you're going and accidentally step off the edge, or you could throw yourself off, thinking you can fly. I did it anyway. This mesa is one of those power places, you know? Medicine men have been going up there for centuries, having visions. There are points in the world, nexuses, where the membrane dividing this plane from other planes is thinner. No doubt that sounds like so much hippie moonshine to you, but I happen to believe it, and so do the Indians round here. And I was feeling kinda stale in my work at the time, like I needed a new approach, fresh inspiration. Some more of those doors of perception needed blowing open, and a power place seemed as good a place as any to do it. Boy, were they ever blown open!'

Creel punctuated with a slightly bitter chuckle.

'I don't know that I can describe what I saw in words. How it was. The *experience*. All the trips I'd ever done before were nothing compared to this one. This was the trippus maximus, the all-time biggie, the one that leaves you in a permanently altered state, the one from which you never completely come down. I saw the world, and the world was wallpaper. Flat, two-dimensional. And then it was as though a giant hand reached out and tore a strip away, and behind was a hole, and through that hole I could see … the Truth. The way things really are. The whole grand plan laid bare. And of course the curse attached to learning the Truth is that there's no easy way of sharing it with other people. It's too huge, too fundamental. Trying to explain it in language is like trying to explain the ocean using only raindrops. Art can come close to getting the idea across. There's Truth in music sometimes, in a passage of Bach or a song by Jerry Garcia. There's Truth in poetry, and also in paintings, and no doubt in sculpture as well, though that's not my particular area of expertise.'

'I know what you're talking about,' said Lucretia. 'We try to put it in, but more often than not it turns up in the bits we do unconsciously, the bits that surprise us when we finally take a step back to view the finished product.'

'I'll drink to that.' Creel poured himself another shot of tequila, downed it at a gulp, and exhaled a hot, contented breath. 'Out there on that mesa,' he said, 'four years ago, I suddenly understood everything. It was like my whole life had been building up to that moment. Like everything I'd done, every choice I'd made, had been designed to get me to that place at that time. As if, without realising it, I'd been through the whole initiation ceremony and vision-quest preparation, all the rituals necessary to become a shaman or a sage or whatever, and now I was being rewarded with my revelation. And as soon as I came down, both literally and pharmaceutically, I headed back here and set about trying to capture on canvas what I'd seen. I painted for a day and a night and a day, thirty-six hours straight through without a break. I *had* to get it right.'

'And did you?' said Lucretia.

'Yeah, I did.'

'So what,' said Piers, 'does *The Pandora Possibility* represent?'

'There's a struggle going on out there.' Creel swept an arm around in a manner that clearly indicated more than just the landscape, the sky, the wheeling buzzard. 'For us. For the soul of humanity. Not between the forces of good and the forces of evil. Nothing so clear-cut, so Manichean, as that. It's a struggle between two sides, both of whom think they know best, and it's been going on since recorded history began, and probably longer. In the shadows. In the spaces between what's believed and what's known.' He barked out a short, self-deprecating laugh. 'Leastways, that's how *I* interpreted what I saw. Drugs are so subjective, huh? I dare say either of you could go up there tomorrow, drop as much peyote as I did, and see nothing more than pretty colours and intense lights. You wouldn't feel, like I did, that you'd been chosen for a moment of perfect insight. That this was the destination you'd been headed towards since birth, and that you'd taken a roundabout route but you'd got there in the end. A bit like this story of mine.' He paused there, shrugging, as if to say more was to risk ridicule.

'Keep talking,' said Lucretia. 'Tell us more about these two "sides".'

'OK, but only because you asked,' said Creel. 'They belong to a superior race, a higher order of being. Not gods, not angels, but a bit of both and something more besides. They're competing over us, and to do that they offer us gifts. I don't think they're supposed to, I think it's against their race's creed or philosophy or whatever, but they do it anyway, surreptitiously. Gifts of knowledge. Things we don't know yet, maybe shouldn't know. That's the egg in the picture. Symbol of life. Of potential. Why the heck I showed it floating and all divided up into sections, perhaps you can tell me, seeing as how you go around with one on your finger. To me it just seemed *right*, aesthetically and instinctively. And one bunch of these superior beings, maybe both, gives us these gifts to

196

help us, or maybe to test us. The distinction's unclear. Everything they do is unclear. Their motives are nebulous. They move, to coin a phrase, in mysterious ways. And please feel free to shut me up if you can't bear to listen to me any longer, because this may be the Truth as I perceive it, but one man's Truth is another man's done-too-many-drugs, read-too-much-Michael-Moorcock baloney.'

'I'm finding it fascinating,' said Piers, who did not believe it was possible to read too much Moorcock.

Lucretia concurred.

'Well, you're very generous people,' said Creel, 'and since you still haven't told me why you're here and what you want with me, I guess it's only fair you pay for your reticence by listening to me yammer on. You'll be relieved to hear, anyway, that I'm nearly done. Once I'd finished *The Pandora Possibility*, you see, I realised I had nothing else to say. I was all self-expressioned out. It was all there on that one canvas, the culmination of everything I'd been groping for throughout my career, everything I'd had instinctive glimpses of before and fumbled to put down in oils but never quite managed to capture properly.'

'Why didn't you sell the painting?' said Lucretia. 'It's a fine piece of work and, from the sound of it, it would have been the capstone of your career.'

'Why would I *want* to sell it? It would never mean as much to anyone else as it means to me. I've always painted for me, and someone buying what I've done has just been a bonus. Oh sure, I've done the occasional commission, but only if I was temporarily short of cash and there were bills that needed to be paid. The best stuff, the truest stuff, has always been for me, and that final picture is the best and truest of them all, in my opinion.'

'But there's nothing to stop you starting again, if you felt like it.'

'Oh, there is, Lucretia. In fact, I think it's safe to say that my long-term career prospects are pretty much

197

fucked up the ass.' Creel frowned, debating inwardly for several seconds before arriving at a decision. 'I guess it won't hurt to tell you two. I've been keeping it from the folks down in town. Don't think I could stand all the sympathy, however well-intentioned. Don't think I could stand everybody offering a hundred different ways to help with their crystals and such.' He drew in a deep breath and let it go as a sigh. 'I'm dying. Got another six months, tops. Probably less. Prostate cancer. Too far gone to be cured.'

'Oh my God,' said Lucretia, sincerely. 'I am sorry.'

'So was I, to start with,' said Creel. 'Mad as hell, too. But I've kind of gotten used to the idea now, and I'm not so mad any more, or sad. Painkillers help me stay green and serene, of course, but I've come to terms with death, I'm prepared for it mentally, and I'm not scared. The only thing that still kinda makes me pissed is it's my fault.'

'Your fault you have cancer?'

'Statistically, there's a high incidence of prostate cancer among men who have a vasectomy while they're young,' said Creel, 'and I had one back in '69, when I was twenty-five. Blame my mother. She loved me to hell, and I couldn't have asked to be raised by a better person, but God rest her soul, she did have some strange notions rattling around inside that head of hers, and one of them was making me swear an oath never to have children of my own. She told me I had to be the last of my line. Said it was important. I don't think I'll ever understand why, but ten to one it had to do with my dad. His death hit her pretty hard, I guess may have shaken a few brain cells loose, you know what I'm saying? Not only was she keen for me not to become what he had become, she didn't even want me to father a child who might become what he had become. My grandfather was also killed trying to perfect some kind of scientific experiment or other. Did I mention that? So I guess my mother must have thought we were cursed. That the men of my bloodline were fated to destroy themselves in the pursuit of scientific knowledge. Which is pretty dramatic-sounding, I appreciate, but anyway, she got me to swear I wouldn't have kids, and after a couple of pregnancy scares with women I'd slept with, I decided – being the dutiful son and all – to go the whole hog and have the snip. I sacrificed everything on my mother's behalf, on account of a father I scarcely knew. Crazy, huh?'

Lucretia leaned forward in her chair. 'Pregnancy scares?'

Creel looked up from pouring himself yet another shot of tequila. 'Sure. We've all had them, haven't we? Time of the month's overdue. You're young, you're not married, the last thing you want is *this*. So you go around hunched over and frowning like a penitent monk for a few days. "Why me, God? Why me?" Then, hey presto, time of the month arrives, and all's right with the world again.'

'Mr Creel –' said Lucretia.

'Listen, if I'm to call you by your first name, the least you can do is return the compliment.'

'All right,' said Lucretia. 'Antony. I don't think there's a delicate way of putting this, Antony, but I'll try anyway. Is it at all conceivable that one of those pregnancy scares *wasn't* a false alarm?'

' "Conceivable",' Piers murmured under his breath. 'An apt choice of adjective.'

Creel drained the shot-glass and sat back, considering Lucretia's question. 'No. No, I don't think so. I mean, I'd *know*, wouldn't I? If I had a kid? I'd have to know.'

'Let me rephrase the question slightly. Would one of those pregnancy scares by any chance have been with a woman called Mary Byrne?'

'Name doesn't ring a bell. No, wait. Hold on.' Creel's gaze lost focus as he looked inward, searching the honeycombed terrain of his memory. 'Mary Byrne, Mary Byrne … Shit, yeah. I do remember a Mary Byrne. Gorgeous creature. Thick red wavy hair like a woman in a pre-Raphaelite painting. Big wide eyes, green as jade.

Face a map of Ireland. Yes, dammit. Mary Byrne. She turned up at the commune I was in, and we just clicked the instant we met. We lived together, as in cohabited, for nearly a year. This would be '68 I'm talking about. She came from a well-to-do Boston family. Sheltered upbringing. Catholic family. Convent education. I think running away to join a commune in San Fran was her way of rebelling against all that, only it was a limited rebellion because her parents still kept sending her money once a month and she always cashed the cheques. She was kind of too delicate to make her way by her wits alone, you know? Although that didn't stop her from thinking she could. And she was one of those people you'd get mad at all the time because you couldn't rely on her to be anywhere at the right time and because she never pulled her weight as a member of the commune, but you could never *stay* mad at her for long. She'd just look at you with her big green eyes and her round, sweet face and you'd have to forgive her. Her head was never quite together but her heart was definitely in the right place.'

'And she became pregnant by you?'

'You know,' said Creel, some of the warmth fading from his voice, 'I'm beginning to wonder why I should be revealing intimate details from my past to a pair of near-strangers.'

'Of course.' Out of the corner of her eye Lucretia glimpsed Piers's hand stealing towards the neck of his shirt. 'If you're uncomfortable talking about this ...'

'As a matter of fact I'm not. I'm just wondering why I'm doing it and why it doesn't feel weird. I guess that's what the imminence of death does for you. Takes away those inhibitions. Now, where was I?'

'Mary Byrne.'

'Yes. My God, Mary Byrne. Talk about a blast from the past. I haven't thought about her in years. Like I said, she was raised a Catholic, and she could never completely shake off her upbringing, so even though she and I were living together in sin, we still had to practise the rhythm method. No prophylactics, no sir. She wouldn't even consider the idea. The Pill? Forget it!'

'Hardly what one would call Free Love,' commented Piers.

'Yeah, well, I did my fair share of screwing around, but on the whole I was a one-girl-at-a-time kind of a guy,' said Byrne. 'A serial monogamist, I think they call it these days. And it was worth making a few small sacrifices for someone like Mary. Like I said, she and I, we had something together. Anyway ... Fall of '68 – I know it was fall because the Bay Area fogs were starting to get thick again – Mary skipped her period. Naturally, I started panicking. I'd broken Mom's Eleventh Commandment: 'Thou shalt not procreate if thy name is Antony Creel.' But Mary was cool. She said if she was pregnant she would do something about it. Have it seen to. Then, a couple of days later, she told me that everything was fine. Back to normal. The thing is, I didn't personally see any evidence of everything being back to normal, but I so badly wanted to believe her that I took her word for it. And a week later she was gone. Fled the commune one night, without even leaving a note. That cut me up pretty bad. I'd thought she and I were meant for each other. But a girl like Mary, who knew *what* was going on in her head? I got over it soon enough. When you're young you're so much more emotionally resilient, aren't you? The blows seem tremendous, but you bounce back quick. And there was another girl in the commune, Julie I think her name was. Dead ringer for Grace Slick. The big hair, the fuck-you attitude. She'd had her eye on me for a while. I got it together with her, and Mary was pretty much forgotten.'

'Then Mary Byrne could have been pregnant with your child.'

'I ... guess so.' Creel frowned ruminatively. 'It's possible. Like I said, I took her word on it that she wasn't, but I never had any proof. And her upping and leaving like that, without warning ... She could have been.' He reiterated the last three words slowly and softly to himself: 'Could have been.'

'You seem to be taking the news that you might have a child remarkably calmly,' said Piers.

'Hey, a year ago I'd probably have pitched a fit. Now? I'm going to die soon. There aren't many shocks left for me.'

'If Mary Byrne was, as you say, a good Catholic girl,' said Lucretia, 'it stands to reason that if she had been pregnant she wouldn't have had a termination.'

Creel squinted closely at Lucretia. 'You know, I'm getting the distinct impression that you know a lot more than you're letting on. Both of you. In fact, I'm betting you knew already, even before you came here, that I might have had a kid by Mary Byrne, and all you needed from me was a few details to confirm it.'

Lucretia's silence was all the answer Creel needed.

'But what I don't get,' he said, 'is why. What's your angle here? You can't be working for some private investigations bureau. You, Lucretia, you're a sculptress, a legitimate artist. And you, Piers, you're ... Well, I haven't got the first clue *what* you are, but you don't look like you work for any official agency I can think of. I'm prepared to accept that I may, without realising it, be a father. And if I'm going to be slapped with a paternity suit, then fine. Go ahead. Be my guest. I'll be six feet under before it ever gets to court.'

'That's not why we're here,' said Lucretia.

'Then tell me why you *are*. No, don't. Not yet.' Bracing himself against the table, Creel clambered to his feet, wincing. 'I've got to go drain the lizard. I may be a while, being as how my tubes are kind of blocked these days. You stay there, and when I come back you can tell me precisely what you want with me, or from me, and why you're wearing a ring that happens to be exactly the same as an object I painted from my imagination. I think I'm owed an explanation, at the very least.'

Lucretia watched Creel make his way slowly and stiffly back into the house. He had the grim, fatalistic bearing of someone going off to be tortured, which, given his condition, was probably not far from the truth. She felt a surge of compassion for him.

'You're going to tell him, aren't you, old girl?' said Piers. 'Everything. The whole bang shooting match.'

'He's dying, Piers. Can it do any harm? Besides, he seems to know most of it already, and what he doesn't know he's guessed.'

'Well, it's your decision, my dear. If it were left up to me, I'd deal with him the same way we dealt with Señor Ramos. We've found out what we came here to learn. And, incidentally, not that you've asked, but everything he's told us has been gospel truth.'

'But he's right. We do owe him an explanation.'

'Pity is such a poor motive.'

'Perhaps. But don't you think, alongside all the acts of violence and destruction we commit as Guardians, there's room for a single, small act of decency as well? And it's not as if we don't possess the necessary countermeasures to deal with him, should he try to go public with the knowledge, which, in my opinion, seems highly unlikely.'

'As I said, it's your decision.'

'Then I've decided. I'm going to tell him.'

And, when Creel came back out on to the deck ten minutes later, she did.

23

They live (Lucretia said) at one remove from us, in a reality that lies adjacent to ours. Its flipside. Its counterpart. Its twin.

What they call themselves is a mystery, but they have come to be known to us as paraterrestrials, and once, a long time ago, their existence was not a secret. Through the many points where their reality and ours intersect an exchange of communication was possible, and we, the human race, regarded them as our allies, our friends. They had watched, with something close to paternal pride, as we took our first tentative, toddling steps out of the cave of ignorance into the dim light of dawning self-awareness; as we picked up crude tools and began to use them; as we fumbled our way to a vocabulary and the first crude interactions of a society. They wanted us to grow up to be like them, to enjoy all the benefits of advanced technology, to live, as they did, in a state of ease, contentment and harmony. We were to be their great project. Like Professor Higgins making a well-mannered, well-spoken lady out of Eliza Doolittle, they were going to make a civilisation out of us.

It was a noble goal, but they failed to take one thing into account: human nature.

It all went wrong roughly 12,500 years ago. By then, with the paraterrestrials' help, we had raised a great metropolis, one that spanned an entire continent in the middle of the Atlantic Ocean. It was a place of wonders and glories, of miracles and marvels. It had shining towers, intricate harbour-mazes, and lush leafy gardens, and its streets were cruised by whispering-wheeled vehicles and the sky above it was filled with silently swooping aircraft. It was to be the cradle of our future, the example that would, in time, be followed in other regions of the globe. The name of this city was Atlantis.

It seemed, however, that the paraterrestrials had tried too hard with us. In their eagerness for us to become like them, they had become carried away and had let us have too much knowledge too soon. Or perhaps we simply weren't ready yet, or deserving of what they had given us.

What actually happened is uncertain. There was a battle, of sorts. An attempt was made to force a way into the paraterrestrials' reality. Having had a taste of knowledge, we wanted it all. We were greedy.

Though they repelled our invasion easily, the paraterrestrials decided we needed to be taught a lesson. They destroyed Atlantis, subjecting the entire continent to a tectonic shift so that the city was engulfed by the ocean. They bombed us, you might say, back to the Stone Age.

It was our Fall.

For some centuries afterwards we struggled on with the tattered remnants of what the paraterrestrials had taught us. The few surviving Atlanteans travelled out into the world and used what they could remember of what they had learned to try to rekindle the spark of civilisation. Ruined monuments from this period still remain: the Sphinx and the Pyramids at Giza, built when the Nile Valley was temperate and forested, before desertification; the Mayan and Aztec cities of South America, with their massive ziggurats and complex, astronomically aligned streets and water gardens; Atlantis itself, now better known as the desolate white waste that is Antarctica, beneath whose mile-thick sheath of ice the city's ancient glories lie crushed and buried. But gradually, inevitably, the knowledge dwindled and was lost. The flame of civilisation guttered and went out, and we were left in the dark.

The paraterrestrials continued to observe us. They still had a fondness for us, but now, too, they were wary of us. They had had their fingers burned. Never again would there be complete openness between our two races. The lustre was gone from their zeal to improve us. Eventually, after a hiatus of some 8,000 years, they decided they would resume the task of educating and nurturing us, but this time they would proceed with far greater caution.

It was a decision that provoked discord among them and led to the formation of a splinter faction. While the majority of the paraterrestrials believed that the human race ought to be given a second chance, a minority felt the opposite. We had shown ourselves to be untrustworthy, unreliable, dangerous. There was no guarantee that, were we to regain sufficient technological capability, we would not try to make an incursion into their reality again. The splinter faction's opinions were heard out, then outvoted and overruled.

A gentle rising arc of Progress was mapped out for the human race. No great leap of knowledge would be permitted before its due time. If it was determined that we were ready for a particular advance in theoretical or practical science, that we had developed a sufficient level of maturity to deal with its consequences, then it would be allowed to go ahead. Otherwise, all traces of the idea or invention would be erased, and fate would decree whether it would be rediscovered at some later date or lie forever forgotten. Each stage of our evolution would be carefully assessed and monitored, and should it look as if we were about to overreach ourselves, a system of checks and balances would be brought into play.

It was decided, too, that there would no longer be any direct contact between us and them. Trace memories of the time when our race and theirs shared close communication could not be deleted. The days when mankind conversed freely with superior beings, with gods, would always, through oral tradition and genetic memory, be recalled as a golden age. But now the channels between the two realities would be one-way only, from theirs to ours, and used sparingly.

Because they had elected to pursue a hands-off policy in dealing with us, the paraterrestrials realised they would need human agents to act on their behalf. And so the Guardians were created – a loosely knit, clandestine, worldwide cabal of men and women dedicated to the task of regulating the pace of Progress.

('And that's who you and Piers work for,' said Creel, and Lucretia nodded.)

The Guardians (she continued) operate behind the scenes, amid the cogs and circuitry of the world, beneath the façade of all that is generally perceived. For six millennia they have ensured that the blueprint for the human race's technological evolution is not deviated from and that no major scientific or social advance occurs before it is meant to occur. Their motto: 'Every idea in its time.'

('Or alternatively,' said Piers, ' "All according to plan." ')

As for the disgruntled splinter faction of paraterrestrials, although their objections had not been effective, they refused to admit defeat. Firmly convinced that the human race was a wild animal that needed at the very least to be muzzled, but preferably to be put down, they set about proving their point to the rest of their own kind.

At first, in accordance with their race's self-imposed rule prohibiting direct intervention in human affairs, they confined themselves to whispering ideas to men and women in their sleep, planting seeds of thought in fertile minds. The Ancient Greeks called them 'daemons', creatures of inspiration. In other cultures they were faeries, imps, djinns, brownies, kobolds ... They offered tempting titbits of knowledge, steering people towards insights that led to discoveries, or else guided unwitting victims towards actual items of contratemporal technology that had been left in strategic places, waiting to be found.

Numerous references to the splinter faction's machinations can be found in myth and folklore. In almost every old story, buried at some level, their hand can be discerned. They are, classically, slippery customers. Their gifts are almost invariably double-edged. The insights they grant seldom come without a price attached.

And whenever the splinter faction attempted to disrupt the carefully ordered plan for mankind, the Guardians were there to counteract their efforts. For every action they took, the Guardians supplied the appropriate equal-and-opposite reaction. By and large they were successful, and the status quo was maintained.

However, with the end of the Renaissance and the dawning of the Age of Reason, things began to change. The splinter faction, having grown increasingly impatient with the repeated thwarting of their schemes, decided the time was right to adopt a new approach. Instead of hoping to demonstrate, by means of isolated incidents here and there, that mankind was not to be trusted, they set about spurring us as a race towards greater and more daring leaps of intuition, rationalisation and achievement, in the hope of rushing us towards the same level of technological capability that the Atlanteans achieved when they made their catastrophic error of judgement.

'And so,' Lucretia concluded, 'what up until two and a half centuries ago was a series of skirmishes has escalated into a full-blown war, with nothing less than the future of the human race at stake. If the splinter faction's tactics succeed and we, like our early ancestors, lack sufficient collective maturity to deal with what we know and are able to create, then we'll either destroy ourselves, or need to be destroyed.'

She sat back, finished.

Creel was silent for a moment. Then he said, simply, 'Wow.'

'Indeed,' said Piers.

'So how many of you Guardians are there? I mean, how far does this reach?'

'It's hard to say precisely. Our networks are extensive. We have numerous affiliates, some of whom do and some of whom don't know the full story. Some of them aren't even aware they're working for us at all.'

'What's so weird is I *knew* this all along.' This was said by Creel, not in a tone of perplexity, but with a slowly unfurling sense of wonderment. 'It's like a secret we all carry inside us, hidden from ourselves.'

'Which makes recruiting new members easier than you might expect. You're simply showing a person that what they suspect to be true *is* true.'

Creel took a sidelong look at his guests. 'Are you trying to recruit *me*? Is that what all this has been in aid of?'

'No, Antony,' said Lucretia, 'we're merely satisfying your demand for an explanation.'

'Oh. Good.' Creel did his best to appear relieved, but it was obvious that, deep down, he was a little disappointed. 'Well, I wouldn't have been much use to you, I suppose. In my condition. Unless you'd wanted a volunteer for a suicide mission.'

'Your condition, as a matter of fact, is the only reason we're revealing any of this to you at all.'

'Ah, I get it. This information normally comes on an if-you-tell-me-you'll-have-to-kill-me basis, but I'm dying anyway so it doesn't matter. Correct?'

'When it comes to guaranteeing silence,' said Piers, 'our methods are, on the whole, more refined than killing. We have misinformation specialists working for us – people who can ruin a reputation with a few well-placed words and make even the most reasonably and rationally presented argument look like the rantings of a madman.'

'There's also "grey" propaganda,' added Lucretia. 'A known crackpot endorses what you say, and immediately your credibility lies in tatters.'

Creel held up his hands, palms outward, in a pose of surrender. 'Whoa. Enough already.'

'Murder would only be a last resort,' Lucretia went on, feeling the point had to be made.

'OK, OK,' said Creel. He made a zipping gesture across his mouth. 'I'll carry your secret to my grave. Which shouldn't be too difficult, given how I'm going to be heading there real soon. But I do have a couple more questions I'd like answered, if I may.'

'Go ahead,' said Lucretia.

'Is everything the human race has ever achieved down to these "paraterrestrials"? Every step forward we've taken thanks to them prodding and nudging us? 'Cause if so, that's kind of a depressing thought.'

'No, not everything,' said Lucretia. 'Far from it. We're a naturally ingenious species, born problem-solvers, but unfortunately we're as *ac*quisitive as we are *in*quisitive. Offer us a tempting shortcut, a way of gaining knowledge without having to struggle to come up with it ourselves, and by and large we'll take it. It's not a conscious thing. It's a flaw in our makeup, one the Anarchs can and do exploit.'

'The Anarchs?'

'That's our name for the splinter faction. The ones who are more kindly disposed towards us we call the Librans. Arbiters of balance.'

'And do these ... "Anarchs" have their own equivalent of the Guardians?'

'No, the Anarchs prefer to use disparate individuals, who in turn employ others to do their dirty work for them. That way, the Anarchs' machinations are harder to detect, both for us and the Librans.'

'And they're busier than ever, aren't they?' Creel said. 'The Anarchs. That's why the planet's in the state it's in. The population's booming because our medicines work and people are living too long and breeding too success-fully. We're growing too well for our own good. Heh. Like a cancer cell. And our weapons are getting bigger and better all the time, and the environment is deteriorat-ing because we keep coming up with brilliant new ways to screw it up.'

'And behind it all are the Anarchs,' said Lucretia. 'They're hoping to push us into committing racial suicide.'

Creel fell silent again, trying to absorb the implication of all he had just learned. The afternoon had worn on. The tops of the pine trees had begun to cast arrowhead shadows across the deck. The buzzard had flown off some time ago to search for prey elsewhere.

Lucretia said, 'Perhaps Piers and I should be on our way.'

The two Guardians rose. A moment later so did Creel.

They walked through the house, Lucretia and Piers maintaining a slow pace so that Creel would be able to keep up.

As they made their goodbyes at the front door, Creel said to Lucretia, 'I've probably had enough world-shaking revelations for one day, but I can't *not* ask. This child I had. Have. Girl or boy?'

'Boy,' she replied. 'Mary even named him after you.'

Creel half-smiled. Lucretia could see in his eyes that he was trying on the mantle of progenitor for size and finding he liked it and it fitted. He had lived in the belief that his bloodline ended with him and that his art was all he would leave to posterity, all he would be remembered by. Now death no longer carried with it the threat of extinction. Somewhere out there in the world was a person who bore his forename and – more important to him at a basic, instinctual level – his chromosomes, his genetic heredity. His future in the flesh. He would live on.

'I don't suppose there's any way you'd let me know where I could get in touch with him? Just to, you know, say hi.'

Lucretia shook her head. 'Out of the question.'

Creel shrugged manfully. 'Ah well. Easy come, easy go. How about Mary? It'd be nice to catch up with her.'

'Mary died in 1988.'

'Oh. That's sad.'

Lucretia nodded and turned to go.

'Lucretia?'

'Yes?'

'He's doing something he shouldn't be doing, isn't he? This son of mine.' Creel's tone was unhappy but not resentful. 'That's why you're interested in him. He's "tampering with forces he does not comprehend".' This was spoken in the sonorous, doomy tones of a movie-trailer voiceover. 'Like my dad and my grampa did.'

'We believe so.'

'And you're going to stop him.'

'We are.'

'And is he ... Does he have to die?'

'No, Antony. No, he doesn't.'

Creel seemed satisfied with this answer, and Lucretia, as she and Piers walked back up the steps to the car, regretted that the exceptional honesty with which she had treated the terminally ill artist should have to have been marred by that one last lie.

24

For a day and a night, MacGowan and Arnold staked out Nowhere.

They found a suitable observation position half a mile to the north of the town, atop an outcrop of rock as upthrusting and solitary as the one in whose shade MacGowan and Rattray had sheltered the day before. This outcrop ran for a hundred metres in an undulating ridge like the spine of some legendary lake-monster, and in cross-section was wedge-shaped, sheer on the side that faced Nowhere and gently sloped on the other, so that the two combat-grade Guardians were able to lie on their bellies in the lee of its crest, hidden from sight and in relative comfort. From this vantage point, and with the aid of binoculars, they had a clear view of the town's central junction and its triumvirate of establishments that offered bodily or spiritual refreshment, the diner, the grocery store and the chapel.

Taking it in turns, sleeping in shifts, they noted the comings and goings at the Brilliant Bagel. Over the course of twenty-four hours, beneath a hard sun and an icy moon, they watched the townsfolk visit and leave the diner, and assessed the ebb and flow of clientele like a pair of entomologists studying an anthill, trying to perceive a pattern to the seemingly random droppings-in and departings.

There seemed to be no clearly defined system of shifts or rotas at the diner, but it became apparent that 'customers' turned up as and when they were needed, in the kind of numbers that were needed. At no point during the daytime were there fewer than eight people on the premises, not counting the waitress and a cook, the latter of whom made occasional appearances in the eating area when business was slow.

When a refrigerated delivery truck turned up around 3 p.m., its arrival 'coincided' with a mid-afternoon rush. Patrons crowded the tables while supplies of burgers, buns, bread and suchlike were unloaded around the back of the building. Clearly the delivery drop-off was considered a security hazard, because as soon as the truck drove off, the patrons began to drift away again in dribs and drabs.

As evening wore on the diner became increasingly less popular, until by midnight its clientele had dwindled to just five, four patrons and a waiter who had relieved the waitress and the cook of their duties at 6 p.m. These five remained put all the way through until dawn.

At the first sign of dawn – a gradual greying of the sky, an incremental leaching of tone from the blackness of night – the two Guardians decamped and made their way back to the Dodge, which they had left parked not far from the turnoff from US 95. To get there, they retraced the route they had taken twenty-four hours earlier, a long, circuitous, town-shunning arc that added several extra miles to their journey but kept them out of sight of Nowhere. As they walked, a cold, mean breeze pricked goosepimples from their skin and rattled the scrubby underbrush around them.

By the time they reached the car, a red and unwarming rind of sun had risen above the eastern horizon. They drove back to the roadside motel, and there, in their adjacent rooms, showered away the accumulated stiffness and grime that came from lying almost motionless on dusty rock for twenty-four hours.

Rattray took his laptop from its leather carrying case and plugged it into the phone jack in the wall. With

MacGowan and Arnold watching over his shoulder, he went online. Before coming round to visit Rattray in his room, the two combat-grade Guardians had crossed the road to the mom-and-pop store and bought themselves breakfast. MacGowan was busy glugging down a bottle of pink grapefruit juice and chewing on a microwaved hamburger wrapped in greaseproof paper, while Arnold was cutting chunks from a Slim Jim salami sausage with a pocket knife and popping them into his mouth.

To the accompaniment of their munches and slurps, Rattray called up the URL of Kawai Kim's Koven from the computer's memory and dialled. His US service provider patched him through to the designated Web site address. To the accompaniment of a sampled koto plangently plucking out the famous five-note musical motif from *Close Encounters of the Third Kind*, Kawai Kim's Koven manifested itself on the screen. One of the many reasons why this particular chat room was celebrated among 'Net-users was its introductory sequence, which downloaded in record time, no matter what the baud-per-minute rate of your modem. Within seconds, the sequence was up and running.

The laptop screen displayed an empty night-time road, as seen from the point of view of a person of average height walking along it, the horizon and the star-spangled sky bobbing slightly to convey a loping sense of motion. Only the slightly too smooth textures betrayed the fact that this was not filmed footage. The graphics were richly detailed, the animation almost seamlessly fluent.

Suddenly a cone of bright light flared down from above. The subjective viewpoint veered up to reveal that the light was emanating from a hovering UFO – a standard silver Adamski saucer, as featured in countless science-fiction B-movies of the 1950s, all sleek lines and smooth, rounded contours.

The UFO descended, giving the impression that the viewer was being drawn into its belly. The light intensified and spread to fill the entire screen, then dissolved to reveal the craft's interior. Now the viewer was being ferried along on a conveyor belt, up to a sliding door, through, and into the main cabin. The decor here, too, was retro: shiny-clean surfaces, oscilloscope displays wowing and wavering, valves glowing, banks of tiny lights flashing in preset patterns, even an early wardrobe-sized computer spinning its reels.

Seated in a swivel chair at the main console at the far end was the UFO's pilot, facing away from the viewer so that only a pair of bare arms could be seen working the controls. Swinging around, the pilot revealed herself to be a young Asian woman clad in a clinging black Lycra bustier, a black micro-skirt and thigh-high black suede boots. She had bobbed hair, westerner-wide eyes, and a pneumatic physique of the kind not naturally found on any human being. She looked like a character out of a *Manga* comic, an artist's impression of an adolescent boy's wet-dream ideal of how an Oriental woman should be.

'Hi there, funky saucer boy!' said the digital Kim in a cheesy Japanglicised accent quite unlike her real, American-inflected English-speaking voice. 'You come to play with Otaku Queen?' To complete the cliché, she was even transposing her l's and r's – 'play' came out as 'pray'.

There the sequence ended, cross-fading into an options menu listing the various chat rooms that were in use and the topics currently under discussion.

One of the most frequently hit Web sites in the whole wide wire-world, Kawai Kim's Koven was a haven for conspiracy theorists, saucer enthusiasts and eccentrics of every stripe, many of whom were lured in by the perky Asian-babe stereotype Kim publicly presented. The Koven was moderated with a veneer of irony just thick enough to enable participants to feel safe in indulging their deepest, darkest paranoias. Consequently users were emboldened to embark on flights of fanciful speculation that they might not otherwise have had the courage to make. Kim herself frequently took part in the debates. She liked to spice the conversations with a dash of a lie here, a pinch of misinformation there, and stir to see what resulted. If a rumour was gaining currency and coming too close to what she knew to be the truth, she would hype it up and elaborate on it and inflate it until it was too absurd to be plausible. The more outlandish a rumour grew in the 'Net (and in that sweaty, hermetic atmosphere, rumours could grow to the baroque proportions of hothouse orchids), the less likely it was to go down well in the world outside.

The background to the options menu was filled with vertical strings of Japanese characters picked out in blurry, garish, fluorescent colours reminiscent of neon advertising hoardings. To anyone who knew the language, the phrases made no sense. One read, 'Warrior dog eating bonsai tree', while another conveyed the useful warning, 'Mountain karaoke harvests curse Toyota'.

Rattray used the laptop's tracker-ball to guide the arrow button over to a sapphire-blue character-string which contained an ideogram that bore a distinct resemblance to a man standing to attention with a barb-tipped spear in his right hand. The phrase itself was something nonsensical about insurance companies. The ideogram, however, was a syllable that served many purposes, including that of being the first syllable of the Japanese word for 'guardian', *hogosha*.

Rattray positioned the cursor arrow over the ideogram and double-clicked. Were anyone other than a Guardian to have done this, their computer – lacking the requisite 'handshake' identification software – would have immediately suffered a drastic systems crash. Rattray was rewarded with an empty page unfolding on his screen and a text message appearing, icon-led by a small, animated cameo of Kim's face: 'Hello, John. How may I help?'

A list of option headings unfurled beneath:

Emergency Assistance

Rattray selected 'Node Location', and a simplified Mercator map of the world manifested on the laptop's screen, land in green, sea in dark blue. He clicked on the Americas. A larger and more detailed map of the continent appeared. Zeroing in on the south-western corner of the United States, he clicked on the state shaped like a guillotine-blade and marked with the abbreviation NV. Another, yet more detailed map appeared, this one of Nevada and environs. Rattray used the cursor to etch a square around the spot marked Las Vegas, referring to the scale-bar at the top of the screen in order to make sure that the area covered was no more than a hundred miles long on each side.

Yet another map formed onscreen, this one topographically detailed, showing roads, lakes, contour lines, towns large and small, and all other instances of human habitation in the region. There were two small, bright blue ovals on the map, linked to each other by a single blue line. Further blue lines radiated like spokes from the ovals, disappearing offscreen.

Using the laptop's built-in printer, Rattray ran off a hard-copy of the map. He then typed a quick thank-you message to Kim, which he signed using his first name and the emoticon ':- Ì '. Going offline, he shut down the computer and unplugged it.

'There are two Nodes within a hundred-mile radius of here,' Rattray informed his colleagues. 'The closer of the two is less than twenty miles away, but it's within the boundaries of Ballard air force range, so it might be better to head for the one further away.'

'Ah, screw that,' Arnold said. 'Goddamn military's got so much land, even *they* don't know how much land they got. Doubt there'll even be a perimeter fence.'

'Nevertheless, the Node is quite a hike from the nearest road,' said Rattray, pointing to the hard-copy. 'Best part of ten miles. And chances are it'll be somewhere under-ground. Do they sell torches at that store across the road?'

'You mean flashlights?' said Arnold. ''Spect so.'

'Then it might be as well to go and buy one. And some iron rations.'

25

Nodes, the points at which the human and paraterrestrial realities intersected, were evenly distributed across the planet. Some were the sites of shrines and pagan temples (many of those now supplanted by churches and mosques). Some lay buried or hidden as a result of natural or manmade disasters. Some were in such inaccessible regions that they had fallen into disuse. Some had simply been forgotten about.

Before the Atlanteans launched their ill-advised and ill-fated bid to wrest further knowledge from the paraterrestrials by force, it was possible to visit a Node and converse there with representatives of humanity's twin race. The curious were even allowed glimpses into the distant yet adjacent counterpart-reality that the paraterrestrials called home, and the images that were projected into their heads filled them with amazement and awe (and perhaps, also, with envy, as they saw how the other half lived and wondered why they should not be able to live that way, too).

After the paraterrestrials embarked on their 8,000-year period of 'radio silence', Nodes became sad, broken places of half-remembered happiness, like abandoned cinemas or demolished theatres. People would make pilgrimages to them and carry out rites and celebrations in the hope of winning back the paraterrestrials' favour, so that everything might be as it was before, innocent and sublime. After a while, these ritual events became formalised into religious mysteries, and these in turn became the cloistered preserve of priests, druids, sibyls and initiates, who hoarded for themselves what had once been freely and openly available to all. As the original purpose of the Nodes faded from memory, so the residual aura of importance that clung to them was all the more zealously and jealously guarded.

When the paraterrestrials elected to re-establish contact with the human race, they reactivated only those Nodes that had not been commandeered as sites of special sacred or secular interest. They limited the Nodes' function to the depositing of contratemporal materials for the Guardians' use and fitted them with defensive measures to inhibit unauthorised access. Guardians, meanwhile, camouflaged and disguised the Nodes in order to lessen the likelihood of accidental discovery.

Two classes of Node existed, major and minor. Each of the major Nodes (of which there were few, on average two per inhabited continent) was managed by a human curator, was in or close to an urban area, and was concealed beneath a large, imposing house whose cellars delved deep into the Earth but also *beyond* the Earth. Bretherton Grange stood on just such a Node.

Minor Nodes, the more common variety, were less formally situated and less well stocked. They were automated, and the defensive measures that protected them were not of the order of magnitude of deadliness of, for example, the Domestic, the roving, inhuman entity that prowled around beneath the Grange.

The Node towards which MacGowan and Arnold were hiking was definitely a minor one. Being in such an inconvenient location, it could not be otherwise.

Having travelled as far as they could along a dirt track, they had parked the car and set off on foot into the arid wilderness, Arnold toting a small knapsack which he had purchased at the mom-and-pop store and into which he had put some bottled water, some non-perishable foodstuffs for emergency rations, and a flashlight.

221

They walked at a fast marching pace, Arnold determined to impress MacGowan with his physical fitness and MacGowan – ten years younger and only just managing to keep up – determined not to be impressed.

Using a compass (also bought from the store), the printout map and his orienteering skills, MacGowan kept them on course. Where the dotted line on the map marked the boundary of the Ballard base, the two Guardians found no fence or other indication that they were about to trespass on to the US Air Force's land. They took this as a sign that the authorities at Ballard considered this corner of the range too remote to be worth guarding. They continued walking, keeping an eye out for patrols but feeling confident that if they *were* spotted and arrested, the lack of proper signposting would give an added ring of authenticity to their claims that they had not been aware they were on military property. The sole evidence they saw of aeronautical activity was a pair of F-15s swooping across the northern horizon several miles away, trailing the distance-dimmed roar of their jet engines a few seconds behind them.

Finally, having passed over a series of low hills, the two Guardians entered a broad, shallow, sheer-sided valley that reminded MacGowan, uncomfortably, of a desert *wadi*. Halfway along the valley lay the entrance to the Node. It had been tricked out to resemble the mouth of a disused silver mine, complete with chainlink gates and a fence made up of sheets of corrugated iron on which hung official-looking signs warning of DANGER and PROSECUTION. The tunnel burrowed perpendicularly into the wall of the valley, its entrance fitted with lopsided beams and struts that seemed in peril of giving way and collapsing at any moment. A set of rust-caked, narrow-gauge tracks disappeared into the darkness within.

The huge padlock that secured the chainlink gates would have thwarted the efforts of even the most skilful locksmith and its hasp would have defied anything but the heaviest-duty set of bolt-cutters. For a Guardian, however, it presented little problem.

Arnold unbuttoned his left shirtcuff to reveal a gold bracelet composed of chunky links forged into curved, irregular polygons. No sooner had he slipped the bracelet off his wrist than, of their own accord, the links reassembled themselves, with a series of quick, soft snicks and snaps, into a complete, solid puzzle-egg. Held up to the padlock, the egg silently extruded a single slender segment, serrated like a key. This Arnold inserted into the padlock, and, with a deft twist of his wrist, the padlock fell undone. (MacGowan could have performed the same operation with his keyring.)

The gate's long-unused hinges squealed as Arnold hauled it open.

'After you, Mr MacGowan,' he said, with a bow and an exaggerated sweep of his arm.

'No, I insist, Mr X,' said MacGowan. 'After *you*.'

'Yeah, yeah. You British are so polite.' Sliding himself sideways through the opening, Arnold added, 'When it suits you.'

MacGowan followed him through and pulled the gate shut behind.

Pausing at the tunnel entrance, Arnold took out the flashlight from the knapsack, switched it on and aimed it into the gloom. Its conical beam picked out the tracks, bedded on rotting, splintered sleepers, and the rough rock walls ribbed with vertical props. Spider's webs hung in tattered veils from the ceiling braces.

Squaring his shoulders, he ventured in. MacGowan followed, ducking under the entrance's precarious-looking lintel.

The tunnel sloped downward at a gentle incline into ever cooler and danker darkness. The two Guardians trod gingerly from one sleeper to the next, Arnold tearing aside the spider's webs as they went. Arnold was short enough to be able to walk along the tunnel without stooping, but MacGowan had to go hunched over into order to keep from braining himself on the ceiling beams.

As the light from the tunnel mouth receded and the flashlight became their principle source of illumination, the air seemed to grow staler and thicker, harder to breathe.

'What kind of deterrence will there be?' MacGowan wondered.

'Who knows?' came the reply. 'Some kinda phantom Miner Forty-Niner?'

'Yeah, right. If this was an episode of *Scooby-Doo*, maybe. "So it was Mr Johnson all along. He dressed up as the Phantom Miner to scare people away from the mine so that he could keep printing his fake bank notes." '

' "Yeah," ' said Arnold, ' "and I'd have gotten away with it if it hadn't been for you meddling kids." '

Their laughter rang hollow, as laughter in the dark often does.

Then they came across an old miner's cart lying athwart the tracks, and for some reason Arnold's suggestion didn't seem so funny any more.

It was as they were circumnavigating the cart that MacGowan first heard the faint scratching sound. He could not be sure it had not just been an echo of his and Arnold's footfalls ... but it had sounded very like something small scuttling across the tunnel floor.

He said nothing, and he and Arnold continued along the tunnel.

A few yards further on, both of them glimpsed a sudden movement at the edge of the flashlight's focal circle. Something close to the ground, something small and many-legged, scurried into the shadows of a crevice to escape the light – and MacGowan heard the sound again, and this time it was distinctly the tickle of tiny feet on stone.

'All right,' he said, 'what *was* that?'

'Rat?' replied Arnold. 'Whatever it was, it looked way too small to give us any trouble. But you can turn round and go back if you want to.'

'I'm all right,' said MacGowan, peeved not so much

because of what Arnold had said but because turning back *was* an attractive proposition.

Not long after, they came to a rockfall. One of the ceiling beams had snapped and given way, although there remained a gap between it and the rubble generated by its collapse that was large enough for an agile person to clamber through.

The flashlight beam waved crazily around as Arnold slid one leg over the pile of rubble and negotiated the obstacle. MacGowan followed.

On the other side Arnold was standing, shining the flashlight beam ahead.

'Bill?' he said.

'Yup?' said MacGowan, straightening up as far as the restricted headroom allowed.

'Take a look.'

MacGowan peeked over Arnold's shoulder.

At first he thought there must be a stream flowing across the floor of the tunnel, beneath the tracks. But what appeared to be rippling water turned out, on further inspection, to be writhing creatures.

MacGowan saw myriad clusters of tiny, bright eyes glinting in the flashlight.

He saw countless small, dully gleaming, carapace-covered bodies – brown backs, yellow undersides.

He saw jointed legs and curving, segmented tails held aloft, each tail tipped with an uptilted barb.

And he realised that he could hear the scratching, scuttling sound again, only now it was magnified many times, a massed susurration that filled the tunnel with sinister, whispery sibilance.

'Scorpions,' he said. 'Buggeration.'

There must have been hundreds of them, perhaps thousands, most of them contained within a shallow depression in the tunnel floor, a few spilling out over the sides and crawling up the walls. The depression, which was about three metres across, appeared to have been caused by the subsidence in the floor. The tracks, their sleepers fallen away, spanned it like a pair of rusty iron bridges.

'You OK about this?' Arnold enquired. 'You ain't got a phobia about insects?'

'They're arachnids, not insects,' MacGowan replied tersely. 'And no, I *don't* have a phobia about them. I just don't much fancy getting stung.'

'You'll be all right,' said Arnold. He handed Mac-Gowan the flashlight and set off towards the scorpion-filled depression. 'Keep that trained on me.'

MacGowan directed the flashlight beam ahead of Arnold as Arnold stepped up on to one of the tracks and bounced on it, testing it for stability. Then, arms outstretched like a tightrope walker, Arnold traversed the depression, placing one foot carefully in front of the other. Reaching the other side, he turned. 'Piece a cake,' he said. 'Throw the flashlight over.'

MacGowan lobbed the flashlight to Arnold, who caught it and aimed it at the track.

'Come on, we ain't got all day.'

'Yeah, yeah, all right.' MacGowan recalled Daisy Holman-Fisk describing him as the sort who did not back away from a challenge. It was true, but that did not mean he was necessarily happy doing things he did not want to do. There were times when he resented the unwritten codes of manly conduct and resented, more, his own blind obedience to them. There were times when he wished he had the courage to do something cowardly.

Taking a deep breath, he stepped up on to the same length of track Arnold had walked along. With Arnold illuminating his path, he made his way slowly over the milling carpet of scorpions, his boot-soles mere centimetres above the forest-throng of uplifted, poison-bearing tails.

'Oops,' said Arnold, when MacGowan was a little over halfway across. 'Looks like we got ourselves a conflict of interests.'

A scorpion had climbed up on to the same track

MacGowan was using and was marching bullishly towards him.

MacGowan stopped and waited for the scorpion to come near. The temptation to try and crush it underfoot was strong, but he resisted, fearing that stamping on the scorpion might cause him to lose his footing and slip off the track. Instead, when the scorpion came within reach of his toecap, he lifted his foot and tentatively nudged at it. The scorpion raised its pincers like a boxer's gloved fists and shrank back, bunching its legs.

'Whoa, another one coming up behind you, Bill,' said Arnold. He chuckled. 'Heh. What you might call a classic pincer movement.'

'You're enjoying this far too much,' said MacGowan, glancing over his shoulder. The second scorpion was a big bastard, getting on for the size of a small lobster.

He returned his attention to the scorpion in front, which was heading remorselessly towards him again. With a swift, sideways swipe of his foot, he knocked it from the track, sending it tumbling into the midst of the scorpion multitude. It landed on its back, legs wriggling.

He started shuffling forwards again.

Something dropped on to his shoulder with a light thump.

A glimpse of dull-brown carapace out of the corner of his eye was all he needed to see. He gave a violent, reflexive jerk of his shoulder, and the scorpion, dislodged, rolled down his chest, bounced off his stomach, and plunged flailing into the swarm below. The sudden involuntary movement, however, threw MacGowan off-balance. He teetered for a moment, arms waving. He pictured himself crashing face-first into the crawling carpet of arthropods, being pin-cushioned by hundreds of needle-sharp stings. He fought desperately to recover his equilibrium, but then, realising that he was not going to manage it, that he was going to fall, he thrust his body-weight forwards instead, translating his downward momentum into a headlong lunge for the far side of the depression.

He just made it. One foot landed on bare tunnel floor, the other sank into the scorpions, ankle-deep. He felt pulpy bodies crunching and popping beneath his sole. Then Arnold had him by the arm and was pulling him out.

'Damn! Sod it!' MacGowan hissed, angry with himself. 'That was so fucking clumsy!' He stamped his foot, dislodging a single scorpion that was clinging tenaciously to his bootlace. The scorpion scuttled away.

'Hey,' said Arnold, patting him on the shoulder, 'don't matter how you get there, long as you get there.'

MacGowan gave him a chagrined look. 'It's all right for *you*. They weren't blocking *your* way or dropping on to *you* from the ceiling. Those buggers had it in for me.'

'Maybe they *liked* you. Did you think about that?'

'Yeah, well, the feeling's not mutual.' MacGowan scraped his boot-sole along the floor, leaving a sticky smear of mashed arachnid.

Arnold let MacGowan have a minute to catch his breath, and then they resumed their journey.

Two hundred metres further on, the tunnel rounded a corner, and at that point all pretence that this was an abandoned mine was dropped. The tracks ended abruptly, and the rough texture of the walls, floor and ceiling gave way to a fine, marble-like smoothness, as though the rock had been vigorously sanded and polished. The timbre of the two Guardians' footsteps changed as they passed on to this new surface, becoming dull and echoless. It seemed to both of them that they were not so far underground any more. No longer were they conscious of a weight of rock above them. Rather, they could have been in a corridor somewhere, anywhere. In the basement of some building, perhaps, just a staircase-length down from ground-level. That was how much lighter their surroundings seemed, how much less claustrophobically oppressive.

Presently they arrived at a dead-end, a smooth, solid wall blocking the tunnel. Into this was set a circular door composed of wedge-shaped metal plates screwed tightly together like the iris of a camera aperture. At its base there was a lock with a geometrical opening.

Arnold's gold puzzle-egg did the honours, extending an appropriately shaped segment of itself to be slotted into the keyhole. The door dilated with an abrupt, steely rasp.

Lights flickered on in the chamber beyond. Arnold extinguished the flashlight and stepped through the doorway.

The chamber was fashioned in the shape of a perfect ovoid, some seven metres high at its vertical axis and five metres across at its broadest diameter. A pattern of grooves divided up the rounded walls into close-fitting sections – squares and rectangles of varying dimensions – which reached all the way up to the circular recessed light at the chamber's apex. The floor bowed down in a gently concave hollow, at the lowest point of which stood a podium, roughly a metre in diameter. At the centre of this rose a chrome column, waist-high and looking not unlike a thicker version of a traffic bollard.

Arnold and MacGowan strode down to the podium and stepped up on to it. Set into the hemispherical crown of the column was a series of graduated, concentric circular depressions designed for the insertion of puzzle-eggs ranging from chicken-egg-sized to thrush-egg-sized.

'The world's fanciest eggcup,' MacGowan remarked.

Arnold held his gold puzzle-egg over the column. Having determined which was the correct-sized depression, he solemnly lowered the egg in, base first.

For a moment nothing happened, and then the light altered, growing muted and bluish, and the two Guardians became aware of a dim, distant throbbing. Not a sound, exactly. More a fluctuation in air-pressure, accompanied by a pulsing shimmer at the periphery of vision. The walls began to expand and contract in time to the throbbing, as though the chamber were a giant, breathing lung. Everything, every solid, every surface, became flexible and membranous – even the column, which both men were gripping on to tightly. There was a brief, dizzying sense of dislocation, of being *there* and at

229

the same time *elsewhere*, and then the light was restored to its former brightness and the throbbing and its attendant unpleasant sensations vanished.

MacGowan and Arnold exhaled involuntarily held breaths.

With barely a sound, several sections of wall slid discreetly and discretely out, revealing themselves to be drawers, racks and shelves loaded with items of contra-temporal equipment. There were lightweight one-piece armoured suits, comms-link headsets, night-vision goggles, gas-masks, and bandoliers and belts. There were hand weapons suitable for all forms of combat, from close-quarter to long-range. There was a selection of grenades, mines and bombs, laid out in compartmental-ised trays like chocolates in a box. The Node even thoughtfully supplied large black backpacks, each of which, as a precaution against paraterrestrial technology falling into the wrong hands, was fitted with an entropy accelerator. When triggered, the entropy accelerator emitted an enhanced-tau field that sped up the natural processes of ageing and decay, affecting everything within a set radius. In an emergency, the backpacks and their contents could be reduced to dust in a matter of seconds.

The Node had made available a whole host of hardware. It was up to MacGowan and Arnold to choose what they thought would be needed for the infiltration. With a brief exchange of grins, they set about doing just that.

The return journey along the tunnel was uneventful in as much as there were no surprises waiting for them. Recrossing the scorpion swarm was no less daunting and precarious than it had been the first time, but at least this time there were no mishaps.

When they emerged from the tunnel mouth, it was twilight. The sun had left bruises on the western horizon, and one or two stars were glimmering overhead in the violet of oncoming night.

By the time darkness fell completely, they had put two miles between them and the mine. Donning pairs of lightweight paraterrestrial night-goggles, they were able to negotiate the terrain as easily as though it were day.

It was Arnold who first spied the lighted cigarette-tip. In the ghostly, green-hued world of the night-goggles, it stood out like an emerald flare. Motioning MacGowan behind him to halt, he brought two fingers to his eyes, then pointed ahead. MacGowan followed the direction of the gesture, and nodded.

By silent consent the two Guardians moved cautiously closer, until they were within a hundred metres of the cigarette glow. Crouching down behind a rock, they saw three figures sitting on the brow of a ridge, silhouetted sharply against the starry sky. A patrol. Three cadets in fatigues, none of them older than eighteen. They were sharing the cigarette between them, each taking a few drags before passing it on. Their rifles, M16s, lay propped up against one another in a tripod formation, butts to the ground.

'Nice outline there,' said MacGowan, *sotto voce*. 'Not making much of an effort to avoid being seen.'

'Good vantage point, though,' replied Arnold, eyeing the lie of the land. 'We wanna take a detour around them, we're going to have to go a good two or three miles out of our way.'

'So do we wait here till they move on, or what?'

'Nah.' Arnold eased the black backpack off his shoulders. 'Let's have some fun.' Opening the backpack, he delved in, groped around, and produced a black metallic cone the size of a Roman Candle. 'Your basic, handy, all-purpose, indispensable, accept-no-substitutes paraterrestrial diversion device. Don't know 'bout you, but *I* never leave a Node without one.'

MacGowan's grin was a white crescent in the darkness that almost rivalled the moon for breadth and brightness.

Five minutes later the three-man patrol was startled by the sight of a blue fireball that came bobbing towards them like a child's party balloon wafted along by a breeze, following the contours of the ground at a height of roughly a metre. With a clatter of gunmetal the cadets grabbed their M16s and took aim at the fireball. Each urged one of the others to shoot at it, but each was too alarmed and afraid to pull the trigger himself.

Silently blazing, the fireball wafted right up to the patrol. It circled them twice, then came to a halt directly in front of them, hovering at waist-level and bathing their faces in its azure glow.

After a full minute of staring at the fireball, one of the cadets plucked up the courage to take a step towards it.

It darted back, and so did he. Then it drew close again.

The cadet took a step to the left.

The fireball copied the move.

All at once the three cadets started laughing.

'Whoa, this is freaky shit,' said one. 'It's like that thing's, you know, *alive*.'

'I heard about this,' said another. 'It's called St Elmo's fire, I think. Somethin' like that.'

'Wasn't that that dumb Rob Lowe movie?' said the third.

'You don't need to say "*dumb* Rob Lowe movie",' said the first. 'You only need to say "Rob Lowe movie". The "dumb" part is taken as read.'

They laughed again, and the fireball danced and quivered as though in on the joke.

The cadets spent a further, happy quarter of an hour interacting with the fireball, testing the limits of its sentience and agility and jabbering incredulously all the while. They poked at it with their toecaps and rifle barrels and threw pebbles at it, and each time the fireball jinked and dodged out of the way, avoiding being touched or hit and always hovering just out of reach.

Meanwhile, MacGowan and Arnold slipped past, behind the cadets' backs, unnoticed.

At last the fireball, apparently deciding it had had enough, flew off. One of the cadets, in a fit of bravado, gave chase, but the fireball accelerated until it was travelling faster than he could run, and then the cadet's foot caught on a rock and he stumbled and fell flat on his face, at which his two cohorts dissolved into fits of giggles.

The fireball swooped out of sight over the next ridge, and vanished.

26

MacGowan and Arnold made it back to the car without further incident, and drove back to the motel, where they deposited the *matériel* they had collected from the Node. They showered, dressed in clean clothes, and went round to Rattray's room.

In their absence, Rattray had been eating plentifully, storing up energy for the forthcoming mission. His room was littered with empty packets and wrappers from junk food which he had consumed not for reasons of taste or healthfulness, obviously, but for sheer calorific value – raw fuel to stoke up the biomechanical furnace of his body.

Rattray was regaled with an account of the trips to and from the Node, MacGowan and Arnold supplying a dual-perspective narrative interspersed with insults at each other's expense. When they had finished, Rattray offered them, in return, a précis of a telephone conversation he had had with Lucretia while they had been out. She had called from near Santa Fe to say that she and Piers had successfully tracked down the reclusive Antony Creel and had established that he was, indeed, the father of Tony Byrne, but that he was not at work on an antigravity drive of any description. They had learned, also, that he was dying of prostate cancer.

'So the antigravity engram thingy is inactive in Creel,' said MacGowan.

'It would appear that way,' said Rattray.

'And I bet you have a theory as to why that might be.'

Rattray did. 'We assumed that Creel failed to follow in his father's and grandfather's footsteps because he was a young man in the 1960s and that was something that most young adults were doing at the time, rebelling against tradition and that embodiment of tradition, their parents. But it's likely Creel, without realising it, was conforming to another agenda, one the Anarchs set for him. He told Lucretia and Piers about a drug-induced hallucinatory experience he had up on a nearby mesa, a site the local Indians regard as a power place.'

'A Node,' said Arnold.

Rattray nodded. 'Historically, Nodes have been known to exert an influence over those with natural psychic sensitivity, particularly if their abilities have been enhanced by the ingestion of psychoactive substances. The priestess at the Oracle at Delphi, for example, would inhale the smoke from a brazier of burning eucalyptus leaves before making her prophecies. The paraterrestrials would sometimes take advantage of this as means of conveying messages and information.'

'Evidently it still works today.'

'Quite,' said Rattray. 'Clearly Creel's proximity to the Node, in combination with the hallucinogen he ingested, awakened an understanding inside him. He described it, Lucretia said, as the moment to which all his life up until then had been leading. It's as though the Anarchs wanted him to know what they had done to him. They were taunting him, in a way, and through him, us.'

'But I still don't get why the Anarchs wanted Creel to break with the family tradition,' said MacGowan. 'What did they hope to achieve?'

'Think about it,' said Rattray. 'If successive genera-tions of Krilovs had kept coming up with antigravity technology, we or the Librans would have twigged soon enough. The Anarchs designed the antigravity engram to remain inactive – recessive – in Creel in order to throw us off the scent.'

'But the engram was still passed on.'

'It was, but we couldn't have known that. Even Creel didn't know that he had fathered a son. According to Lucretia, this Mary Byrne woman, the one who bore Creel's child, was naïve, fey, innocent, idealistic. In other words, perfect for the Anarchs' purposes.'

'They used her to wrongfoot us,' said MacGowan, 'and possibly the Librans also.'

'And now we have an opportunity to rectify the error,' said Rattray.

'So the action-to-suppress is going ahead?' said Arnold. Rattray nodded.

'When?' MacGowan asked, sounding not so much eager as relieved.

'I'd suggest we've delayed long enough,' said Rattray. 'We go in first thing tomorrow morning.'

27

Tony Byrne, unable to sleep, called his wife, using the facility's one and only external phone-line (outgoing calls only).

He woke her up – he had suspected he was going to – but she wasn't annoyed. She was glad to hear his voice.

'I was dreaming about you,' Ruth said.

'Something nice and pornographic, I hope.'

'No, I don't think it was that.' She thought for a moment. 'You were flying, that's all I remember.'

'A flying dream,' he said. 'That symbolises escape, doesn't it?'

'Yeah, maybe. How are you doing, Tony? You sound ... I don't know. Nervous.'

'I am. You know I can't tell you what we're up to here, Ruth, but I *can* tell you that we're nearly there. We've nearly done it.'

'That's great, Tony. So why the nerves?'

'Stage fright, I guess. You know – what if it doesn't work, what if I've been chasing a phantom all this time?'

'It's going to work fine, Tony. I have every faith in you.'

'Thanks, hon. I needed to hear that.'

'Tony?'

'Yeah?'

'I love you.'

'I love you, too, Ruth. More than anything. And give

that junior Picasso in the next room a big kiss from his daddy, OK?'

'I'll give him dozens.'

'Good. He'll hate that.'

They laughed. They said goodbye. They hung up lingeringly, regretfully, each letting the receiver come to rest on its cradle slowly, prolonging the act of disconnection, the severance of their frail electric contact.

And as Tony Byrne headed back to his sleeping quarters, he wished he could have shared with his wife the real reason for his nervousness. When it was discovered that he had been using military funding for a secondary purpose of which the military were unaware, there was going to be trouble. Sure, Colonel Clayton was going to get his antigravity drive, but if things went the way Byrne intended, the world was going to get more. Much more. And Ruth was better off not knowing about that until after it happened.

PART 3

PART 3

28

The graveyard shift at the Brilliant Bagel consisted of four war veterans and a cook who had worked for thirty-five years in the kitchens of several military training academies, including West Point.

The most senior of the veterans, both in rank and age, was a wily, wiry septuagenarian who had served in General Patton's Third Army. He never tired of reminding the others how he had helped contain the Germans' Ardennes offensive in 1944 and how Patton himself had pinned a Silver Star to his chest. He had been a colonel when he received his honourable discharge in 1979.

The other three veterans were in their sixties and had all fought in Korea, and one in Vietnam as well. The highest-ranking among them had attained the silver oak leaf of lieutenant-colonel.

Although in theory retirement from active duty renders all old soldiers equals, uniformly demoting them to civilian status, the colonel none the less assumed a certain authority over the other graveyard-shift regulars and they, in turn, accorded him a certain deference. In the discussions that kept the four of them awake and entertained through the small hours, the colonel's were the only opinions that could be stated without fear of contradiction; his the only arguments that were listened to with full attention and never challenged. The habits instilled by a lifetime of military service were hard to break.

As for the cook, while he might never have seen action, he had served his country in his own way. An army, as the saying goes, marches on its stomach, and skill with a skillet was just as valuable, in strategic terms, as an ordinary infantryman's ability to shoot straight. Or so the cook firmly believed.

His job at the diner was to keep the other four men fuelled with snacks and coffee. He took part in the discussions, but only as long as the topics under debate remained non-martial. Politics, sports, favourite movie actresses of all time – these were subjects in which the cook's input was as valid as anyone's. But whenever the four veterans got around to swapping combat tales, as they inevitably did at some point each night, that was the cook's cue to make a tactical withdrawal and go wash up some dishes or tap out and replenish the coffee-machine filter.

Other townsfolk might drop by the Brilliant Bagel at various times during the night and stay for a while to chat before returning to their homes and beds, but these five were the core members of the graveyard shift, the ones who could regularly be found there between midnight and breakfast-time.

And it was these five who were at the diner when the wounded white-haired stranger came staggering in early that Saturday morning.

The four veterans were sitting in their usual place, one of the banquette tables by the front window. The cook had just finished pouring out refills of coffee for them and was returning the coffee pot to its warming stand behind the counter when he heard a sound coming from the kitchen. A sound like a sack of frozen peas being emptied out on to the floor.

None of the veterans appeared to notice. The cook's hearing, having not been subjected to as many reports, detonations and fusillades as theirs, was that much sharper.

Before he could investigate the noise, however, or even

remark upon it to the others, his eye was caught by movement out in the parking lot.

There was a man out there, stumbling towards the diner door.

With a cough and a surreptitious gesture, the cook alerted the four veterans.

Immediately a hand that was gnarled by arthritis but still capable of holding and firing a sidearm reached under the table and clasped the grip of a Smith and Wesson 9mm that was stowed there in a specially constructed holster. Another hand, this one dappled with liver spots and belonging to the colonel, groped along the underside of the bench-seat for the Desert Eagle .357 Magnum that was held in place there by spring-clips.

The stranger came reeling up to the diner door and opened it more by colliding with it than pushing it. The door slammed back against the wall and swung slowly shut on its hinge-spring. The white-haired man took a few tottering steps across the floor, then fell to his knees, groaning. Half his face was masked with blood from a deep, ugly gash in his forehead. His left shirtsleeve was shredded and blood-drenched, and there was torn flesh visible through the crimson-stained tatters.

'Car,' he mumbled, waving his intact arm in no particular direction. 'Lost control. Came off road.' Then he slumped over on to his side, the last of his energy seemingly sapped by the effort of talking.

On a nod from the colonel, the two veterans who were not secretly holding guns beneath the table stood up and approached the wounded man. They were cautious – it was their job to be cautious – but they were also concerned for the welfare of a fellow human being. The latter consideration marginally outweighed the former.

One of them crouched down beside the man and examined his injuries. The man's left arm was a mass of straight, deep slashes, while the skin had peeled back from the gash in his forehead to expose a shiny white sliver of skull. His blood was spilling over the diner's floor tiles in loops and spatters.

The veteran looked up at the colonel. 'He's cut up pretty bad, Doug. What should we do?'

The colonel deliberated a moment. 'Fella's obviously been in an accident. Guess we don't have much choice but to call an ambulance. Georgie?'

The colonel had to speak the cook's name twice more before the cook realised that he was being addressed. In the past the veterans had all seen wounds similar to, and worse than, the white-haired man's. The cook was new to such sights, and was finding it a distinctly unnerving and unmanning experience.

'Yes?' he said, queasily.

'Use the phone in the kitchen,' said the colonel. 'Call some paramedics.'

'Uh-huh.' The cook nodded. 'OK.' But he did not move.

'Georgie,' said the colonel firmly, 'this is a normal situation, understand?'

The cook did understand, even though the situation, to him, was anything but normal. Rousing himself into action, he turned towards the swing door that connected the diner to the kitchen.

And found the door already open and two men standing there, framed by the doorway.

One of the men was short, black and slim, the other tall, white and bulky. Both were dressed in one-piece grey suits that were like overalls but with sections of ribbed, rubbery black material covering their chests, crotches, arms and legs. They were wearing combat boots and black bandolier/belt arrangements that bulged with buttoned-in ordnance, and each sported a wristpad on his left arm that had buttons and a small display-screen on it like a miniature videogame. They looked like they belonged to some kind of high-tech SWAT team.

The cook had time to wonder how these two had managed to get in through the locked back door to the kitchen. Then the larger man took a step towards him, raising a matt-black device that resembled an electric gas-hob lighter, a handle-grip fitted with a hollow stalk that tapered to a narrow tip. Before the cook could even think of yelling a warning to the others, the man brought the device up under his chin and depressed its thumb-trigger. There was a brief, all-but-inaudible hiss as a bullet-velocity bolt of super-compressed air drilled a hole up through the cook's mouth and into his brain. The man caught the cook's body as it fell and lowered it gently to the floor.

The other man was moving before the cook was even dead. Skirting around his comrade, he vaulted the counter and made for the two veterans still seated at the banquette.

The colonel caught sight of the man darting across the room and managed to get his Desert Eagle up above the level of the table, but was not given an opportunity to fire off a round. Humming metal scythed through the air, and the colonel's neck was sliced clean through to the vertebrae. His head tumbled sideways under its own weight, tearing free of the remaining cervical tendons and the flap of skin that tethered it in place, rolling on to the fake-leather upholstery of the banquette bench and bouncing off on to the floor. His decapitated body fell forward, spraying blood across the tabletop.

The veteran sitting opposite, face measled with the colonel's blood, could only stare at his colleague's severed neck. He did not even see the colonel's attacker draw his arm back or the blade of the short sword he was wielding swing around in a vibrating blur. The Smith and Wesson fell from his limp fingers with a loud clatter as his head was cleaved vertically from crown to chin.

At the same instant, the white-haired 'car-crash victim' on the floor reached up with his right hand to grasp the face of the veteran who was kneeling over him. The last thought that went through the veteran's mind was how strong the man's grip was. His fingers felt like steel claws. Then the white-haired man tightened his grip, clenching the veteran's cheekbones and temples, crushing his skull.

The taller of the two grey-garbed, black-bandoliered

figures approached the fourth, and last remaining, veteran. The old man had survived four tours of duty in Korea and a fifth in Vietnam. He had watched villages burn and men he called friends die. He himself had cheated death on several occasions. Once, while out on jungle patrol, the PFC walking a few yards behind him had stepped on a landmine which his own foot must have missed by mere inches. Another time, an enemy grenade had landed next to him and failed to go off.

Now, unarmed, and with no hope of being able to defend himself, he looked passively into the eyes of the man who was about to kill him. He recognised a fellow soldier, someone who was merely doing what he had to do.

He felt the tip of the black wand the man was carrying being pressed against his temple and, with a click and a hiss, twice-thwarted death finally came to claim him.

MacGowan and Arnold deactivated the pressure-wand and the sonic knife, the close-combat weapons that each, respectively, had employed to make cemetery-fodder out of the graveyard shift. They stowed the weapons away in the appropriate sheaths in their bandoliers, then set to work moving the corpses, dragging them behind the counter, out of sight.

Rattray, meanwhile, picked himself up off the floor, favouring his injured left arm. He had cut himself with Arnold's pocket knife, trying not to think, as he had gouged the blade repeatedly into his flesh, that the last time he had seen the knife Arnold had been using it to hack off bite-sized chunks from a length of highly spiced salami sausage.

The injuries had anaesthetised themselves immediately but, with a mental command, Rattray had put his body's autonomic healing ability on hold. A countermand now set the process in motion.

It was not so much a conscious thought as an envisioning of the need to heal. Rattray only had to see, in his mind's eye, his arm and forehead regaining their integrity, and his body obediently began making that thought a corporeal reality, knitting sundered flesh, lacing together divided skin.

The itching came, inevitable and exquisitely unpleasant, and with it a dizzying drain on his energies. The wounds had had to be deep in order to look authentic, but repairing them was going to cost him, depleting his physical reserves.

Rattray gritted his teeth and demanded adrenaline, and the dizziness cleared.

He cleaned the blood from his face and left arm as best he could, using a tea-towel from behind the counter. Then he drew a comms-link headset out of his breast pocket and donned it one-handed. He inserted the audio-receiver plug into his ear and adjusted the slender mic-arm so that its pick-up was an inch from his lips. Clipping the base-unit to his belt, he hit the OPERATE switch.

'Kim?'

Thousands of miles away, and yet there in his ear, inside his head, Kim replied, 'Hiya, John.'

Rattray checked with MacGowan and Arnold. They were both wearing their comms-link headsets already, and both nodded to indicate that the signal they were receiving from Kim was good. Kim was patched in through a universal channel, so that she could hear everything the three Guardians said. They themselves could contact each other simply by saying the name of the person they wanted to speak to. Word-recognition software in the comms-link base units, programmed with the waveforms of each man's forename, would assign the signal appropriately.

'You're coming over loud and clear,' Rattray told her. 'The initial phase of the infiltration is complete. We are proceeding with the second phase. Now would seem to be a good time to assume control of the Ballard mainframe.'

'Say no more.'

Kim, in the early hours of a Tokyo morning, prepped her computer to penetrate the system at the air force base again. She reopened her trapdoor with a few keystrokes and sat back while her software insinuated its invisible, intangible tendrils into the network like some electronic nerve-parasite.

At the Brilliant Bagel, Arnold took up sentry position by the entrance to the passageway that led to the men's room. He was now armed with a pistol manufactured from the same matt-black metal that was a common component of almost all paraterrestrial hardware. The pistol had strange, runic detailing engraved on it in bright blue, and it was skeletal, like the framework of a gun, an outline sketch rather than the finished article. It weighed under two pounds, and Arnold bandied it about like a child's toy.

Inside the men's room, MacGowan stood back while Rattray pushed open the door to the OUT OF ORDER lavatory-cubicle and entered. On any other occasion MacGowan might have sniggered at the sight of the dignified erstwhile police inspector reaching up to pull the cistern chain. Might have made some joke about plumbing new depths, or the mission being a load of crap. Might have said that penetrating the security at Nowhere was a piece of piss. Something along those lines. But he held his silence. The thought of wisecracking did not even cross his mind. The time for that sort of thing was past. This was business now. Deadly serious.

With a clunk and a whirr, the floor of the men's room began to descend, taking the two Guardians with it.

29

All across the world they were waiting ...

In Bogotá the morning mist had not yet cleared. It clung to the buildings and the slopes of the Eastern Cordillera mountains like shreds of torn gauze.

In a well-appointed house set in its own compound on the outskirts of the city, a middle-aged man whose face was not the face he had been born with stood gazing out through the bulletproof panes of his study window at the cable car moving in shallow arcs between the pylons that stalked up the side of the highest peak of the range, Montserrate. Behind him, on the leather surface of a vast teak desk, a computer softly hummed.

Once an accountant, the middle-aged man had amassed a small fortune administering the financial affairs of certain Colombian 'businessmen', all of whom were now either dead or behind bars. These days, in spite of the cosmetic surgery that had altered his features, the man rarely ventured beyond the walls of the compound. There were a dozen separate bounties on his head, and no lack of hitmen keen to claim them.

Physically imprisoned, the erstwhile accountant had found a kind of freedom, a virtual globe-roaming existence, on the 'Net. He had also found a second calling, one that (he hoped) would never put him through the same agonies of conscience that his previous job had, and one that would never lead him again to do anything quite as foolhardy as selling out a cocaine cartel to the police.

Waiting …

In the same time zone as Colombia, in a cybercafé in New York's Greenwich Village, a young woman glanced furtively to her left and right to make sure that no one else was watching the screen in front of her. She was half convinced that she ought to get up, pay the bill for her breakfast and her downtime, and leave. She felt uncomfortable here, out in the open, among people, even though the café was all but empty.

Outside in the street, cars, buses and yellow cabs growled by. Commuters on their way to work milled past the café windows, a few of them glancing in, most lost in their own grey thoughts. All the commotion out there, all the activity, all the Real Life, filled the young woman's head with noise, desecrating the sanctity of her inner thoughts with the cacophony of the mundane. She knew she ought to head back home, where there were not all these people about, where it was safer. But she did not think she would be able to do what was expected of her on her terminal back home. Not with her mother there – her mother bustling and clumping around the tiny apartment they shared, asking her what she thought she was up to, sitting in front of that goddamned computer screen all day, she was going to make herself crazy that way, she was going to make herself go blind …

Hunching down, her knobbly elbows resting on the table in front of her, her twig-thin fingers splayed against her temples and holding back her long, auburn fringe, the young woman steeled herself to stay put.

Waiting …

It was mid-afternoon in Lagos, and a briny, truculent wind was blowing onshore from the Gulf of Guinea, its gusts causing windows and doors to rattle in their frames and palm-tree leaves to slap together like circus seals clapping their flippers.

In one house, a two-storey colonial residence on Victoria Island, these noises were making an already worried Nigerian teenager even more nervous. Above the wind-generated racket, it was possible he might not hear his father and stepmother returning home. The teenager was not supposed to be using his father's computer, and the consequences, if he were caught doing so, would be dire.

His father and his loathed stepmother were currently out on one of their all-day shopping sprees. Normally the thought of that gold-digging tramp blowing his father's money on vulgar, trashy clothes and jewellery would have made the teenager feel sick with disgust, but today he found himself praying that she would keep on shopping and spending. The longer she and his father were out of the house, the longer he could stay online.

His stepmother was the reason the teenager had been forbidden to use his father's computer. After that time when he had broken into the Lagos police database and falsified a criminal record for her (eleven convictions for prostitution, and it was no better than she deserved), he had been banned from even entering his father's study. If his father came home and discovered him there, he would receive a severe thrashing.

It was a big risk he was taking, but the teenager, keen to be of service, was determined to stay online as long as possible.

Waiting ...

The young man in Tel Aviv, likewise, was not supposed to be using the computer. It was a Saturday and, while his family were not Orthodox Jewish, they did observe all the various proscriptions of Shabbat. Were the young man to be discovered in his bedroom, sitting at his terminal, there would be trouble. He would not be punished, but his parents' disappointment would be as bad as a punishment. He had lied to them, telling them he had a headache so that he would not be disturbed. His mother disapproved of many things, but she frowned on lying most of all.

The young man, a sophomore law student at Haifa University, lived with his family in a beachfront condominium overlooking the Mediterranean. From his bedroom window he had an enviable view of the strip of white sand that ran along the city's entire western edge, and of the gleaming sea beyond. Today, the beach was packed with people sunning themselves, picnicking, and playing *matkot*, Israeli beach tennis. Swimmers bobbed in the shallows and, further out, waterskiers and windsurfers zipped to and fro, criss-crossing one another's wakes.

The sun was still several degrees above the western horizon, the ocean reflecting its light with a dazzling, gemlike blaze. When sundown arrived and Shabbat ended, the young man would no longer feel bad about what he was doing. Until then, though, he was going to suffer agonies of self-recrimination and anxiety.

Whoever said Catholicism was the religion of guilt had clearly not tried being a Jew.

Waiting ...

The arrival of evening in New Delhi had brought with it some relief from the sweat and swelter of the day, and the professional programmer, in his well-appointed apartment near Connaught Place, was glad that he could at last switch off the ceiling fans and throw open the windows to let in some fresh air.

He had been indoors all day, and the combination of tedium and confinement was beginning to grate. To relieve the tension he began pacing around the tiled floor of his living room, keeping one eye on his computer in case the message from the man in Paris should appear onscreen. The programmer was not certain how much success, if any, he and his colleagues around the world were going to have with the action they were intending to take. He did know, however, that he was not getting paid for this work, which was bad enough, and that he was stuck inside on a Saturday evening, which was worse.

'Something had better bloody damn happen soon, that's all I can say,' the programmer muttered to himself, still pacing. Otherwise this would be the last piece of *pro bono* hacking he ever did for de Sade and his *Société Pour la Vérité*.

Waiting ...

It was midnight in Alice Springs, and the Australian widow was in the middle of her umpteenth game of computer patience and for once not minding that, at her advanced age, she seemed to require so little sleep. Tonight the insomnia that habitually kept her up and awake into the small hours seemed not a curse but a blessing.

Two years ago, not long after she and her husband had celebrated their ruby wedding anniversary, her husband had collapsed and died while out mowing the back lawn. (A subdural haematoma, the doctor had said. Could not have been predicted.) She could recall little of the numb months that had followed, except that at some point, acting on the advice of a similarly bereaved acquaintance who had recommended that she find herself a hobby to give herself something to focus on other than her loss, she had gone out and impulsively purchased a computer. She had taught herself how the thing worked, and then she had gone online and found out there, in the 'Net, company and a strange sort of solace. It had not been long before she had begun teaching herself rudimentary hacking skills, and these she had honed by repeatedly invading the system at the US communications base at nearby Pine Gap. She only ever caused mischief there – the occasional loss of data, the occasional rude message, nothing drastic. She felt she was doing the Yanks a favour in a way, keeping them on their toes, relieving the monotony of their job.

Almost everyone who lived at Alice Springs resented the presence of the Americans, mainly because the base made the town a priority target in the event of nuclear war. Such a war might not be as likely as once it had been, but the resentment still simmered. Hence the widow, who in her day had been a vigorous anti-nuclear protester and campaigner, seldom missed an opportunity to inconvenience the Yanks.

Tonight, however, she was going to be inconveniencing someone else. An enemy whom, if this French bloke de Sade was to be believed, was infinitely more dangerous and insidious.

Waiting ...

Out of a shifting roster of twenty who had been contacted on de Sade's behalf by Xavier Barraud three days ago, these half-dozen hackers were the ones who happened to be online when the Guardian infiltration of the Nowhere facility began. United by the copper, fibre-optic, coaxial and etheric strands of the global telecommunications network, they stood by, poised to act as soon as the command came through from Paris.

And in Paris, Xavier himself was also waiting. Using the software he had been sent anonymously a few days ago, he was back inside Kim's system, lurking, a ghostly telepresence. He had sent the others copies of the software, too.

And now, at last, shortly after lunchtime, Xavier registered that Kim was re-entering the mainframe at the US air force base. He reacted swiftly, informing his associates around the world with a simple, one-word command:

Go

And with this message flashing out to six separate terminals in six different latitudes, the first-ever act of anti-Guardian sabotage to be carried out by the *Société Pour la Vérité* was under way.

30

'Kim,' said Rattray, 'we're downstairs standing in front of the main door to the facility. There's an alphanumeric code-lock mounted on the wall beside it.'

'Gotcha, John. Let me see. OK, the lock is alarmed. If you enter the incorrect code, you'll set the alarm off. The door itself isn't wired up. You can break through.'

MacGowan needed no further prompting. He already had a freeze-mine in his hand, a squat metallic tube with a ring of suction cups at one end. He used the suction cups to attach the mine to the door, set a calibrating dial, then depressed the activating plunger.

The mine squirted out a blob of a blue fluorescent jelly, which impacted against the door like a wad of expectorated phlegm. The jelly was a paraterrestrial substance which some Guardian – no one could quite remember who it was – had dubbed 'gelidnite'.

No sooner had the gelidnite made contact with the door than it was absorbed into the metal and the door began to emit the creaks and crackles of solid matter undergoing a precipitous drop in temperature. A sheen of frost spread out around the freeze-mine as atmospheric moisture condensed and turned to ice on the door's surface. When the entire door was coated with glittery whiteness, MacGowan detached the mine, then raised a grey-gloved fist and rapped on the door, once, hard.

A lacewing lattice of hairline cracks radiated out from where his knuckles had struck, spreading swiftly to the four corners of the door-jamb. Steel having been rendered as brittle as spun sugar, the door crumbled away in a chattering hail of tiny chunks, leaving a jagged aperture like a monster's fang-fringed maw. MacGowan bashed or kicked away the remaining shards that hung in place and stepped over the heap of door debris, which had started to give off a thin, spectral vapour as the effects of the gelidnite wore off and the shattered steel warmed.

An empty concrete corridor stretched ahead, lit for night-time by a single red light bulb mounted on the ceiling inside a wire cage. MacGowan, moving with surprising grace for such a big man, proceeded along to the junction at the far end. He was carrying a pistol identical to the one with which Arnold, upstairs, was armed – matt-black and skeletal, with bright-blue detailing.

At the junction MacGowan checked both ways before beckoning to Rattray to join him. They were not anticipating armed resistance within the facility itself, but it was better to err on the side of caution.

'End of the first corridor, Kim,' Rattray said *sotto voce* into his comms-link. 'Right or left?'

'Left leads to the bathrooms. Right's the way to the sleeping quarters and the laboratories.'

MacGowan indicated that Rattray should head down the corridor. As Rattray moved off, MacGowan took out a limpet charge, a small black disc the size and shape of an ice-hockey puck. Reaching as high up the wall as he could, he held the charge in place and let it attach itself, its weirdly flesh-like underside forging a molecular bond with the concrete.

On either side of the corridor there was a row of a dozen-odd doors, each sporting a number and a name-card in a slot. Rattray moved along, glancing at each one, looking for Byrne's name. He had just gone past one door when it opened inwards. He turned around. A man in a towelling bathrobe stepped out through the doorway, carrying a shaving kit in one hand and rubbing his other hand through his unkempt, slept-on hair. Yawning, the man glanced at Rattray, looked away, and then did a textbook double-take, looking back again, this time with an expression of puzzlement. There were smears of blood encrusted on Rattray's face and his torn shirtsleeve was soaked with the stuff. He still looked as though he had been in an accident of some sort.

Rattray took advantage of the man's surprise and confusion. Rushing at him, he clamped a hand over his mouth. Nerve-receptors working at an elevated speed, muscle fibres thickening and strengthening, he thrust the man backwards into the room from which he had emerged, and there judo-wrestled him to the floor. A sharp upward jab with the heel of his palm drove the man's nasal cartilage into his brain, killing him instantly.

Returning to the corridor, Rattray waited for someone else to emerge from one of the other rooms. The commotion had been slight but could have disturbed a light sleeper. MacGowan, at the other end of the corridor, stood still.

No doors opened, no heads poked out.

Rattray nodded to MacGowan and resumed his search for Byrne's room. He soon found a door marked 'Byrne, A.'.

MacGowan remote-armed the limpet charge using his wristpad, then rejoined Rattray.

Standing back from the door, Rattray grasped the handle with one hand and raised the other. MacGowan, facing the door, steadied the black and blue pistol at waist-height.

Rattray showed MacGowan three fingers. Two fingers. One. None. Then thrust the door open.

MacGowan lunged into the room, Rattray following close behind.

The room was empty. Rattray went over to the bed, threw back the covers and laid a hand on the bottom sheet. Still warm. Byrne must have got up within the past quarter of an hour. They had missed him by moments.

'I'll try the bathrooms,' said MacGowan.

He returned a minute later.

'No luck. He must be in one of the laboratories.'

He saw that Rattray was peering at the child's pictures that were affixed to one wall of the room. MacGowan had not noticed the pictures before.

'He has kids,' he said.

'One son,' Rattray replied.

'You didn't tell us that.'

'Would it have made any difference if I had?'

'No,' said MacGowan. 'No, I suppose not. It's just … It brings it home, you know? When you're confronted with it.' He tightened his grip on his pistol and his resolve. 'Ah well. Fuck it. Let's get this over with.'

31

Kim did not see her Koven suddenly become engulfed by a vast flood of raw data. She did not see the onscreen conversations-in-progress disappear amid a welter of facts, statistics and columns of figures, or the graphic interfaces and users' avatars dissolve and break down into pure, basic ASCII code. To the exclusion of all else she was concentrating on her mother-screen, where the Ballard schematic of the Nowhere facility was displayed.

Haiiro No, however, was cognisant of the danger, and swung into action, setting about containing the data-deluge the way he would a power surge or a junkmail-borne virus, isolating the affected areas and re-routing essential functions elsewhere.

But before these countermeasures could be successfully executed, a second wave of invasive software came crashing in from outside, this one lousy with bugs. A digital locust swarm was unleashed on Kim's system and rampaged through sector after sector, devouring RAM and leaving swathes of bald, deleted memory-space in its wake.

Haiiro No, overburdened and unable to cope, signalled his distress by flashing up on the mother-screen and jumping up and down there, waving his arms and informing Kim, with a panicked inflection in his synthes-ised voice, what was going on.

Kim looked up to see the images on the lesser monitors

that surrounded the mother-screen one by one being reduced to gibberish and sizzling snow.

Who could this be? Who would even dream of attacking her, Otaku Queen, in her own lair? How *dare* they!

Outrage swiftly gave way to the urge to retaliate, but she knew that she could not afford to divert her energies elsewhere, not while the action-to-suppress was still in progress. The three men in Nevada were relying on her to guide them safely through the Nowhere facility. All she could afford to do right now was shut out the intruders and limit the damage they were inflicting. She would, however, make sure to run a trace on these digital vandals, so that vengeance could be exacted later.

Without extricating herself from Ballard, she switched back over to her main CPU, summoned up her most potent viral-extermination packages, and let them loose.

The viral-extermination software went to work, tracking down and neutralising every byte of externally introduced contamination. She watched as sector after sector was fumigated, the ratio of corrupted data to uncorrupted gradually stabilising.

Finally a synthesised trumpet voluntary rang out and Haiiro No came onscreen to announce that the damage had been contained and the system was clear. He mimed wiping sweat from his forehead, and Kim, puffing out her cheeks, copied the gesture.

Otaku Queen triumphant, no problem. Better luck next time, losers!

She was in the process of calling the Nowhere schematic back up when the third attack began.

32

Beyond the subterranean facility's sleeping quarters lay an open-plan canteen-cum-recreation-room. At one end there were cooking and dining facilities, at the other a pool table and a set of armchairs clustered around a TV set and a VCR, with a selection of prerecorded video-tapes stacked on shelves behind. Articles and cartoons clipped from newspapers were pinned to a cork bulletin-board, a Kermit the Frog doll sat, slumped but grinning, atop a chilled-water dispenser, and travel-company posters of tropical beauty-spots were tacked to the walls, the scenic paradises depicted seeming somehow all the more remote and unattainable for being displayed here, in a windowless chamber below ground.

MacGowan finished setting another limpet charge, attaching this one midway along the exposed load-bearing joist that bisected the ceiling. He clambered down from the chair that he was using as a stepladder and crossed over to join Rattray at the entrance to another corridor that led off into the laboratory area of the facility.

Along this corridor the doors were half-glassed, so that it was possible to identify the purpose of each room at a glance, even in the red-lit gloom. One contained an industrial lathe and other items of heavy-duty metal-working equipment. Another was furnished with an oval pine table surrounded by plastic chairs and a free-standing wipe-clean whiteboard whose display surface was covered with complicated mathematical equations scribbled in marker-pen. Another room was filled with rack-mounted testing apparatus, each unit sporting a profusion of knobs, potentiometers and buttons and an array of readouts, diodes and dials, all of them blank and unlit.

The only solid door in the corridor lay at its far end, and was marked LAB 1. Along its threshold a strip of light shone.

Halting at the door, Rattray held MacGowan back by the elbow. 'Kim?' he whispered.

There was no reply, only a sizzle of satellite static in his ear.

'Kim?' he repeated. 'Do you read me?'

MacGowan looked at him questioningly.

'Kim, if you do read me, we've reached the door to the main laboratory and are preparing to enter. Kim? Do you copy?'

'John, yes, sorry, what was that?'

'We may be getting some ground-interference with our signal. I said, we're at the door to the main laboratory.'

'OK.'

'Kim, is everything all right?'

'Everything's fine. I'm just ... There's a slight problem.'

'What sort of problem?'

'Nothing I can't handle.' But Kim's usually confident tone sounded forced, unnatural.

'Should we abort?' asked MacGowan.

'I'll have it under control in a moment.'

MacGowan covered the mouthpiece of his comms-link mic. 'We don't have a huge time-window,' he said to Rattray. 'Somebody's bound to turn up at the diner at some point, and there's no guarantee Arnold'll be able to deal with them before they can raise the alarm. We can't just stand around with our thumbs up our bums waiting for Kim to sort herself out. Either we move now or we abort. It's your call.'

'Kim,' said Rattray, 'do you still have control of Ballard?'

'I – I think so.'

Rattray heard a furious tapping of computer-keyboard keys. 'Be more certain.'

'I can't. Give me three minutes and I'll know.'

'We don't have three minutes,' said MacGowan. 'It's now or never.'

Rattray glanced at the door. 'Byrne could hit a panic button as soon as we enter. Can you be sure of neutralising him straight away, if necessary?'

MacGowan raised the pistol and thumbed a switch. The pistol, faintly, began to whine. 'If he so much as twitches,' MacGowan said, 'he goes down.'

'All right, then,' said Rattray. 'It's a risk, but an acceptable one. Let's do it.'

MacGowan took one pace back and kicked open the door.

33

Byrne was enjoying his first coffee of the day with Hansen, who was seated at her terminal, getting ready to run yet another computer simulation.

Both scientists' heads snapped round as the door was booted open. Both scientists' expression went slack with shock as a large man strode into the room, clad in some sort of bizarre quasi-military uniform and carrying a handgun that looked like something out of a science fiction movie.

'Oh Christ,' Byrne breathed, and the coffee mug slipped from his fingers, fell to the floor and smashed, splashing his and Hansen's shoes with hot brown liquid.

MacGowan moved swiftly over to the two scientists, holding the pistol at chest-height, covering them both. 'Hands where I can see them,' he said.

Slowly, Byrne and Hansen raised their hands.

'Who the hell are you?' Byrne asked. The bold phrasing of the interrogative was belied by a quaver in his voice.

'None of your business,' said MacGowan.

'Tony Byrne?'

A second man had entered the laboratory. With a supreme effort Byrne managed to tear his gaze away from the man holding him and Hansen at gunpoint and look at the new arrival.

He was white-haired and dressed in ordinary clothes.

The sight of the torn and bloodied shirtsleeve put a frown on Byrne's face.

'What *is* going on here?' Byrne said. 'And how did you two get in?'

Rattray ignored the questions. 'The blinds,' he said, pointing to the row of windows that ran along one wall. 'Open them.'

'Move slowly,' warned MacGowan, training the pistol on Byrne's head. 'So slowly I'll think you're going backwards.'

Like someone wading armpit-deep through a swamp Byrne crossed over to the switch that controlled the blinds. 'Please,' he said. 'I have a family. A son.'

'We know,' said MacGowan grimly.

'British,' said Hansen.

MacGowan flicked a glance in her direction. 'What about it?'

'You're British, aren't you? But you guys are supposed to be on the same side as us.'

'What are you on about?'

'Or is this industrial rather than international espionage? Is *that* why you're here?'

MacGowan, deciding the less said the better, returned his attention to Byrne.

Rattray joined Byrne at the windows just as Byrne hit the switch. The blinds retracted with a hissy, metallic rattle. At first there was nothing to be seen through the thick windows but shadows and darkness. Then Byrne hit a second switch and several batteries of floodlights came on, revealing the adjoining chamber to be a large hangar-like space. The floor was substantially lower than that of Lab 1 and the walls rose all the way up to ground level. Fitted into the ceiling, and filling most of it, were a pair of large, hydraulically operated, downwards-hinging doors.

Byrne's invention rested on a raised metal platform whose perimeter was demarcated with black and yellow hazard-warning stripes. The antigravity craft was circular, nearly eight metres in diameter, and consisted of a fat

265

outer ring surrounding a central hemispherical dome. What appeared to be large ball bearings could be glimpsed through the narrow join between the two sections, gleaming with lubrication. The external shell was constructed entirely from moulded panels of dull-grey anodised steel. There were no viewing ports, nor was there any obvious means of access into the craft. It balanced on three jointed, heavy-sprung legs, and a length of thick, rubber-insulated cable snaked out from underneath it, connecting it up like an umbilicus to a power-supply socket on one wall.

'Looks about as aerodynamic as a tractor tyre,' was MacGowan's verdict.

'She may not look much, I grant you,' Byrne replied, with the defensive air of a father who has just been informed by a complete stranger that his child is ugly, 'but she can achieve faster-than-sound speed without creating a sonic boom and she can dance in the air like a dragonfly. Or at least,' he added, somewhat more humbly, 'so the computer models say. She hasn't yet been field-tested.'

'Function determines form,' said Rattray, peering down at the craft.

'As far as the prototype goes, yes, that's correct.' Byrne saw here an opportunity to stall for time and evaluate the situation. If he could work out what it was these two men wanted, he might be able to figure out a way of giving it to them that would ensure that he and Hansen were not harmed. He decided to adopt a tactic similar to the one he had used on Colonel Clayton: baffle with techno-babble. 'The outer hull has to be toroid to accommodate the lift coil of superconducting niobium/tin electro-magnets,' he said. 'That's how the anti-mass field is generated. The lift coil's magnetic core is moved along its field lines and the hull is rotated in the counter direction, rendering the entire vehicle weightless and generating a considerable vertical thrust. In later models, of course, the propulsion system could be incorporated more aes-thetically into the design of the craft.'

Predictably, the soldier-type Englishman with the gun looked nonplussed. The other Englishman, however, appeared not only to be interested in what Byrne was saying, but also to understand it. 'The anti-mass field generator must give off quite a bit of radiation,' he said.

'The interior of the cabin is well shielded. As is this laboratory.' Byrne tapped the window. 'Lead-impregnated glass.'

'And despite her lack of aerodynamic elegance, she can do everything you say she can?'

'When the anti-mass field is generated, the layer of air immediately surrounding the hull becomes charged plasma, a mixture of positively charged atmospheric ions and negatively charged electrons. The plasma particles flow around the surface of the craft at immense velocity without touching it, thus eliminating aerodynamic drag and allowing her to turn on a dime.'

'And she's ready to fly?'

'Today was going to be her first scheduled test-flight.'

'She's quite an achievement. I congratulate you.'

'You'll understand if I fail to be flattered,' said Byrne, with as much rancour as he dared. 'Seeing as how you're probably about to destroy her.'

Rattray, ignoring the remark, turned away from the windows. 'Blueprints,' he said. 'Where are they?'

Byrne indicated a computer workstation in one corner of the laboratory. 'Everything's stored on hard disk there.'

'Back-up diskettes?'

Byrne shook his head. 'Too much of a security risk. Everything there is to know about her is on that computer.' It seemed to him now that Hansen's second guess had been right. This *was* industrial espionage. Whether that meant he and Hansen were in more danger or less, Byrne had no idea, but at any rate he *felt* more confident that they were somehow going to emerge from this situation unscathed, as long as they did not cause any trouble or put up any resistance.

He leaned close to Rattray, lowering his voice. 'Listen.

You seem to me like an intelligent and reasonable man. I'll give you the password you need in order to access the files. You can take it all, the plans for the propulsion system, everything. Just please don't hurt us. I've no reason to be noble about this. Like I said, I have a wife and son. They're more important to me than anything.' At that moment Byrne realised this to be true, and he regretted all the weeks he had spent away from Ruth and Ant and the precedence he had given, over their needs, to his work. 'And my colleague here's got family in Iowa. Isn't that right, Hansen?'

Byrne glanced over at the engineer.

His eyes widened.

Hansen had lowered one hand and was groping furtively around the side of the desk. Her attention was fixed on MacGowan, who was standing sideways-on to her, concentrating on Byrne. Her eyes, behind the thick lenses of her spectacles, were narrow and resolute.

Byrne cried out, 'Hansen! No!'

MacGowan wheeled around and took aim with the pistol. 'Don't do it,' he warned.

For a split-second Hansen hesitated, then, gritting her teeth and squeezing her eyes shut, she made a desperate, fatalistic lunge.

At precisely the same moment that Hansen's stubby fingers found the panic button hidden along the side of the desk, MacGowan squeezed the trigger and a ribbon of coruscating blue light erupted from the pistol's barrel, zipping across the room to strike the engineer in the face. She threw back her head, mouth gaping in a soundless scream, body twitching and spasming in a brief, brutal dance of death. Her skull was lit up from within, filled with an azure glow that silhouetted her teeth through her cheeks and her eyeballs in their sockets, and then spread out under her skin, dispersing over her neck and torso in vein-like patterns that rippled and crackled and dissipated. She toppled forwards, her forehead crashing down on to her keyboard, her spectacles snapping in two at the bridge. The mashing of multiple keys at once halted the virtual test mid-run and prompted an onscreen message of 'ERROR! Invalid Command – Please Retry'.

'Stupid move,' said MacGowan, lowering the gun.

And then a klaxon began to sound, filling the corridors of the facility with its braying whoop, and all over the town telephones started to ring, letting out a long, continuous trill that had dozens of old men leaping from their beds and reaching for their boots and their firearms.

34

Through her headphones Kim heard the klaxon go off. Seconds later she heard Rattray's voice, superficially calm but with urgency compacted into every syllable.

'Kim, cancel the panic alarm in Lab 1 and send an error-override message to Ballard.'

Kim looked up at her screens, the majority of which showed either fizzing snowstorm static or fast-scrolling strings of random characters. Her hands were lying inert on either side of her keyboard like a pair of exhausted animals. She had abandoned her resistance. What was the use? A lone intruder she could have coped with, but this was a concerted effort, at least five, maybe six hackers punching their way into her system at once, a tag-team assault. Every time she saw off one of them in one sector, another would start causing trouble in another sector. She had used every trick she knew, deployed every piece of software she had in her possession, all to no avail. There was nothing left for her to try. All possible avenues had been exhausted. It was hopeless. Even Haiiro No, in order to protect his code from harm, had been obliged to retreat to a corner of the mother-screen and curl up there inside an impregnable egg. Kim wished a similar foetal refuge was available to her.

Back in the school playground again, surrounded by sneering tormentors. Hands reaching out to pinch her and punch her and pull her pigtails. Mouths calling her

*names, the least ugly of which was 'ugly'. Everyone
ganging up against her, mocking her, laughing at her.*

She had thought she had conquered these fears. She
had thought she had buried them safely away where they
could not hurt her. But not so. They had just been lying
dormant, waiting to resurface at the slightest excuse. It
had all been a joke, a cruel trick. The status she had
achieved, the respect she had earned – these things had
been granted her purely so that they could, at a later date,
be stripped away again. All along, the world had been
secretly, silently conspiring against her. It was an apt
revenge on someone who spent so much time playing on
and preying on the conspiracy fears of others.

'John,' she said quietly, and she was close to tears, 'I've
lost control. There are people in my system. It's all gone
wrong. I can't help you.'

'Kim.'

The way Rattray spoke her name then flew through the
panicked memories of playground humiliation, through
the paralysing fear, through the despair, homing deep
inside to a still, quiet corner of her soul. Rattray was
thousands of miles distant, yet it was as though he was in
the room with her, standing at her shoulder, laying a
heavy, reassuring hand on her, leaning close, whispering
intimately in her ear.

'Listen to me.'

Tranquillity came over Kim, as cool and thrilling as a
wave at the beach cresting and breaking over her
shoulders. The klaxon at Nowhere was still sounding.
Arnold was demanding to know what in Christ's name
was happening, because the goddamn phone in the
kitchen had started ringing like a bitch and was not
stopping, and MacGowan was replying angrily that the
whole situation had gone arse over tit and then telling
Tony Byrne to stay absolutely still and do nothing
because otherwise he was next. But Kim was tuned in to
Rattray's voice, and was listening to him and him alone.

'No one is better than you at what you do,' Rattray
was saying. 'Whoever's inside your system, get them out.

Fry their printed circuits. Make it so that they'll wish they'd never laid eyes on a computer. You are Otaku Queen. You can do it. I know you can.'

Things had gone terribly awry. The Guardians at Nowhere were counting on her to put them right again.

Kim settled herself forwards in her chair. She did not have any clear idea what she could do. Perhaps an all-out purge-and-reboot? It was a drastic step to take, and she was not sure she had sufficient control of her system to initiate the necessary command-sequence and, even if she managed it, she might not be able to get back inside Ballard in time to be of any use. Still, for everyone's sake, including her own, she had to try.

At that moment, just as Kim's index fingers were instinctively locating the home-keys on the keyboard, a parchment scroll appeared mid-centre of her mother-screen, and unfurled downwards to reveal a message written in an elegant script, Roman-alphabet characters rendered in Japanese brush-pen style:

Need some help?

Three simple words of English, and Kim stared at them, and blinked hard a couple of times, as though she was in a desert and an oasis had shimmered into existence on the horizon and she had to be sure that she was not seeing things, that it was not a mirage.

The message remained where it was. Stirring herself, Kim called up an answer-window and typed in, 'Who is this?'

The message reappeared, reiterating its offer.

She tried again – 'Who is this?' – and again all she got in the way of a reply were those three short words: 'Need some help?'

Finally, after her third enquiry as to the identity of her mysterious would-be ally, the message was amended to: 'If you don't want my help, just say so and I'll leave you alone.'

Like most in her profession, Kim was by nature a

loner. The very thought of working in tandem with anyone else was anathema. It was an admission of failure, of inadequacy. Newbies sometimes ganged together, making up in numbers for what they lacked in ability, but a pro took pride in his or her solitary skill. Dogs hunt in packs. A tiger stalks alone. (And this, to a large extent, was the reason why the multilateral attack had caught her so by surprise. A group of evidently talented individuals operating in unison – it was such an unlikely occurrence that she simply had not been prepared for it, practically or psychologically.)

Now, here she was, being asked if she wanted assistance, and just when she could really do with it.

But how could she tell if this stranger's offer was genuine or not? It might be a trap, a deceit – one of her attackers pretending to be a friend in order to gain her trust, only to turn around a moment later and mock her for her gullibility. Giving the knife a further cruel twist.

The stranger must have guessed what she was thinking, because the present message was erased and a new message appeared: 'Consider this a token of my sincerity.'

Three seconds later, the klaxon at Nowhere fell silent.

35

As soon as he understood that the mission had been compromised – had gone from covert to overt – and that there was going to be trouble, Arnold took refuge behind the counter, where he and MacGowan had laid out the bodies of the graveyard shift in an untidy, gangling heap. As he hunkered down beside the dead veterans the stench of their blood pervaded his nostrils, accompanied by the fainter smells of faeces (death-trauma had caused one of the old men to void his bowels) and stewing coffee.

He noticed that the veteran whose head he had cleaved in two was still holding on to the Smith and Wesson 9mm, right hand rictus-clenched around the grip. Tucking away his own paraterrestrial pistol, he unpicked the dead man's fingers from the gun. The warmth had almost gone from the man's flesh. The stainless steel of the Smith and Wesson was only slightly cooler.

He checked the ammo clip and drew back the slide, chambering the first round (a smooth action – this was a well-looked-after sidearm). The paraterrestrial pistol was as lethal as any earthly handgun, but its toy-like lightness made it somehow less reassuring to hold. There were times when this raygun shit just did not cut it, when you needed the solid weight of an American-made man-stopper in your fist, something that did not merely snap and spit a blue beam, something that boomed and recoiled. The Smith and Wesson nine-mil, a favourite among cops, was a good, straightforward, reliable weapon. Like the Colt .45 Arnold used to carry in his Green Beret days, you could bash it and bump it, dash it and dunk it, and it would still fire.

Abruptly, the telephone in the kitchen stopped ringing. The silence throbbed.

Then: faint footsteps outside. Several sets. Boot soles scuffing on dust-covered asphalt.

Arnold raised his head above the countertop and saw half a dozen old men emerging from around the side of the chapel opposite the diner. All were holding a handgun – both revolvers and automatics – and all appeared to have dressed in a hurry. Shirts were incorrectly buttoned and tucked imperfectly into waistbands, and the wrinkled collar of a pyjama jacket flopped over the neck of one man's sweater.

A pair at a time, the old men loped across the road to the parking lot, their colleagues keeping them covered with their guns. There was a drilled precision about their movements, but in some cases an unlimber slowness, too, as worn old leg-joints failed to match up adequately to the demands being placed on them.

All safely across the road, the veterans crouched down between the parked cars, chests heaving from the exertion. One of them – the stocky ex-Marine who had followed Arnold into the men's room on his first visit to the diner – unhooked a walkie-talkie from his belt and spoke into it while, squinting, he scanned the interior of the diner for activity. Fortunately for Arnold, either the erstwhile Leatherneck's eyesight was poor or a reflection of the low sunlight was flaring off the window. Either way, he was having trouble seeing through the glass.

As Arnold watched, a second wave of old soldiers arrived at the side of the chapel. One was carrying a shotgun, a Remington 12-gauge. Another toted an aged carbine whose make Arnold could not identify at this range.

It was roughly ten metres from the line of parked cars to the Brilliant Bagel's front door. Not a vast distance to dash across, even for an old man. Sooner rather than later, Arnold reckoned, one of the veterans was going to make a bid for the door. For now, however, the old men did not appear to be about to move. In fact, they looked to Arnold like they were waiting for something.

Of course.

The front door was not the only entrance to the diner. There was the way he and MacGowan had got in, the less exposed access-point, the back door, which MacGowan had reduced to a heap of fragments with the freeze-mine.

Lowering his head below the level of the counter, Arnold crawled around the five corpses, placing his hands and feet gingerly to avoid the puddles of their blood and breathing through his teeth. Above his head the coffee machine let out a hissing gurgle, as though mocking the corpses (and, perhaps, Arnold as well) by mimicking the guttural croak of a death-rattle.

Reaching the swing door that led to the kitchen, Arnold went down flat on his belly and nudged the door slowly open a few inches. Holding the Smith and Wesson close to his cheek, he peered through the gap, past the deep-fryers, the stoves, the refrigerators and freezers, the racks of cooking utensils, to the empty frame of the back door.

There, darkening the ground just beyond the shallow mound of door debris that littered the threshold, he saw the elongated shadow of a man's head and shoulders. The shadow was moving slightly, and Arnold glimpsed the silhouette of a walkie-talkie antenna held next to the shadow head. Cupping a hand behind his left ear (the one not plugged with the comms-link earpiece), Arnold was able to detect the faint murmur of a lowered voice. Then a second shadow appeared beside the first, and then a third.

OK, he thought, nodding to himself. Fine. Not a problem.

Arnold had been in enough fubar situations before – the Oregon fiasco sprang to mind – to know that there was nothing to be gained by apportioning blame while everything was still in the process of going down the pan.

All you could do was adapt to events as they unfolded, be flexible, make the best you could of the altered circumstances, and hope to survive. Afterwards was the time for recriminations, for should-have-done-thises and shouldn't-have-done-thats. All the same, he could not help feeling just a little bit aggrieved that the computer whizkid had screwed up, the Brits had screwed up, and yet he, Arnold X, the only one who had *not* screwed up, was the only one who was in any immediate danger. There would be strong words later, you could count on that. Assuming, that is, he got out of this alive.

Propping the swing door ajar with his shoulder, Arnold laid down the Smith and Wesson, undid one of his bandoleer pouches and drew out a black cylinder the size of a shotgun cartridge. Printed on the side of the cylinder was a blue symbol, a circle with arrows radiating out from its epicentre. At one end there was a cap, which Arnold popped off with his thumb, to expose a spring-loaded detonating catch. Extremely carefully, he inserted the catch end of the cylinder between the swing door and its jamb, then, equally carefully, eased the door shut, trapping the cylinder in place. Only when he was absolutely certain that the cylinder was secure and the detonating catch still depressed did he let go of the door, snatch up the gun and scramble back on all-fours to the other end of the counter, clambering hastily over the bodies this time rather than easing himself around them.

He slithered across to the entrance to the passageway that led to the restrooms, hauling himself over the floor tiles with his knees and elbows. Once safely ensconced inside the passageway, he sat up on his haunches, leaned back against the wall, knees up to his chest, and activated his comms-link.

'Bill?'

'Arnold. What's your status up there?'

'We got ourselves two teams of old-timers converging on the diner, one out front, the other out back. Front team are wary about comin' in, and the rear team have a heavy-g surprise waiting for 'em. What's the plan?'

'How long do you think you can hold them off?'

'I'm in a defensible position, but as far as exiting the way we came in goes, I'd say we're pretty much fucked.'

'All right. Stay put for now. We're working on an alternative escape-route.'

'Work fast,' said Arnold.

From the direction of the kitchen door came the sound of something round and metallic rolling, released, and someone saying, 'Mother.' The first half of a well-known Oedipal oath? The beginning of an invocation to the Virgin Mary? Or the plea of a suddenly terrified old man for a return to the security – the maternal certainties – of his infancy? Which of these interpretations was the correct one would remain for ever undetermined, because the next instant the 'white dwarf' grenade that Arnold had lodged inside the swing door detonated.

The grenade emitted a pan-directional pulse of ultra-dense gravity waves that compacted every solid object they touched within a three-yard radius. It was as though a large, invisible globe abruptly manifested itself in the diner, squashing and displacing extant matter in order to make itself fit. A neat hemispherical crater appeared in the floor, lined with pulverised tile. A matching rounded section of the wall was dented inwards, as was a section of the counter opposite, plywood and Formica splitting and splintering along the cleanly curving perimeter of the damage. With a wrenching crack of wood and brick the kitchen doorway bulged as though an unseen elephant had squeezed through. The door itself, blown inwards, snapped free from its hinges and flipped sideways across the room.

The veteran who had opened the door, thus releasing the grenade, was instantly crushed to inch-thinness, becoming a shapeless upright mass of powdered bone and liquefied organ that collapsed to the floor in a wet, slithering gush. The pair of veterans who had been standing immediately behind him were thrown backwards with as much force as if they had been hit head-on by a ten-ton truck travelling at a hundred miles an hour.

Their mangled bodies sailed across the kitchen, trailing blood from every orifice, to smack brokenly against the rear wall.

A second's silence followed the grenade's detonation, and then there were yells of horror and disbelief from the men still positioned by the back door, who had watched some inexplicable, virtually soundless explosion take the lives of three of their colleagues.

You've sampled the *hors d'oeuvres*, thought Arnold. Now try the main course.

He drew out a pair of hi-ex grenades from his bandoleer. Leaning out from the passageway entrance, he lobbed one towards the front of the diner and the other into the kitchen through the warped, distended doorway, then ducked back to safety, pressing his hands over both his ears.

The floor beneath him rocked and jolted as the two grenades went off in quick succession.

The first explosion blew the entire front of the diner outwards, hurling shattered glass, lumps of brick and other debris over the startled veterans crouching between the cars. Parts of chairs, salt and pepper pots, paper-napkin dispensers, even a whole table, sailed from the building and thudded down into the parking lot and the street beyond. The old men stationed by the chapel scurried for shelter around the side of the locked House of God.

The explosion in the kitchen, meanwhile, tossed cookers, refrigerators and microwave ovens about as though they weighed nothing, and sent knives, utensils and saucepans flying in a storm of culinary shrapnel.

Outside the back door old men ran as hard as they could, hurdling the fence at the rear of the building and taking cover there. At the front of the diner, the ex-Marine shouted, 'Fall back! Fall back!' But the order was superfluous, for the veterans were already beating a retreat from the parking lot, those who had not been injured by flying debris assisting those who had. The gaping, roughly rectangular hole that had been the

Brilliant Bagel's façade formed an appropriately shabby frame for their limping and scurrying efforts.

Arnold watched the fleeing veterans gain the sanctuary of the chapel's side and regroup there, and he saw the ex-Marine engaged in an animated discussion, via walkie-talkie, with his counterpart on the second team. Then a smell of burning reached him.

Leading with the Smith and Wesson, he leaned out from the passageway and peered along the length of the counter to the kitchen. There, he saw to his dismay, a fire had started. A ruptured gas-pipe that had been connected to one of the displaced stoves was sending out a jet of blue flame several feet in the air, and orange flames were springing up around it, coiling and licking over the floor and the work surfaces and snaking up the walls, blistering and blackening wherever they went.

This was not good, Arnold thought. It would not be long before the fire was raging out of control. Whatever evac-plan Rattray and MacGowan had in mind, they had better put it into action pretty goddamn soon.

36

'Well, this is a turnabout, isn't it?' said Byrne. 'Your asses are on the line and all of a sudden you need my help. And if I refuse? Do I end up like her?' He pointed over at the lifeless form of Hansen, sprawled in front of her computer, which was still patiently awaiting a response to its onscreen prompt. They had worked together for so long and so closely, he and Hansen, that Byrne had come to think of her not just as an associate, not even as a friend, but as a physical adjunct, a part of himself that gave shape to his abstract mental processes. Losing her was like losing a limb. He was in shock, both numbed and pained at once, disbelieving and strangely reckless.

'Do you wish to see your wife and son again?' Rattray replied evenly.

Byrne looked deep into the Englishman's grey eyes, searching them for some flicker of expression that might give the man's true thoughts away, but his eyes were as blank and impenetrable as stone. He might be bluffing. The big guy with the beam-firing pistol (some kind of coherent-light weapon?) had killed Hansen without batting an eyelid. Doubtless he would feel as little conscience about killing Byrne. There was no reason for Byrne to trust either of these industrial spies or terrorists or whatever the hell they were. Yet Ruth; Ant …

His shoulders slumped. 'OK,' he sighed.

If there was a chance he might get to see Ruth and Ant

again, no matter how slim it was, how remote, he had to take it. Besides, it was just conceivable that he might be able to turn this situation around to his advantage.

Two muffled explosions resounded from overhead, causing thin clouds of displaced dust to drift down from the laboratory ceiling. MacGowan, who was in the process of attaching an EMP mine to the housing of the computer on which the blueprints for the antigravity craft and its propulsion system were stored, cast a glance upwards. 'Party going on upstairs,' he said.

'Bill,' said Rattray, 'how much longer are you going to be?'

'I just have to set this' – MacGowan pointed to the EMP mine – 'and lay another charge, then I'm done.'

'All right.' Rattray turned to Byrne. 'Come on, then.'

With a shrugging show of reluctance, Byrne crossed over to one end of the row of windows, where stood a heavy, lead-lined, airtight door marked with a yellow and black radiation-warning sign. The door, opened by a latch lever, gave on to a metal staircase that descended to the floor of the hangar. Byrne headed down the staircase, Rattray followed, and together they approached the raised platform.

'Getting in's a bit undignified,' Byrne said, stepping up on to the platform and ducking under the hull of the antigravity vehicle. 'Something we'll have to work on in later models.' Stressing a sense of continuity, emphasising to the other man that he was thinking of a future beyond today, seemed a good idea to Byrne.

He and Rattray crawled on their hands and knees until they were beneath the centre of the craft. Here, there was a round hatch set into the saucer's belly; next to it, a recessed panel where the umbilicus-cable was attached. Twisting around so that he was lying on his back, Byrne checked a gauge on the panel, then, nodding in approval, unplugged the cable. He grasped the locking handle of the hatch, rotated it one full turn anticlockwise, and swung the hatch downwards and outwards. A similar inner hatch opened upwards and inwards. With a grunt of effort, Byrne reached up with both arms and hauled himself awkwardly into the craft. He barely had time to pull his legs clear of the hatchway before Rattray followed. Though it might not even have occurred to Byrne to slam the inner hatch shut in his face, Rattray was not about to give him the opportunity. In one fluent motion, he manoeuvred himself up and in.

The cabin's interior was, perhaps predictably, circular, and the domed ceiling allowed sufficient headroom for Rattray to stand without stooping, although he did not think MacGowan would be so fortunate. A pair of seats were positioned back-to-back on opposite sides of the hatchway. Each seat was foam-padded and contoured to the human form, with a canvas lap-belt secured by a metal buckle, and each faced a curved control console with an array of instruments, readouts and displays. The craft evidently required a crew of two, a pilot and a navigator.

Byrne seated himself in the navigator's chair and activated the craft's radar scope and GPS. He then moved around to the pilot's chair and began pressing buttons and throwing switches. One by one indicator dials lit up – airspeed, altitude, ground attitude, false horizon, pitch, trim and so on. Also facing the pilot's chair were four viewscreens, which, when Byrne activated them, relayed black and white images from videocameras flush-mounted equidistantly around the craft's central dome, providing a 360-degree view of the hangar. On each viewscreen a bar was superimposed along the top, incremented in numbered degrees and with a letter indicating one of the four cardinal points of the compass. A fifth screen, positioned centrally between the other four so that together the five of them formed a plus-shape, showed two schematic views of the craft itself – one from above, the other a horizontal elevation – and was marked 'AMF Status'. Directly in front of the screens there were a joystick, a lever and various other controls.

'How long is this going to take?' Rattray enquired.

'Approximately six minutes,' came the reply.

'You can't make it any quicker than that?'

'The coil needs that long to warm up to full operating capacity. One of you guys, by the way, is going to have to play navigator.'

'I'm sure one of us can manage that. Bill?'

Byrne glanced round and saw that the Englishman was now talking into his comms-link mic.

'We're going to be off the ground in six minutes. I repeat, six minutes.'

'Roger that,' said MacGowan.

'Get Arnold down here.' Rattray pushed the mic-arm aside again. 'Might I ask a question?'

Byrne, not realising that he was being addressed again, did not respond.

'Mr Byrne?'

'Oh. Yeah. What?'

'I'd like to ask something. If it won't distract you.'

'I've been through the prep-procedure dozens of times,' said Byrne, nodding at the console. 'I could do it in my sleep. Fire away.'

'What sort of power source does this vehicle use? I have a feeling it takes more than a mains-charged storage battery to keep something as large as this off the ground.'

'D'you know,' said Byrne, 'that's the one thing nobody at the Pentagon has asked about. All they want to know is how fast can she go, what are her manoeuvrability specs, what weapons payloads might she be able to carry. How much energy she consumes? Doesn't bother them.'

'And you've been counting on that, haven't you? No one asking that question.'

Now Byrne did pause. He turned round in his chair again and looked hard at Rattray. 'How did you guess?'

'I didn't. It merely seems the logical conclusion to be drawn from the available evidence. You've cracked zero-point energy, haven't you?'

'I wouldn't say "cracked",' said Byrne. 'The idea just sort of evolved out of my early researches. Throughout the relatively brief history of antigravity research there's been a long-standing theoretical link between a massless propulsion system and free energy. If you had a couple of hours spare, I could go over the basic principles involved, tell you all about Black Hole evaporation and virtual particles and energy wells. But as we're on a tight schedule ...' He shrugged. 'Maybe you could get your fellow-countryman Dr Hawking to explain it all to you some time.'

'Maybe I will,' said Rattray. 'Dr Hawking and I have some unfinished business. We met several years ago. He's not been the same man since, although you can't help but admire his resilience.'

Byrne searched the Englishman's face for some hint that he was joking, but his expression was impassive, inscrutable. Was this the famous dry British sense of humour? 'For our purposes, at any rate,' he said, turning slowly back to the pilot's controls, 'all you need to know is that I have found a practical means of tapping that resource of free energy. Once this craft is off the ground, she generates all the power she needs herself. She can stay airborne virtually indefinitely.'

'I take it, then, that an antigravity drive was merely the bait you dangled in front of the military's noses in order to obtain the funding you needed. All along you had an ulterior motive.'

'It's time for a change. I've known this since I was a kid.' Byrne threw a lever, and a low, sine-wave pulse began emanating from the craft's toroid hull, a vibrant throb of sound that circled clockwise around the cabin, gradually gaining speed. 'Our present methods of generating energy are killing the planet,' he went on. 'Killing *us*. Burning fossil fuels isn't only hopelessly inefficient, it creates untold quantities of waste and pollution. As for nuclear fission – well, Three Mile Island and Chernobyl. Need I say more? What we have here is an endlessly renewable source of clean, efficient power which, once it's set going, puts out more energy than it consumes.'

'So why throw your lot in with the military? Why not apply to some civilian research-and-development agency for a grant?'

'I know. It goes against every belief my mother inculcated in me. But the military have the money and the resources to risk on a long-shot like this, and they don't ask too many questions. As long as they think they're going to get a new weapon or weapons-carrying system out of it, they pretty much leave you be. Deep pockets, shallow aims.'

'But they still get this' – Rattray indicated the craft around them – 'to use for non-peaceable purposes. How does that square with your ideals, your noble goals?'

'A trade-off,' said Byrne. 'You might even say a gamble. You see, it's my belief that the advent of free energy, if it's made openly available to everyone, won't just change people's habits and lifestyles, it'll change our entire way of thinking.'

'Literally *free* energy.'

'Exactly. Because once the concepts of "rich" and "poor" cease to have any meaning, then the boundaries and animosities arising between nations as a result of differences in wealth and resources will be eliminated at a stroke. Not only that, but energy production without unwanted by-products will awaken in us a new-found respect for the planet, and with that there will come a global shift in consciousness that'll see old modes of behaviour abandoned in favour of newer, better ones. Out will go war and social inequality and the uneven distribution of wealth. In will come peaceful coexistence and mutual co-operation between nations. Liberated from the constraints of the past, we will arrive at a better understanding of ourselves and our fellow human beings. In short, free energy will free us.'

'What you're talking about is nothing short of a worldwide revolution.'

'This is revolutionary technology,' Byrne replied, simply.

'But revolutions don't always come off as planned. More often than not they just bring a period of chaos and suffering, followed by a resumption of the status quo.'

'I have more faith in humanity than that.'

'Besides, once your employers realise what they have on their hands, they'll never share it with the public. They'll keep it to themselves.'

'I know.'

'So what were you intending to do? Post the blueprints on the Internet?'

'That,' said Byrne, 'and also something similar to what you're doing now.'

'Hijack your own invention.'

Byrne nodded.

'And then what?'

'Land her somewhere very public, in the full glare of the media spotlight.'

'Having alerted the TV stations and the press before-hand. And where would you set her down?'

'Where else? The White House lawn. Can you imag-ine? The biggest breaking-news story in history. "Space-ship Lands On White House Lawn." Except, the pilot's human, and he wants to share his technology with the world.'

Rattray was reminded of the film *The Day the Earth Stood Still*, where the Christ-like alien Klaatu lands his flying saucer in Washington and proceeds to try and warn humanity of the dangers of atomic weapons, only to be martyred by the military. There had been a hint of self-deprecating irony in Byrne's voice just now, but not enough to disguise the messianic import of his words.

It never ceased to amaze Rattray how naïve idealists could be. Everything was so simple to them, so straight-forward. He debated whether or not to break it to Byrne that, even if the Guardians had not shown up, his plan would have been doomed to failure. For one thing, it was unlikely anyone in the media would believe him when he contacted them. He would be dismissed as a crank. If he was lucky, he might be able to muster a token presence of reporters at his proposed landing site, a few bored hacks with nothing better to do, but that would be all. And, even assuming he did get as far as Washington without being shot down by the air force, the military would see to it that the world never found out what had happened. Film footage would be destroyed. Eyewitnesses would be intimidated into silence, and permanently silenced if they could not be intimidated. Official denials would be issued, and sightings of the antigravity vehicle explained away as a freak atmospheric effect or (tried and tested) a rogue weather balloon. There was no event so great that it could not be hushed up by the appropriate authorities and treated as if it had never occurred, something the Guardians were increasingly using to their advantage in the modern era, as the margins in which they could operate anonymously grew ever narrower and secrecy became less a matter of concealment and more a matter of disinformation and misdirection. Rattray could have reeled off a list of recent headline-grabbing massacres and disasters – Jonestown, Bhopal, the downing of Korean Airlines Flight 007, the *Challenger* explosion, the *Exxon Valdez* catastrophe, Waco, the gas attack in the Tokyo subway system, – and asked Byrne if he accepted the official version of any or all of these incidents and then offered him an alternative, and factually more accurate, explanation for each.

Instead, he decided that Byrne would remain more amenable and co-operative if he was allowed to continue to believe that there was some hope of his dream achieving fruition, as he obviously still did. So he said, 'Well, it could work, I suppose. How long till we're ready?'

Byrne glanced at the AMF-status screen. 'Couple of minutes.'

'Good. Kim?' The comms-link patched Rattray through to Tokyo. 'How are you getting on?'

37

Together, Kim and her unknown ally were picking off the intruders one by one, rousting them from her system and sending them back where they had come from. Her ally had programs of considerable complexity, as well as above-normal bandwidth and access to substantial processing power. Those alone meant nothing, but he/she had ability, too, and plenty of it. Not to mention (Kim grudgingly had to admit) a certain panache.

The main thing, though, was that collaborating with this stranger had given Kim back her self-confidence. In the old days, Japanese houses used to be built from wood and paper, and many still were even now, the idea being that, because they were made from such flimsy materials, it was of little consequence should an earthquake or a hurricane or a tsunami come along and flatten them. The philosophical-shrug school of architecture: what could be brought low without too much trouble could be raised again without too much trouble. And so it was with Kim's self-confidence, which she had not known was such a brittle, fragile construct until the unexpected, unprecedented assault on her system had so easily (all too easily) shattered it. It had taken first Rattray's faith in her and then, when she and her ally had begun working together, the realisation that she was in the company of a near-equal, to restore her nerve, and now that it was back, it was as though it had never been away.

As her fingers flew furiously over the keyboard, Kim

overheard snatches of dialogue between the Guardians at Nowhere, but was too preoccupied to listen closely. Onscreen, a spirited defence had burgeoned into a devastating counterattack, carried out, it must be said, with a vindictive glee on Kim's part. Not content with hounding the intruders out of her mainframe, she dogged them back to their lairs, her ally penetrating gates and clearing the way for her so that she could wade straight in and inflict even greater harm on her assailants' systems than they had on hers.

Down went a terminal somewhere on the west coast of Africa (and a teenage boy, staring at a suddenly blank screen, and at the same time hearing the sound of a key in the lock of the front door, felt a terrible, aching dread start to uncoil, python-like, in the pit of his stomach).

Down went another terminal, this one in New York City (and a sensitive young woman, hearing groans of frustration and irritation from the other users around her as every other computer in the cybercafé also went dead, wished she had never ventured out from her apartment that morning, and wished she could click her heels three times and be magically transported back there right now).

Down, crashingly down, went a terminal somewhere in Israel (and a young law undergraduate, shocked though he was at the utter obliteration of his operating system, none the less felt deep down that this was a fair and just punishment, no less than he deserved for violating the Shabbat).

Down went a terminal Down Under (and an elderly widow would be up for the rest of the night, cursing like a navvy as she attempted, in vain, to resuscitate the machine bought with a portion of her late husband's life-insurance settlement).

Down, high in the Eastern Cordilleras, went a terminal purchased – albeit indirectly – with the profits of illegal narcotics trafficking (and a former accountant would thank God that evidence of police payoffs and back-handers, which was probably the only reason his whereabouts had so far not been leaked to the people who wanted him dead, was safely backed up on diskettes).

Down, down, down went a terminal in New Delhi (and a professional programmer was left amazed, wondering just how it had happened, how this catastrophic reversal of fortunes could have come about when he and his colleagues had had Kawai Kim on the ropes, had had her reeling and ready to throw in the towel).

And down, on the outskirts of Paris, went a seventh and final terminal, that of the ringleader of the assault, Xavier Barraud, who watched with a wearying sense of *déjà-vu* as his screen smeared and ran, and realised, with dismay, that for all the disruption he and the others had caused the *Japonaise*, they had clearly not done enough to distract her from her task. This was the news he was going to have to break to Gérard de Sade: that they had tried and failed, that even seven of them were no match for her. And he did not think de Sade was going to like hearing that. De Sade did not strike him as the sort of man who handled disappointment well.

And when all this downing was done, Kim sat back in her chair with a sigh of satisfaction. Had there been time, she might have gone further, delivered the *coup de grâce* by tracing the intruders' private telephone accounts and adding several thousand yen's worth of calls to their bills. Later, perhaps. Right now, she had more pressing matters to attend to.

She rattled off a quick message to her nameless partner. The Otaku Queen could never stoop to saying thank you (gratitude was beneath her). Instead, she proffered congratulations on a job well done and expressed a wish – purely out of politeness, not intending that it would be fulfilled – that the two of them might communicate again some time soon. She also attached a secret tracer-tag to the message, which would report back the user's name and Real Life location.

Her ally's response was swift and tart:

I do not appreciate your feeble attempt to track me down. It is insulting to us both. I will overlook the lapse as an error of judgement born of relief. There are only two things you need to know about me: that my name is EMPEROR DRAGON, and that you are in my debt.

The words remained onscreen long enough for Kim to read them and take them to heart, and then the parchment scroll on which they were written was incinerated by a jet of fiery breath from the maw of a large, ornate dragon whose eyes flashed like rubies and whose scales glistened like jade as it roared and writhed across her screen, claws slashing, long tail lashing.

And no sooner had the dragon departed than the Nowhere schematic came back up, and Haiiro No emerged from his protective egg, stretching out his slender limbs and blinking his jet-almond eyes and asking how he might be of service.

Irritably Kim banished the sprite from the screen.

It was then that Rattray's voice came through, asking how she was getting on. Struggling to keep her anger out of her voice, she replied that she was up and running again. Rattray said that he was glad to hear it and that he, MacGowan and Arnold were themselves going to be up and running very shortly.

The attack had left Kim with approximately a quarter of her normal processing power – enough to be getting by with, just. A considerable quantity of data had been irretrievably lost, although, as far as she could tell from a cursory inspection, nothing vital. Restoring the damaged sectors was going to take several days. This she could accept. What she could not accept was the contemptuous and condescending manner in which she had been treated by Emperor Dragon. The way he had used her, taken advantage of her in a moment of weakness. How long had he been waiting for a chance to pull this stunt? How many days, weeks, months, even, had he been hiding out inside her system, silent, undetected?

She should never have accepted his help. Would not have, either, if she had known who he was and if others had not been depending on her.

In his debt? She would see about *that*.

38

Smoke was coming in from the kitchen in dense, dark, acrid billows, the flames being fanned by a through-draught. Arnold estimated he had three to four minutes before the fire spread to the eating area.

Batting aside his mic-arm, he took out a respirator from his bandoleer and fitted it over his nose and mouth, feeling the rim of the pliant, pear-shaped cup mould itself to the contours of his face to form an airtight seal. The respirator's membranous material filtered according to the direction of his breathing, extracting good air from bad as Arnold inhaled and expelling excess carbon dioxide as he exhaled. The smoke was making his eyes sting, but he had no paraterrestrial remedy for that.

Through the shifting, now-thinning, now-thickening curtain of fumes he watched the veterans outside equipping themselves with some high-power hardware. The building that looked like a closed-down grocery store was, it transpired, an armoury, and weapons were being fetched from it and distributed among a grimly eager throng of the elderly that now numbered at least fifty, including several women. Seeing M16s, Barrett 82A1 semi-autos, stubby little Heckler and Koch G11s, and even a tripod-mounted M60 being hauled out of the building, Arnold realised that, in his efforts to make the veterans overestimate the strength of their opposition, he had succeeded rather too well.

He was more than a little relieved, therefore, when

MacGowan contacted him and summoned him down-stairs.

'We've chartered ourselves a flight out of here,' MacGowan said.

'Byrne's antigravity machine,' said Arnold.

'Correct.'

'It works?'

'No, it doesn't. We just thought it'd be fun to sit in it and make brrrm-brrrm noises.'

'Cute.'

'John says it'll be ready to go in six minutes.'

'Copy that. I'll be right down.'

Arnold headed along the passageway to the men's room. He tried the door but found that, though the handle turned, the door would not open. What the hell was this? MacGowan and Rattray could not have been so stupid as to bolt the door behind them, could they? Actually, considering the way things had gone, it would not have surprised him if they had.

Then, from the other side of the door, he heard the sound of a motor thrumming up from below, and a muted babble of worried voices, growing louder.

The elevator, rising. The scientists were evacuating the facility. Which, obviously, was the SOP if the alarm sounded. And the men's-room door must automatically lock itself while the elevator was in use.

He would have to take the ladies'-room elevator.

Turning to face the door marked WOMEN, Arnold hesitated. This was no time for fine feelings, he knew, but still, it was such an ingrained taboo that he could not help himself. Forbidden territory. Females only.

What the hell. It was not as if anyone would ever have to know ...

Just as he grasped the door handle, a thought struck him.

The original plan had been to invalidate all the scientists and technicians in the facility along with Byrne. That plan might have gone to hell in a handcart, but the scientists still could not be allowed to walk free, not if between them they could cobble together enough knowledge to reproduce the antigravity technology at a later date.

Arnold turned around and bounded back towards the eating area.

From the passageway entrance he looked out through the diner's ruined façade. Rifle-toting veterans were moving in, approaching the parking lot from both sides. The M60 had been set up on the chapel porch, its muzzle trained on the diner. Two veterans were lying prone with the gun, one to aim and fire, the other to make sure the magazine-belt fed cleanly into the breach.

Glancing around the ruined eating area, Arnold could see only one place where he would be able to conceal himself.

Going down on his belly, he slithered across the floor to the counter and crawled over towards the bodies of the graveyard shift. Oddly enough, he was not nearly as daunted by the prospect of snuggling up to five fresh corpses as he had been by the thought of entering a ladies' restroom. He wondered what kind of pervert that made him.

Reaching the pile of dead veterans, he stretched himself out alongside them, face-down so that his respirator would not be visible, then drew one of the bodies partially over him like a kind of macabre eiderdown. He felt the cold, congealed blood on the floor soaking through the fabric of his suit, but at least, thanks to the respirator, he could smell nothing.

Lying as still and breathing as shallowly as he could, Arnold listened as the men's-room door opened and the scientists began filing out. Straight away one of them mentioned the smoke, and then they all began to cough. Einsteins that they were, it did not take them long to deduce that something somewhere was burning, and from this effect they extrapolated the cause of the alarm going off in the facility. From there they were able to arrive relatively swiftly at the conclusion that, smoke or no smoke, their best course of action was to head for the front door of the diner and out into the open air.

They moved along the passageway, spluttering and choking. As they entered the eating area, one of them exclaimed, 'What the hell happened here?' Another, catching sight of the jumble of bodies behind the counter, let out a horrified gasp that elicited a chorus of similar gasps from the others, as well as appalled moans and a couple of brief prayers.

But there was no time to stand and stare. Picking their way through the rubble, hacking and retching from the smoke, only just able to see where they were going, the scientists made their way towards the front of the diner and the light of day.

Arnold judged his moment carefully, estimating from the scientists' coughs and shuffling footfalls how close they were to the front of the building. Just before they emerged through the smoke on to the parking lot, he sloughed off the corpse on top of him, rose up from behind the counter, loosed off three rounds from the Smith and Wesson in quick succession, then lunged for the restroom passageway.

At the sound of the gunshots the scientists flinched and shrieked. Some froze in their tracks, others threw themselves to the floor. None of them was hit, but then that had not been Arnold's intention. What he had been hoping to do was provoke a response from outside, and this he achieved.

The veterans' reaction to the clear-and-present show of hostility from the diner was as extreme as it was immediate. It was, one might hazard, an over-reaction, but then this was what Arnold had been counting on. His three shots reaped a deafening, devastating whirlwind of return-fire. Bullets whooped and whopped and whip-cracked into the Brilliant Bagel's exterior and interior. Already damaged walls shuddered and spat chips of plaster; already ruined furniture splintered, twitched and jumped. The diner came alive with death, and the scientists, caught in the teeth of a bullet-blizzard, were helpless to evade it. Those who had frozen in shock when shots were fired from behind them were mown down by shots fired from in front of them, and fell reeling and flailing to the floor. Those already on the floor writhed and screamed as they were struck by direct hits and ricochets. Some cried out to the ex-soldiers who were supposed to be protecting them and were, instead, killing them. They begged for the firing to stop, but their voices were lost amid the din of the guns – the eardrum-battering volleys of rifle reports, the gnashed-teeth rattle of the M60.

Arnold sprinted down the passageway to the restrooms without a backward glance, away from the cacophony of screams and bullet impacts.

The gunfire continued long after the screaming had ceased, but as Arnold descended in the men's-room elevator the noise grew fainter until it was a distant echoing crackle, like a Fourth of July fireworks display a few streets away, and as he hurried through the doorway into the facility, leaping the pile of freeze-mined fragments, it faded from earshot completely.

Reaching the first junction of corridors, he removed the respirator and informed MacGowan of his location.

'What the hell kept you?'

'I got held up. Tidying up loose ends. Which way?'

MacGowan told him to take a right. Arnold ran past open doors, glancing left and right into rooms that showed evidence of hasty departure – unmade beds, open drawers, strewn clothing. As he entered the recreation area he relayed his position to MacGowan.

'Corridor opposite,' MacGowan replied. 'Keep going.'

Arnold ran.

'Open door at the far end,' said MacGowan.

MacGowan was standing on the far side of the laboratory next to the entrance to the hangar. His face fell when he saw the patches and smears of coagulated blood all over Arnold's suit, head and hands.

'Christ, mate, are you all right?'

'Just peachy,' snapped Arnold, striding across the room.

'We're on a bit of a tight schedule. Come on.'

Together MacGowan and Arnold clanged down the metal staircase to the hangar floor. As they reached the bottom MacGowan tapped a button on his wristpad, triggering the EMP mine. At a stroke the blueprints and every other scrap of data stored on the computer were erased, the memory core wiped clean. Then, in quick succession, MacGowan remote-detonated the first two limpet charges. They exploded, bringing down the ceilings of the corridor and recreation area, along with several tons of concrete and rock. He waited until he and Arnold had reached the antigravity vehicle before remote-triggering the third limpet charge. The ceiling of Lab 1 came thundering down, crushing furniture, equipment and the body of Hansen beneath it. The windows, buffeted in their frames, were thick enough to withstand the blast, although a few of them craze-cracked like car windscreens, turning frosty white. A landslide of rubble spilled through the hangar doorway and down the staircase.

Byrne's invention was throbbing loudly. MacGowan and Arnold – directed by Rattray, who had seen them enter the hangar on the cabin viewscreens – crawled beneath the vehicle and climbed up through the hatchway.

Byrne, without looking round from the control console, told the two new arrivals to close the hatches.

'Yassuh, boss,' drawled Arnold sarcastically, and pulled up the outer hatch and twisted its locking handle, then lowered the inner hatch and locked it, too.

'OK, baby,' Byrne said to his invention. 'Show us what you can do.'

He eased a lever forward and the toroid hull began to turn ponderously anticlockwise. Immediately the clockwise throb of the AMF generator increased in frequency and intensity, the two forces resisting each other, trying to cancel each other out. The craft lurched and swayed on its sprung legs, torn this way and that by counter-vailing torques. Each of the three Guardians grabbed hold of the nearest solid-looking object for support.

Gradually the hull's rotation gained momentum, and the throb mounted to a skull-trepanning groan. Digits on a gauge marked EXTERNAL RADIATION (BECQUERELS) began to count upwards from zero, while a faint glow became visible at the lower edge of all four viewscreens.

The craft began bobbing like a child keen to leave the room, as Byrne reached for a switch on the console marked HANGAR DOORS.

39

The veterans were none too concerned that, after the initial brief salvo from the diner, no further shots were fired at them. High on adrenaline and the smells of cordite and gun grease, reliving with flashback-clarity every firefight, every close-quarter battle they had ever been engaged in, inebriated with a fierce nostalgia for those old, bold days, all they could think of was delivering a response so awesome, so devastating in its ferocity, that it would leave their foe in no fit state to fight back. And in this goal, it seemed, they were successful. Hundreds upon hundreds of rounds were loosed off into the Brilliant Bagel. Scything arcs of bullets brought down the figures that had been glimpsed moving amid the smoke and taken for the enemy, and long after those figures lay still the firing continued, until the building was riddled inside and out with holes, pitted and pocked all over. Even when three deep-booming detonations reverberated from underground, the veterans kept shooting. It was only when the bell in the chapel belltower began to chime that the gunfire petered out, dwindling to intermittent bursts, then the odd sporadic single shot, and finally ceasing altogether.

For several tolls of the bell the veterans exchanged puzzled glances, as though unsure what this repeated note – such a pure, delicate, melodious sound to have brought to a halt such a sonic holocaust – could signify.

Then they remembered. The bell was ringing not, as most chapel bells do, to summon, but to warn away.

The two veterans on the porch picked up the M60 between them and staggered with it down the steps. Anyone who was close to the wooden building began backing away.

The bell continued to toll and then, abruptly, let out a tuneless, truncated clonk, as a fissure appeared along the apex of the chapel roof and, with a low mechanical rumble and an almighty creaking heave, the wooden building began to divide.

The chapel was hinged along the bases of its two longer walls, each of which was attached to one of the end-walls and a half-section of roof. These two interlocking sections separated like a pair of praying hands unclasping. Each opened out, swung cumbersomely through a ninety-degree arc and came to rest with a juddering bounce, eaves and gutters touching the ground. Simultaneously the hangar doors, for which the chapel had been no more than a disguise, a camouflaging shell, caved downwards and inwards, flooding the hangar with daylight.

There was nothing the veterans could do but stand and watch with a mixture of wonder and chagrin as Byrne's antigravity vehicle emerged from the gaping, sundered chapel and rose majestically into the air. A few of the old men and women, observing the roseate halo that shimmered around the craft's hull, realised that the diner's somewhat eccentric name had, all along, been a sly reference to the invention that had been taking shape below it.

As it continued to ascend the craft sucked up a swirling vortex of dust beneath it. Tresses and curls of smoke from the burning diner were also drawn into the vortex and, mingling with the dust, formed a dirty, inverted cyclone of suspended particles whose spout grew thinner and more attenuated the higher the craft rose, until finally it fell away from the craft like a rope cut loose, and the dust and smoke came drifting back down in a thin, fine mist that swept over the town and over the faces and heads of the veterans – a strange, arid benediction.

40

The moment Byrne's invention lifted off from the platform, its shuddering and lurching ceased. Gravity had not surrendered it without a fight but, in defeat, was magnanimous, relinquishing all claim. Smoothly, noiselessly, without turbulence, the antigravity craft glided up through the hangar doors into the wild blue yonder.

Enveloped in its anti-mass field, the four men inside experienced none of the customary effects of acceleration. Indeed, apart from the abrupt halt to the craft's violent rocking, the three Guardians might not have known they were airborne at all, had it not been for the images relayed by the external videocameras to the cabin viewscreens, which showed first the hangar walls rushing downwards, then a glimpse of the interior of the split-open chapel and the veterans standing around, then suddenly the rooftops of Nowhere, and then the entire town, which disappeared swiftly out of sight to leave vistas of rugged desert reaching to the horizon in all directions beneath an empty sky. It was like being in a cockpit simulator when the pistons that artificially generate the bumps and inclines of flight are not functioning. There was no feeling of motion at all, merely a mild and not at all unpleasant sensation of buoyancy.

The craft's creator and pilot manipulated the controls with calm, cool efficiency, but Byrne's eyes were agleam with an inner exultation. It was one thing to have believed – known – for several years that one day his brainchild would fly; it was quite another thing, when that day arrived, to find himself actually soaring aloft on the wings of the theoretical principle that he had dreamed up one hot, drowsy afternoon at Cal Tech during a particularly dull lecture on thermodynamics. To think that a few thoughts and sketches scribbled idly down on the inside cover of a ring-binder file could have chrysalised and metamorphosed into *this*!

Even the presence onboard of three men who had, for reasons still unclear to Byrne, come to destroy his creation could not tarnish his moment of triumph. If anything, knowing that this might be the one and only time his antigravity craft flew compelled him to savour the joy of the moment all the more. If there was one other event in his life that rivalled this one, it was that occasion nine years ago when, in a delivery room in the maternity ward of a hospital at Palo Alto, a midwife had looked up and pronounced him the father of a healthy baby boy.

The recollection of Ant's birth served to, as it were, bring Byrne back down to earth, reminding him that his motive in helping steal his invention was not simply to take it for a test-flight; that his goal here was getting back to Carson City and his wife and son. Easing back on the lever that regulated vertical speed, he slowed the craft's ascent and brought it to a halt, hovering at a height of 5,000 feet.

'Why have we stopped?' Rattray demanded.

'Because,' said Byrne, 'before we go any further, I have to establish something. We have a deal, right? I mean, I got you out of a tight corner back there, so it's only right that you give me something in return.' Rattray remained silent, so Byrne went on. 'I know nothing was actually said out loud at the time, but it was pretty much implied that if I saved your necks, you would let me live. That was the unspoken bargain, wasn't it?'

Before Rattray could reply, Kim's voice piped up over the comms-link. 'Guys? I think you may have a problem.'

Arnold, who had occupied the navigator's chair prior

to takeoff, was nodding sombrely. 'I was just about to say the same thing.'

'What now?' groaned MacGowan.

'Company,' said Arnold, pointing at the radar display. 'Coupla bogeys closing in from the north.'

'Those'll be F-15s from Ballard,' said Byrne, with just the merest hint of glee in his voice. 'Scrambled as soon as the alarm was triggered.'

'And their orders?' asked Rattray.

'What do you think?'

'Kim,' said Rattray into his comms-link, 'crash the system at Ballard.'

'Already on it, John.'

'Take us out of here, Byrne,' said MacGowan. 'Supersonic. Now.'

Byrne stared flatly back at the hulking Englishman. 'Make me.'

MacGowan bent down towards the scientist until their noses were almost touching. 'I don't think you'd want me to make you.'

'Oh yeah?' said Byrne. 'What are you going to do? I'm the only one who knows how to fly this thing. You need me. Without me, you're screwed.'

'Bill ...' Rattray made a warding-off gesture.

MacGowan glared at Byrne and backed away.

Byrne turned to Rattray. 'OK, so *now* we make a deal.'

'They're heading straight for us,' said Arnold. 'Twenty-five miles and closing.'

'I get us out of this,' continued Byrne, 'and at the end I walk away. Otherwise I let us sit here and get blown out of the sky.'

'I can't let you walk away, Byrne,' replied Rattray. 'It's simply not possible.'

'I give you my word that I will never build anything like this again.'

'Twenty miles,' said Arnold. 'Let's do something, hey?'

'Ballard is down,' Kim announced. 'Their radar's blind. They won't be sending up any more aircraft.'

Rattray's eyes, in the shadows of his heavy brow, glittered darkly. 'Very well, Byrne. If I have your word.'

'You do. If I have yours.'

Rattray's head inclined a fraction forwards in a near-imperceptible nod.

Byrne turned back to the controls.

'Fifteen miles,' said Arnold.

'All right,' said MacGowan to Byrne, 'thanks to all your farting around you've let them get close enough to get a fix on us. What are you going to do now? If it comes down to a straight race between an F-15 and this tin Frisbee of yours, my money's on the F-15.'

'We may not be able to outrun them,' Byrne replied, 'but there's a chance we might be able to outmanoeuvre them.'

'How big a chance?'

'Does it matter?'

MacGowan shrugged. 'S'pose not.'

'Ten miles,' said Arnold.

'You,' said Byrne to Arnold. 'Navigator. Which way did you say they were coming from?'

'North. Heading almost due south, bearing one-six-niner.'

'Then north we go,' said Byrne, grasping the joystick and angling it to the right. The horizons on all of the viewscreens began to move, the superimposed compass bars scrolling sideways until the letter 'N' was centred on the topmost screen.

'Hello?' said MacGowan. 'Earth to mad scientist. He said *from* the north.'

'What's their altitude?' said Byrne.

'*From* the north, you twat!' said MacGowan. 'That means we head the opposite way. It's called "escaping".'

'Seven-and-a-half thousand feet,' said Arnold. 'Byrne, he has a point. What are you doing?'

Byrne eased the joystick forwards and did the same with the vertical-speed lever, stepping up the intensity of the anti-mass field above the antigravity craft and along the north-facing rim of its hull. On the central AMF-status screen, pulsing field-lines thickened around the corresponding sections of the top and sideways elevations, as the craft increased its velocity and at the same time began to gain height.

'Oh, I don't buggering believe it,' said MacGowan. 'You're going to play chicken. You're going to play chicken with a pair of F-fucking-15s.'

'Trust me,' said Byrne.

On the top viewscreen, two small dots appeared low over the horizon, growing and resolving swiftly into the familiar spreadeagle silhouettes of jet-fighters seen head on.

'I can't watch,' said MacGowan, but found himself unable to tear his gaze away from the viewscreens.

The altimeter in front of Byrne displayed a reading of 7,000 feet and rising. The airspeed indicator showed 300 knots.

The F-15s broke left and right, disappearing off to either side of the forward, north-facing viewscreen. A dark blur flitted across each of the east- and west-facing viewscreens, and a second later the whooshing rumbles of the jet-fighters' engines roared by on either side of the antigravity craft, just as the F-15s appeared in the rearward viewscreen, their afterburners flaring as they moved back into close formation. The engine roar faded while, on the rearward viewscreen, the planes diminished to dots once more and were lost from sight.

'Why didn't they fire?' said Rattray.

'Warning pass,' said Byrne. 'They aren't going to shoot us if they think they can scare us into setting down.'

'They're coming around,' warned Arnold.

'Another warning pass,' said Byrne, as he stepped airspeed up to 350 knots. 'They'll give us at least two. This time we get proactive.'

'I don't think I like the sound of this,' said MacGowan.

'Navigator,' said Byrne to Arnold, 'where are they?'

'Ten miles and closing.'

'OK.' Byrne tightened his grip on the joystick. 'Here we go.'

The F-15s reappeared in the rearward viewscreen. For a moment it was possible to distinguish their twin tailfins and the payloads that clustered beneath their wings like bulbous, lethal pollen-sacs.

'The timing,' Byrne said, through gritted teeth, 'is crucial.'

As before, the jet-fighters peeled off in different directions in order to pass either side of the antigravity craft. The instant the jet-fighters parted company, Byrne canted the joystick to the left as far over as it would go. The antigravity craft veered towards the F-15 on that side on a converging trajectory.

'Ohhh shit,' said Arnold, but his voice was drowned by the jet-fighter's engine-roar, which swelled to an immense, thundering bellow as the two aircraft crossed paths with a height of less than fifty feet between them, the antigravity craft above, the F-15 below.

A second later, the sound died, leaving sudden silence.

'Starboard viewscreen,' said Byrne, breathlessly.

On the starboard viewscreen the jet-fighter could be seen in a slow-spiralling freefall, gracefully pinwheeling about its vertical axis, nose and tail trading places.

'What the fuck happened to it?' said MacGowan.

'The anti-mass field,' said Byrne.

'What about it?'

Rattray was nodding slowly.

On the viewscreen, the cockpit canopy came free as the pilot ejected. His seat-parachute bulged open like a silken jellyfish while the stricken jet-fighter continued its smooth downwards pirouette.

'The AMF disrupted the F-15's avionics,' said Byrne. 'Guidance systems, controls, flight computer – wiped them out.'

'Oh, you git,' said MacGowan, thumping the back of the pilot's chair. 'You could have bloody said something.' He was grinning.

'I wasn't sure if it would work.'

MacGowan stopped grinning.

'An F-15's avionics are "hardened" against electro-magnetic pulses so they can operate in a thermonuclear theatre of combat,' Byrne continued. 'I was hoping they weren't "hardened" enough to cope with a field of the magnitude such as this craft generates. Happily, I was right.'

'Oh, you git,' said MacGowan, coldly this time.

'A gamble, Byrne?' said Rattray.

'I'm a scientist,' Byrne replied. 'A calculated risk.'

'Hey, folks,' warned Arnold. 'Don't wanna rain on anyone's parade, but the second bogey's coming around again.'

'Bearing?' said Byrne.

'Without wishing to get too technical,' said Arnold, 'right up our asses.'

Byrne yanked the joystick towards him and the antigravity craft immediately switched directions, back-tracking on itself, the compass-bars on the viewscreens wheeling through 180 degrees. In any other vehicle the transferred force of such a sudden and violent reverse would have thrown its occupants about like ninepins, but the four men, cocooned from the laws of Newtonian physics by the anti-mass field, felt nothing.

On the viewscreen that showed the craft's rearward view, the second F-15 was visible, closing in. There was a flash of light beneath one of its wings, and the jet-fighter peeled away, leaving an undulating line of white smoke wavering its way towards the antigravity craft.

'Sidewinder!' yelled MacGowan.

Immediately Byrne slammed the joystick back to upright and threw the vertical-speed lever fully forward. The smoke-trail of the heatseeking air-to-air missile vanished downwards from the viewscreen.

'Where is it?' said Arnold. 'Where the fuck is it?'

'Under us,' said Byrne. Then: 'There.' He pointed at the forward viewscreen, where the Sidewinder was visible, a tiny line the size of a hyphen. No longer trailing smoke, the missile was sailing away from the antigravity craft.

'Overshot us,' said MacGowan. 'How?'

'The anti-mass field disrupted its guidance systems,' said Rattray. 'Just as it did the F-15's. Am I right?'

Byrne nodded. 'It's flying along on momentum alone. In a minute it'll start to fall to Earth, like a spent arrow.'

'How very poetic,' said MacGowan.

Byrne reduced the antigravity craft's rate of climb, topping her out at a little over 8,000 feet. 'Right. Strictly speaking, we should be in the clear now. We've shown Tom Cruise back there what this craft can do. If he has any sense, he'll know not to come too close to us, and not to waste any more missiles on us either.'

'Then he must not have any sense,' said Arnold, eyeing the radar display.

The F-15 swung into view on the rearward viewscreen and opened fire on the antigravity craft, letting loose a second-long burst of 20mm rounds from the six-barrel cannon mounted at its starboard wing root.

Byrne thrust the joystick forwards, simultaneously pulling back on the vertical-speed lever. The antigravity craft swooped towards the desert floor, the bullets passing above it. The F-15 lowered its nose in pursuit and accelerated, narrowing the gap between it and the antigravity craft so the antigravity craft's pilot would have less time to respond the next time the F-15's pilot opened fire.

The altimeter read in the low hundreds as Byrne bottomed out the craft's descent. The F-15 levelled out behind. Byrne shunted the joystick forwards as far as it would go. The terrain, depicted on the four viewscreens in lunar-surface shades of grey, sped towards the craft, and to either side of it, and away. The AMF-status screen showed lines of force pulsing at full intensity along the leading edge of the hull. Airspeed again reached 350 knots.

The F-15 gave chase with predatory determination. Its pilot unleashed another short burst of gunfire. Tracer rounds blipped and flashed in the rearward viewscreen. Byrne waggled the joystick, and there was a crazy interchange of ground and sky, sky and ground on the viewscreens as the antigravity craft jinked and skipped in mid-air, dancing around in a series of sharp-angled turns while still maintaining its forward course. All four men braced themselves for the sound of bullets tearing into the hull, but Byrne, perhaps more by luck than judgement, managed to evade being hit.

'I don't think we can keep this up much longer,' said Arnold. 'He's got another seven good blasts left before his ammo runs out.'

'We can keep dodging,' said Byrne, with conviction.

'Or,' said Rattray, 'we can try and lose him.' He pointed to the port viewscreen, which showed a long, deep, snaking gully. 'Go where he can't go.'

Without a word Byrne aimed the antigravity craft for the gully.

'Crazy fucker's following,' said MacGowan, squinting at the rearward viewscreen, which showed the F-15 banking smoothly to port.

'Asshole wants hisself a medal,' snarled Arnold.

The gully walls appeared on the port and starboard viewscreens, rushing by, rugged and steep. On the rearward viewscreen, the F-15 could be seen levelling out.

This time there was no way Byrne could throw the antigravity craft around as he had done a moment ago, not without risk of hitting the gully's sides.

They had trapped themselves. The F-15 pilot had a clear, direct shot. He could take his time and get within close range. Make sure the antigravity craft was securely in his sights. Make sure not to miss.

Rattray leaned over the pilot's chair and placed his own hands over Byrne's hands on the joystick and the vertical-speed lever.

'What the hell are you doing?' Byrne yelled. 'You don't know how to fly her!'

He tried to shake Rattray's hands from the controls, but Rattray merely tightened his grip, exerting enough pressure on Byrne's fingers to make him cry out in pain.

Rattray knew that Byrne's reflexes would not be quick enough to save them. His own might.

He demanded, and got, internal acceleration. Time slowed and slurred around him as his nerve impulses sped up, chemical messengers whizzing back and forth double-quick, synapses sparking faster, neurones and axons stepping up their rate of activity, his entire nervous system becoming one mercurially swift to-and-fro of information, visual input translated into thought, thought into deed almost instantaneously.

This state of ultra-alertness was a tremendous drain on his energy reserves, but he would only need to sustain it for a few seconds. The instant he saw a muzzle-flash from the F-15's cannon, he would throw the vertical-speed lever forwards. With luck – and assuming the antigravity craft responded quickly enough – he might be able to elevate them out of the line of fire.

Just then, on the forward viewscreen, the end of the gully hove into sight.

The gully did not open out onto a plain. Instead, it terminated in a sheer, vertical wall of rock.

Rattray registered this fact, and almost simultaneously saw a bright white spark flicker at the jet-fighter's wing-root. A sliver of a second later he plunged the vertical-speed lever forwards, and the antigravity craft shot upwards perpendicularly from its previous horizontal trajectory.

Not quick enough.

Bullets struck the antigravity craft's underside. It sounded to the men on board as though the hull was being pounded by a dozen jackhammers.

The F-15 pilot, however, did not get a chance to celebrate successfully finding his mark. Having been concentrating to the exclusion of all else on shooting and hitting the antigravity craft, he did not spot the end of the gully coming towards him until it was too late.

There was no time to pull up. The jet-fighter plunged headlong into the vertical wall of rock. Millions of dollars' worth of combat aircraft flattened itself against the rock-wall's craggy face, fuselage crumpling like a beer can, alloy–titanium wings wrinkling and rending like tin foil. There was no spectacular fireball explosion, just instant and catastrophic disintegration. Splinters of wreckage went rebounding back down the valley. Larger chunks rolled down the cliff, fetching up at its foot.

There was no celebrating on board the antigravity craft, either. Warning lights had started flashing on both consoles. A red message was blinking on the AMF-status screen, signalling a breach in the integrity of the anti-mass field. Digital dials were reeling through numbers like crazy. These instrumental indications of imminent disaster were all but superfluous, however, since the antigravity craft itself had begun to shudder and shimmy and shake, and the throbbing that had preceded takeoff was back, only now it was laboured and arrhythmic, like the beating of a heart about to go into arrest.

Rattray decelerated out of ultra-alertness and let go of Byrne's hands. Byrne let his hands fall limply from the controls and looked helplessly round at Rattray. 'We're going to crash,' he said, simply. 'We're dead.'

'Not all of us,' Rattray replied, and grabbed Byrne and hauled him bodily out of the pilot's chair.

'Wait!' said Byrne, as Rattray swung him around. 'What the hell are you – ?'

'The deal's off,' said Rattray. Such was the steely self-control with which he uttered these words that his lips barely moved. 'You didn't get us away safely.'

Byrne, understanding what was coming next, closed his eyes.

Ruth, Ant, he thought. I'm sorry. I'm so sorry. But I did try. For your sakes, I *did* try.

Rattray gripped the scientist by the shoulders and propelled him upwards, with astonishing force, against the antigravity craft's domed ceiling. Byrne's head struck the ceiling with a dull, hard sound that was a cross between a crack and a squelch. His skull caved in. He died instantly.

Rattray lowered the limp, head-lolling body to the

floor and turned to MacGowan. 'Bill,' he shouted, gesturing at the now vacant pilot's chair. 'Sit down and strap yourself in.'

MacGowan frowned, failing to understand what Rattray was getting at.

'It'll afford you some protection.'

Now MacGowan understood. It went against the grain, putting somebody else at risk in order to protect himself, but he realised that what Rattray was proposing was only right and sensible. They were going to hit the ground hard, and whoever was standing up in the cabin, no matter how tightly he held on, was going to get banged about nastily. Of the three of them, only one could afford to break a few bones.

Sliding into the pilot's seat, MacGowan buckled himself in. Arnold, behind him, had already done the same.

The craft was seesawing erratically in the air now, unable to maintain a straight course, weaving and oscillating like a child's top nearing the end of its spin. When the four viewscreens were not stuttering and blanking out they were showing madly yawing desert-scapes and the earth below the craft rushing by ever faster, ever nearer.

'Use the joystick to keep her level, if you can,' said Rattray, pointing with his free hand at the ground-attitude gauge. 'Counter-steer.'

MacGowan tried, but there seemed to be a delay between using the joystick and the joystick having an effect. The craft would pitch one way, he would attempt to compensate by bending the joystick the other way, and by the time the AMF-status screen showed an increase in the field density on that side, the craft would be angling in another direction altogether. The altimeter was counting down too quickly, threatening zero too soon, too soon, and the ground on the viewscreens was coming closer, closer, dangerously closer ...

The impact, when it came, was so loud it might as well have been silent, a roaring noise above and beyond the ability of the human ear to render intelligible. All the lights went out inside the cabin, leaving black turmoil. There was rolling and buffeting and somersaulting and tumbling and turning, and no up, no down, just a blinded, vertiginous loss of bearings, as gravity returned with a vengeance to reclaim the vehicle that had had the temerity to defy it.

And then one long, slithering, gravelly, sideways slide.

And then a final, almighty, thumping bang.

And, at last, stillness.

41

They manhandled him out of cool darkness into bright heat. He knew he was in considerable pain. His body could not completely inhibit the messages jangling in from his nerve receptors. It tried its best, but it was too low on resources. The information kept leaking through: agony, agony, agony ...

They laid him down on the ground, face up to the sun.

Things went black. He must have passed out.

He was woken by the ground jolting beneath him. He heard the crackling of flames, the timpani clangs of hot metal warping. Shortly, he smelled burning.

They picked him up again and started walking, carrying him slung between them, canted at an awkward angle because one of them was so much taller than the other.

He told them to leave him, look out for themselves, he was just going to be a burden to them. Or at any rate he thought he told them this. Perhaps he did and they ignored him, or perhaps the words were spoken only in his head.

Lurching, stumbling, across the relentless paprika landscape ...

And the heat of the sun increasing ...

Several times they had to hide. He was dragged to the nearest cover – a lump of rock, a narrow crevice, a clump of spiny bushes. Each time he heard the pounding of helicopter rotors nearby. Once, the sound passed directly overhead. And the agony, remote like someone else's pain but unmistakably his own, continued. He needed to eat. Because of what had been done to him almost a century ago, he, more than almost anyone, was conscious of the body as an organic machine. Input fuel, output work. And his mechanism, low on energy now, was winding down. His system was failing. He tried to alert his two companions to this fact as they dragged him onwards, but the words came out muddled, and the answers they gave were soothing but meaningless, the sort of things you say to a confused, bedridden grandparent.

And the heat remorselessly simmering ...

They came to a road. He was left in a patch of shade. They told him they would be back soon.

Having no conception of time any more, he had no idea whether or not they were true to their word. For an immeasurable period he hovered in and out of consciousness, and saw visions: phantoms flitting through the heat-haze, the ghosts of people he had known over the course of his long, long life, old friends, old enemies, and a legion of the dead, men and women he had killed, a sullen parade of lost faces and betrayed eyes – eyes that said, more articulately than spoken words might, *Did we really deserve to die?*

How could he explain? How could he justify to them the harsh truth, that sacrifices had to be made for the greater good of the entire race?

And then one last victim, a woman who had not died by his hand.

Who smiled sadly and said, in thickly accented English, *Do you honestly believe that any more, John?*

His two companions returned for him in a car. They bundled him into the back seat. It seemed he had managed to convey his needs to them after all, because as they drove off one of them produced some bars of chocolate. The chocolate had to be unwrapped for him and hand-fed to him a chunk at a time, as though he were an infant.

316

He chewed. He swallowed. Gradually the pain receded. Energy! Gradually he began to heal.

42

They drove all morning and all afternoon, MacGowan
and Arnold taking turns, one at the steering wheel, the
other feeding Rattray. The Dodge's engine developed a
wheeze, the fan-belt began to lollop, and Arnold said he
had a good mind to go back and find the salesman who
had sold him this hunk of junk and kick his sorry lying
ass. But the car only had to get them as far as they needed
to go and no further, and this, it seemed, it would
manage.

They headed south-east, stopping only to refuel and
buy more food for Rattray. They crossed the Hoover
Dam around noon. Continuing through Arizona, they
bypassed Phoenix and reached Tucson around sundown.
The safe-house, where it had been agreed beforehand that
they would rendezvous with Lucretia and Piers, lay fifty
miles to the east of Tucson. By now, Rattray had
regained sufficient strength to sit up and feed himself. His
superficial abrasions were gone as if they had never been,
and his more serious injuries were in the process of
repairing themselves.

Miraculously the crash had left MacGowan and
Arnold, other than the odd bruise, unhurt. Rattray had
come off by far the worst, having broken his left femur
and several ribs. Those, at any rate, were the injuries
MacGowan had been able to diagnose after he and
Arnold had pulled Rattray from the wreckage of the
antigravity craft. To judge by the itching beneath his

scalp, Rattray reckoned he must have received a skull fracture as well. Not only that but several of his teeth had been knocked out. The replacements were budding in his gums, pushing through.

The safe-house was a remote hacienda in the hills. It was looked after by a housekeeper, Señora Gutierrez, who was under the impression that it was the vacation home of a Hollywood producer who never stayed there himself but often rented it out to friends. These friends were liable to turn up at any time, unannounced, so Señora Gutierrez was under strict instructions to keep the refrigerator well-stocked and the beds always freshly turned. Secretly Señora Gutierrez believed that some sort of shady stuff went on at the hacienda, either drug-dealing or sex-movie shooting, but she had no proof of this, and more to the point she was well paid for her work, receiving the kind of salary that encouraged discretion.

Lucretia and Piers had arrived at the safe-house the previous evening, and as the Dodge pulled up outside the front door they came out to greet their fellow Guardians.

From the way Rattray limped feebly from the car, Lucretia inferred that the action-to-suppress had not gone as smoothly as it should have, but when she pressed MacGowan for an account of the mission, all she got in the way of an answer was a bitter, weary, 'Don't ask.'

A cold supper had been prepared and was waiting on the dining-room table. Piers was desperately apologetic that he had not been able to track down a decent bottle of champagne to go with the meal, but both the combat-grade Guardians were more than happy with beer.

The hacienda's dining room had plate-glass windows filling the walls on three sides. Night and the desert surrounded the Guardians as they ate, enclosing them (paradoxically) with space. Somewhere far off, a coyote began baying, and a dog at another house several miles away barked back. It was comforting to be indoors, and have warmth, food and electric light, while outside lay so much darkness and wildness and wilderness.

319

'So?' said Lucretia, when most of the food was gone. 'What went wrong?' From hints gathered over the course of the meal she had been able to piece together for herself a rough outline of what had happened, but so far no one had explained why the action-to-suppress had so nearly resulted in disaster.

Rattray, in a weakened voice like stone scraping on stone, told her about the hacker attack on Kim's system, the event which had unpicked the thread of their plan, the catalyst that had precipitated its unravelling. 'It needs to be determined,' he concluded, 'how Kim's system security was breached, and by whom, and why. And I think Kim, more than anyone else, will want answers to those questions. In fact, I'd be surprised if she wasn't looking into the matter herself, even as we speak.'

(She was.)

'Some Anarch agency was to blame,' Piers suggested.

'It seems likely,' said Rattray, 'and certainly preferable to the alternative explanation, which is that we have a new enemy.'

'The main thing,' said MacGowan, 'is that, in spite of everything, we managed to do what we set out to do.'

'Yeah,' said Arnold, 'we blew that goddamn anti-gravity craft into so many pieces, even Jesus Christ Himself wouldn't be able to resurrect it.'

'I feel it's only fair to mention, now, that there was more at stake than simply the antigravity technology,' said Rattray. 'Byrne made a second discovery, although strictly speaking it wasn't a discovery, in as much as his grandfather had already stumbled upon it back in 1908. A source of energy. The same energy that caused the Tunguska explosion.'

'You mean we were riding in a bloomin' flying atomic bomb?' MacGowan puffed out his cheeks and shook his head. 'Bloody hell.'

'Not exactly,' said Rattray. 'Byrne found a way of harnessing the same thing that the first Anton Krilov accidentally found a way of releasing: zero-point energy.'

'A source of free energy,' said Lucretia. 'Forgive me if

this sounds like heresy, but surely what the world needs now –'

Piers interrupted her by breaking into song: '"... is love, sweet love." '

MacGowan joined in on the next line. ' "It's the only thing that there's just too little of." '

Arnold buried his head in his hands.

'Thank *you*,' said Lucretia archly, and Piers and MacGowan shared a goofy grin. 'If I may continue? Surely what the planet could do with at this moment' – she chose her synonyms carefully so as to avoid a repeat rendition of Bacharach – 'is a source of energy that doesn't deplete natural resources and damage the environment. Why would the Librans not want us to have that? Are we really not ready for it?'

'I know you're just playing Anarch's advocate, Lucretia,' said Rattray, 'but consider the effect the sudden introduction of free energy would have on the world. Can you imagine what nations whose economies depend on oil revenues would do if their principal export commodity was rendered valueless virtually overnight? Energy production and geopolitics are tightly intertwined at present. If free energy came along, whole regions of the planet, many of them already unstable, would collapse into anarchy and war. This in fact may have been what the Anarchs were aiming at all along, from the moment they introduced the engram into the first Anton Krilov. In the future, when the oil starts running out and our political and economic systems are forced to adapt to the demands of the ecology and not vice versa, then, perhaps, we'll be ready, as a race, for an alternative. For the time being, however, we're just going to have to muddle through with what we've got.'

'Something else has been bothering me, actually,' said MacGowan. 'John, you remember in Byrne's room in the facility, when we saw those kid's drawings?'

Rattray nodded. 'I know what you're about to say, Bill.'

'Well, what about it? I mean, the engram is hereditary, isn't it?'

'Byrne has children?' said Lucretia.

Rattray did not correct her in her use of the present tense. 'One son.'

'How old?'

'Nine.'

'And you've known about him all along, haven't you.' This was not a question. At last Lucretia thought she understood why Rattray had been moodier and more saturnine than usual these past few days: because he had known that, for the action-to-suppress to be completely thorough, a child might have to be invalidated as well. This was what had been weighing on his conscience so heavily.

'I have known about him,' Rattray replied, 'and for a while I've been uncertain what to do. But now I think I have the answer.'

'Which is?'

'It would appear that the engram is inactive in Byrne's son, as it was in Creel. The drawings we saw on the wall of Byrne's room were of sufficient quality to suggest that Byrne's son's talents lie in that direction rather than any other.'

'So the kid doesn't have to be invalidated?' said Arnold.

'No,' said Rattray, then, more decisively: 'No.'

'Thank God for that,' said MacGowan, and his relief was echoed to various degrees around the table. 'I mean, I've done some shitty things in my time, but even I draw the line somewhere.'

'Begging everyone's pardon, but what happens when Byrne's son has a child of his own?' said Piers. 'We've already seen that the engram can be inactive in one generation and active in the next. Surely wouldn't it be safer to invalidate the child now? Get it over and done with?'

'Safer and less trouble for us,' said Rattray. 'But I, for

one, find it difficult to countenance such an act. As Bill said, a line has to be drawn somewhere.'

'The North America chapter will keep a close watch on him,' said Arnold. 'Him and every one of his descendants. If that's what it takes, then that's what it takes.'

'Good,' said Rattray. 'It may not be the most practical and expedient solution, but it is, I think, the right one.'

Some time later, Rattray and Lucretia found themselves alone in the hacienda's main room. There was an open brick hearth, and Rattray had laid a fire there. Pine logs were crackling and spitting, filling the air with their sweet scent.

Lucretia sat nursing a bottle of beer and staring out through the undraped window at the night. After the meal had been cleared away, MacGowan, Arnold and Piers had taken the Dodge out into the desert to dispose of it and the paraterrestrial weapons. An entropy accelerator on high setting would reduce the weapons to dust; another entropy accelerator, on a lower setting, would age the car several years, transforming it, in a matter of minutes, from a serviceable passenger-carrying vehicle to an unusable (and fingerprint-free) roadside wreck. It was always fascinating to watch this process, in the same way that it is fascinating to watch speeded-up film footage of fruit decaying. The car's paintwork bubbling and flaking; rust blooming and spreading over its doors and panels; the headlights, taillights and bumpers dropping off leprously; the windows starring and shattering; the seat covers shrivelling and curling like old orange peel; fluid dribbling out from under the chassis as the hydraulic cables perished and the petrol and oil reserves corroded and leaked their contents. This the three men would watch by torchlight, a pagan and cathartic rite, and a way of marking the successful completion of the mission that did not celebrate the deeds actually committed. Lucretia had declined an invitation to go along with them, however, saying she did not feel up to the walk back. MacGowan had assured her that they would not travel very far from the house, but she had insisted that she was quite happy to stay. Another time, perhaps.

'Well,' she said now, turning to Rattray, who was gazing deeply into the fire. 'Back home tomorrow, eh?'

Rattray murmured some unintelligible assent.

Lucretia had breached the silence. She was not to be deterred. 'John, for what it's worth, I think you made the right decision about Byrne's son. The human decision.'

'You mean humane, don't you?'

'No, human. As in not paraterrestrial.'

Rattray stood up and went over to the fire, walking stiffly, favouring his right leg. 'That presupposes that the paraterrestrial psychology is substantially different from ours.' He braced himself against the wall with one hand as he knelt down beside the hearth, the leg not yet up to bearing his full weight.

'Well, isn't it? I mean, if the paraterrestrials *were* like us, surely the choices they make us face wouldn't be so' – Lucretia groped for a suitably euphemistic phrase – 'ethically challenging.'

'But what if the paraterrestrials *aren't* as different from us as we would like to believe?' Rattray offered up another log to the flames. 'What if they're prey to just the same foibles and flaws that make us human? The formation of the Anarchs was, after all, an understandable reaction to the decision to resume relations with mankind after the Atlanteans' failed invasion – understandable in as much as humans would react the same way. We see the same kind of protectionism at work in global politics all the time, don't we? "Why should we share with *you*?" It's a refrain as common in international diplomacy as it is in the school playground.'

'I never had you pegged for a cynic, John. A misanthrope, maybe, but never a cynic.'

She intended this lightheartedly. Rattray took it seriously. 'With all the things I saw as a policeman,' he said, 'you would have thought I would have become cynical. Suffocated newborn babies in East End tenements, killed by their parents because they couldn't afford another mouth to feed. Mutilated tuppenny whores, raped before *and* after they were murdered. Bloated bodies floating in the Thames. People killed over the smallest sums of money. You would have thought that my former job would have turned me into the worst cynic in the world. Or at least, left me as much of a cynic as any other policeman. But no, I managed to retain an essential optimism about mankind. I felt that we *could* be better, that we might stumble every now and then, slip, take a step backwards, but that eventually our intelligence would lead us to rise above our animal instincts. And then I became a Guardian, and learned that even intelligence couldn't redeem us – even intelligence of the purest, most rational, most cerebral kind. Because it was after I joined the Guardians that I started coming into contact with scientists.' He spoke the word with some distaste. 'Supposedly logical, reasonable human beings. Supposedly the smartest of us all. And they were, almost to a man, fools. Making things just because they could be made. Seeking answers to questions that no one had asked. Carrying out experiments regardless of the consequences, not even pausing to wonder whether what they were doing was going to benefit mankind or not. Just going ahead for the same pointless reason that Hillary climbed Everest: because it was there. Byrne is a classic example. He hadn't thought through the consequences of his hoped-for "worldwide revolution". He hadn't thought that there would be casualties: those who couldn't adapt – individuals, entire nations. He hadn't thought that the tides in human affairs don't change overnight, they shift slowly, imperceptibly. He just *hadn't thought*. I became a cynic when I became a Guardian, Lucretia, because it was then that I began to understand that no one on this planet was anything but fallible. And recently I've begun to wonder whether what is true of this planet isn't also true of other places.'

'John,' said Lucretia, in hushed tones, as though the Librans might be listening (and they might be; the safe-house was nowhere near a Node, but nevertheless, somehow, the Librans might be listening).

Rattray nodded. 'Yes, I'm sorry, I know. Please ignore me. I'm tired. Tired and very old. The question of what to do about Byrne's son was bothering me, and I apologise if I've been somewhat standoffish these past few days. I'll be fine.'

'So do you think,' Lucretia said slowly, 'that the Librans are going to be none too pleased with our decision this evening? That they'd rather we invalidated Byrne's son?'

'I hope otherwise, but yes, I think that's what they would have preferred.'

'Well, then.' She sounded resolute, intending for the firmness in her voice to lend Rattray strength. 'They're just going to have to learn to live with it. We're their agents on Earth. They've employed us to carry out their instructions to the best of our abilities, and that's what we've done. Besides, what's the worst they can do?'

Rattray stared into the fire for a long while. The flames flickered, sharp and sinuous as snakes' tongues.

Finally he said, 'What, indeed, is the worst thing the Librans could do?'

43

Two days later, a visitor rang the doorbell of the Byrne residence in Carson City, and Ruth Byrne opened the front door to find a man she had never met before standing there, wearing full military dress uniform and a bleakly grave expression. As soon as she set eyes on him, Ruth knew the news he had come to break.

He introduced himself as Colonel Willard T. Clayton, and Ruth, displaying admirable self-possession, asked him politely to come in, showed him through to the living room and invited him to sit on the couch.

Doffing his peaked cap and clasping it in both hands, Colonel Clayton enquired after Ruth's health and the health of her son. She replied that they were both of them fine, and told the colonel to go ahead and say it. Her husband was dead, wasn't he?

The colonel nodded. There had been an accident at the research facility, he said. A fire. The cause was still unclear, but he assured her there would be a full and thorough investigation, and that Uncle Sam would honour all his financial commitments to her and her son as the widow and orphan of an employee of the US military.

Widow. The word, to Ruth, seemed like a black and heavy suit of clothes that didn't fit. And orphan. Orphan conjured up visions of skinny waifs with smut-smudged cheeks and ill-fitting shoes, like something out of a Dickens novel. It did not apply to her son, to her Ant.

The colonel expressed his sincerest condolences and departed.

Ruth did not cry until after she had driven to Ant's school, taken him out of class and told him what had happened. Then, as she hugged her son to her breast, the tears welled up inside her and came spilling out, and it seemed as if they would never stop, as if they were the first of an eternal tide of tears that would never dry up, and the sobs which racked her body were the first of an endless succession of sobs that would never cease to cause her pain.

The official inquiry into the events at Nowhere, which Colonel Clayton himself headed up, yielded frustratingly few clear facts. It was apparent that some kind of terrorist incursion had taken place, but what was not so apparent was if the terrorists had been in cahoots with Byrne or if Byrne had taken advantage of the confusion caused by their attack to launch his own invention, possibly attempting to save it from falling into enemy hands, and forfeiting his life in the process.

The latter scenario cast the scientist in a favourable and heroic light, which is perhaps why Clayton inclined towards the former, because he had always harboured reservations about Byrne. Whenever they had met, Byrne had always seemed as though he were laughing at Clayton, enjoying some private joke that Clayton would never understand.

In Clayton's report to General Winter, at any rate, the blame for the débâcle was laid tentatively at Byrne's feet. The colonel lamented the untrustworthiness of scientists, saying that in his opinion they were unpredictable creatures, too much in their own heads, prone to fits of idealism and flights of fancy, and thus easily swayed by nice words and empty promises. His feeling was that Byrne had succumbed to the blandishments of agents of a foreign power and, in league with the terrorists, had attempted to betray the US military. Byrne could, therefore, be held directly accountable for the deaths of an air force flyboy, several venerable war-veterans, a cook, and a dozen scientists and technicians; for the destruction of military property and materials to the tune of over a hundred million dollars; and for the loss of all blueprints and data pertaining to his antigravity propulsion system and the prototype antigravity craft itself, which had been recovered from the desert wrecked beyond recognition and redemption.

As for the terrorists, either they had perished in the explosions that had destroyed the facility – the rubble was still being sifted for bodies – or else they had gotten clean away, in spite of a thorough helicopter search of the area.

Ultimately Byrne's guilt could not be proved beyond a shadow of a doubt, and so all Clayton could do was advise that there be a thorough review of safety and security procedures at all US military research installations and that the results of the inquiry into the Nowhere incident be left open, pending further investigation, and thus never have to be made known to the general public.

Shouldering some of the blame himself, in good military fashion, Colonel Clayton tendered his resignation to his superiors. It was accepted without demur or any abundant demonstration of regret.

The veterans, who, in the course of defending Nowhere, had inadvertently killed the men and women they were meant to have been guarding, were relocated to a series of civilian retirement communities dotted all across America. Non-disclosure documents, which all of them had signed upon accepting their pension-boosting positions at Nowhere, constrained them, on pain of imprisonment, never to reveal to a soul what had happened at the facility and what they had witnessed.

The town itself was abandoned and left to the mercy of the elements, and within a short space of time had mouldered and decayed until it was a sun-bleached ghost of its former self, a nowhere by nature as well as by name.

And in his château on the banks of the Loire, Gérard de Sade brooded on the failure of his first attempt at flushing *les Gardiens* out into the open.

He had been furious to begin with, and Xavier Barraud had borne the brunt of that fury, while Madame Laforgue had suffered the fallout. He regretted snapping at his housekeeper now, but believed that he and she had made their peace. As for Xavier, it was unlikely that he would be doing any more work for de Sade in the future. For one thing, he had proved himself to be unequal to the task, and for another thing …

The message was still up on de Sade's computer screen. Brushstroke script on a parchment scroll. A few words in English:

> You do not know me, but I am the one who made it possible for your tragically talentless underling and his cohorts to breach Kawai Kim's system. With my further assistance, you will be able to achieve everything you desire.
>
> — Emperor Dragon

Epilogue

Much as he would have liked to, John Rattray did not attend his own funeral. Valentina advised him strongly against going, even incognito, arguing that since, during his life, he had had few friends outside the force and had been held in high esteem by his colleagues both junior and superior, it was obvious that a lot of policemen were going to turn up at the church to pay their respects, and policemen, as a rule, had a nose for suspicious-looking characters and an eye for physiognomy, so there was every chance he would be identified, no matter how heavy or how skilful the disguise he adopted. She understood perfectly his desire to see who came to mourn him, and to learn how admired he had been during his time on earth, and to know what kind of legacy he had left behind and how posterity was going to remember him. But the risk was too great. It was simply not possible. Out of the question. He could not go. *Nyet*.

This conversation (a distinctly one-sided one) took place in the room in the insalubrious Bayswater hotel to which Rattray had been spirited immediately following his 'fatal heart attack', suffered while he had been performing his ablutions on the morning of 19 February 1902. He had been cooped up in the hotel room for four days, and though he had never suffered from claustrophobia before, he was beginning to feel the flock-papered walls closing in on him. Two days ago his landlady had discovered his body sprawled half-naked at the foot of the basin in the bathroom of his flat, chin still smeared with shaving foam, cut-throat in hand. An autopsy had been performed, the cause of death established. Tomorrow, at last, the body would be interred at a small churchyard near Lincoln's Inn. But he did not think he could wait to leave the hotel until then.

The body. He had caught a glimpse of it while Valentina and a colleague had been busy positioning it in a suitably corpselike pose on his bathroom floor. It was a horribly exact replica of himself, the sole difference between him and it being that *it* was dead of a stopped heart and he was still alive. He could not bear to look at it for more than a few seconds, and did not dare ask how it had been made. He understood that it must have had something to do with the sample of blood which Valentina had drawn from him a couple of weeks earlier, but more than that he did not care to know.

Eventually Valentina's resolve that he was *not* going to the funeral wore him down. He conceded that she was right and that he should not be there when the counterfeit John Rattray was lowered beneath the sod, but he begged her, as a personal favour, to go in his stead and come back with a report on the proceedings. This she agreed to do.

Black suited her. Rattray intimated as much when, the next morning, she paraded in front of him in full funeral regalia of black brocade bodice, black crêpe-de-chine skirt and bustle, black bonnet, black lace veil and a sable muff.

'I look like a Nihilist,' she replied, inspecting herself in the hotel room's small mirror. 'Crop my hair, put on some blue-tinted spectacles and some big black boots ...'

'All the same,' said Rattray. 'Very fetching.'

Valentina smiled at him, obliquely flattered. 'Perhaps people I know should die more often.'

It had dawned cold, gusty and wet, and as the morning wore on the weather failed to improve. In one respect Rattray was glad that nature was responding sympathetically to the ritual of his burial by laying on ink-stain clouds, an insidious wind and a dismal drizzle, but he would have preferred a crisp, clear day, a blue sky and sharp wintry air, if only for the sake of the funeral-goers.

Valentina, when she returned, told him that the crowd had numbered close to a hundred and fifty, which was a pretty decent turn-out by anyone's standards, and that several sets of mutton-chop whiskers had been dampened by more than just the rain. The ceremony had been dignified but quick, the vicar hurrying through the last rites and apologising to all for doing so but saying that it was in the interests of everyone's continued good health. He did not want anybody to catch their death of cold. And after the handfuls of earth were thrown, as the crowd began to disperse, Abberline had come over to offer his condolences.

Valentina's impersonation of the former Chief Inspector, correct down to the lingering Dorset burr which his nearly forty years of living in London had failed to erase, made Rattray smile.

'We've lost a good'un, Miss Popkova,' Abberline had said. 'Coppers like John Rattray don't come two-a-penny, y'know.'

'Good old Fred,' Rattray said, on hearing this.

Abberline had gone on to describe to Valentina the high regard in which Rattray had held her. Even though the two of them had known each other for just a couple of months, it had been clear to Abberline that Rattray's feelings towards her had run deeper than Rattray himself would ever have made out.

(At this, Rattray had to turn away in order to prevent her seeing him blush, and muttered something about Abberline and an overactive imagination.)

Abberline had then delivered a eulogy that took in Rattray's many successes but hinged principally on his famed final pursuit of Dr Roderick Greatorex, the notorious Bad Doctor, back in 1890, which had culminated in the demise of that criminal mastermind in a burning warehouse on Cheapside.

'And a more fitting death it would be hard to conceive,'

Abberline had said, by way of a sombre conclusion. 'We may not have caught the Ripper, but if John is remembered for nothing else, he'll be remembered for ridding the world of another devil in human guise.'

'I assume he didn't neglect to tell you about the pivotal role he himself played in the Greatorex investigation,' said Rattray.

Valentina said that it had been mentioned.

'Good old Fred,' said Rattray again, this time shaking his head. 'Put him in front of a pretty lady, and he'll say or do anything to impress her. And him a married man, too.'

'That seems to be a common practice among British policemen,' said Valentina slyly. 'Flirting with me.'

'You mean *ex*-policemen,' said Rattray. 'Fred took the brass carriage clock back in '89. Works for Pinkerton's now.'

'Yes, ex-policemen,' said Valentina. 'And sometimes they aren't even aware that they're doing it.'

'Really?' said Rattray, raising an eyebrow.

A day later, he and she caught a train all the way up to Fort William in Scotland, from where they were driven north in a hansom cab to a grim, grey granite castle in a grim, grey granite region of the Western Highlands. And there, the operations began.

What ensued was a nightmare period of bandages and fitful sedations; of bedpans, uneaten meals, and journeys down into the darkened castle cellars and beyond, into a deeper darkness of chemically induced oblivion; and of waking up from anaesthesia to find himself once again in an iron-headed bed in a velvet-curtained room, with every fibre of his being racked with excruciating agony, and no real sense of where he was, only a vague notion that it was somewhere he did not want to be; and of respites from the pain, interludes when he would be wheeled out in a bathchair into the sunshine to sit and stare dazedly at the dark greenery of the castle gardens; and of days that seemed like weeks and weeks that seemed like months; and of never seeing his surgeons, never actually meeting the Frankensteins who were committing this slow, savage, miraculous rape of his body while he was unconscious, able only to speculate as to how they might look, speak, hold themselves; and throughout it all, by his side for almost his every waking moment, his rock, his anchor, Valentina.

He realised that she was there because she had been instructed to be there, to see him through the ordeal. None the less, without her, he doubted he would have endured. If not for her constant presence, her constant reassurances, he would probably have gone mad. As it was, he repeatedly found himself begging to be put out of his misery, recanting his decision, asking for this gift to be taken back, he did not want it any more, he did not want to live for ever ...

And each time this happened Valentina would calmly remind him why he had agreed to submit to the treatment, once again describing the nature of the clandestine war into which he had been enlisted to fight. And, with each reiteration, she would refine and hone her explanation, until it took on, for Rattray and perhaps for her as well, the familiar cadences of a child's favourite bedtime story.

She told him that from the time of our ancestors' first faltering steps out of their caves, certain beings had been observing us and guiding us. Superior beings. Supernal beings. Not creatures from another planet, like the Martians in Mr Wells's fantasy, but similar. Not the Ancient Masters that Madame Blavatsky and her Theo-sophist cronies went on about, but closely akin. Not gods, but very like gods. A higher order of life, as elevated over humans as humans were over, say, cats and dogs. Entities capable of feats of thought and technology of which we could only yet dream.

All of this she had explained to him already, prior to his 'death', while trying to recruit him. And initially, of course, he had not believed her. It had sounded like the most arrant nonsense. But her sincerity, and the evidence she had presented in the form of various devices of mind-boggling provenance, had eventually convinced him. He had been selected for recruitment, she had told him, because of his mind. His mind was incomparable, a great asset, one that would serve the Libran cause well. All that was needed was for it to be preserved in an all-but-indestructible body, and this, if he was willing, she could arrange.

And this he, facing retirement, with little left to look forward to but years of rehearsing former glories and dusting his citations, had agreed to submit to.

And this, finally, in late 1902, was achieved.

And when his time at the castle was over, he and Valentina, without either of them formally acknowledging it, realised that they had reached an understanding. Perhaps he had babbled to her during one of his drug-hazed rages of pain, told her things he might otherwise have refrained from admitting, things that originated in the region of emotions he was most unfamiliar with: the uncharted, unpredictable topography of his own heart. Perhaps. It did not matter. They had reached an understanding, and nothing needed to be articulated in words, for what now existed between them was plain enough in gestures and glances and small courtesies and brief, delicate instances of physical contact.

It was mooted that Rattray might go to Russia for a while, to live with Valentina in St Petersburg. It was a good idea that he stay away from London, at any rate. Even though he looked a good decade younger and his once-black hair had turned pure white – an unavoidable by-product of the operations, he was told – it was still possible that an old acquaintance, passing him in the street one day, might recognise him. In a few years' time, when memories had dimmed and acquaintances were dead, he could go back to the capital. Until then, either he lay low in the countryside, or he left the country altogether.

He chose the latter option, but, in the event, did not go to Russia. For the best part of 1903 he and Valentina travelled extensively throughout Europe and North

Africa. Rattray had never set foot outside the British Isles before and had always wanted to see the world. Besides, he needed time to become accustomed to the changes that had been wrought on his body. Changes such as the fact that the slightest nick in his skin healed up almost instantly. Such as the fact that he could summon up sudden, startling turns of speed and strength at will. Such as the fact that he was immune to every kind of illness, from infection to food poisoning, and – a pleasant discovery, this – that he could imbibe as much alcohol as he liked and not suffer from a hangover the following morning.

One might have thought that attributes of this order, all self-evidently advantageous, would not have required much adjusting to, but for the first few months Rattray succumbed to an eerie sense of physical dislocation, as though he were no longer the governor of his own body but a passenger in a flesh-and-blood vehicle that worked independently of him. It helped, however, that he and Valentina were perpetually in transit, moving from one place to the next using every mode of transportation imaginable, from steam engine to horseback, passenger ferry to camel, and even once an airship. That way he was able to ally his internal feelings with his external, geographical displacement, and so merge the one into the other. Gradually he grew comfortable with what he had become, and the bargain he had struck with his new 'employers' came to seem less of a devil's pact and more of a square deal. Immortality at a price, but the price – his continued loyalty to the Libran cause – seeming increasingly less costly.

With his travelling companion, who was learned and multilingual, a one-woman encyclopaedia of cultural history, he saw all the sights. He felt as though he were a wealthy aristocrat taking a somewhat belated Grand Tour, with Valentina assuming the role of mentor, and filling it much more appealingly than some stuffy, elderly tutor steeped in the classics and brandy. He was also, at the same time, exploring new countries inside himself, regions his obsessive dedication to his job had hitherto led him to neglect or avoid. Beliefs and prejudices were being overturned, maps were being redrawn in his head ... and in this, too, Valentina acted as his guide.

1904 found them settled in Salzburg. By now Rattray was entirely content with his new self and was half forgetting that he had been surgically transformed for a purpose and half hoping that the Librans would never find a use for him, so that he could continue his idyllic life with Valentina indefinitely. Rationally he knew that this was not at all likely. *Ir*rationally he yearned that it might be.

Valentina took time to outline what was going to be expected of him as a Guardian. First, the benefits: he would never want for money, for he would be living on a generous stipend donated by various benefactors; he would have plenty of opportunity to exercise his talents for detection and deduction; and he was part of a worldwide organisation, so that no matter what continent he visited, he would always find allies there. Then, the drawbacks: he had new enemies now, and they were ruthless, subtle and dangerous, so he would never be able to lower his guard for an instant; he was no longer master of his own destiny, and there would be times when, indeed, he felt quite the opposite, like a leaf being tossed by a tornado, a twig being twirled along on a torrential flood; and he would have to kill, frequently in cold blood, without compunction, without apparent justification, and without the moral safety net of the Law.

He would only realise it later, but in a way she was telling him these things in order to prepare him for the time when she would have to leave him.

That time came at the beginning of 1905, with the delivery of a telegram.

The telegram, which gave no point of origin, stated that Valentina was to depart for Moscow post haste. There, by the usual means, she would receive further instructions. It was expressly stipulated that she go alone.

There was nothing to be said, and both Rattray and

Valentina said it eloquently, with heavy silences. She packed her bags. She gamely tried to smile whenever their gazes met. He yearned for her to reassure him that she would be back, but knew she could not.

They enjoyed one last night together. The small hours were long, the taste of their kisses bittersweet.

He did not expect to fall asleep – did not want to – but eventually did.

And when he awoke, she was gone.

She left a note.

Nearly a century later, he still had it. It was kept on the upper floor of his Kensington maisonette, in a small, windowless room where all the documents and correspondence he had accumulated over the past century were stored, in chronological order, on shelves labelled by year and arranged around the walls, clockwise from one corner. The papers were filed in every form of stationery-holding device invented over the past ten decades, starting with musty, tattered leather wallets and finishing with plasticised, dayglo box-binders.

Now, a day after returning from the States, Rattray was sitting in his living room, with Valentina's farewell note in his hands. He had dug the letter out the previous Tuesday morning, shortly after receiving and reading Kim's e-mail, when that faint click of connection that he had heard at the fast-food restaurant the day before had returned as a resounding, full-blown chime of comprehension.

The paper the note was written on had once been pliant and white; now it was brittle and yellow. The words had once been black; now they were a faded brown. This was the only tangible evidence Rattray had of Valentina's existence. The rest was memory and imagination

The letter said:

24th January 1905

My dear John,

This moment was inevitable, much though we both

pretended that it was never going to arrive. In truth, how long could we have lasted together? While I aged and you stayed forever young?

Ours is a lonely business. You will learn that. And yours will be a more solitary and more difficult path than most. Our masters, though, would not have selected you had they not thought you up to the task. I, too, have perfect faith in you.

I do not believe in an afterlife, John, but I do believe that we live on after we die for as long as someone, somewhere, remembers us. For the majority, that means two, perhaps three generations. For the famous and the notorious, a little longer, but even then, only until the records of history crumble to dust.

I, remembered by you, will live on eternally.

My love,

V.

Having learned, from Kim's e-mail, that the explosion in Tunguska had not been caused by a meteor impact after all but by the destruction of an antigravity vehicle created by a certain Professor Anton Krilov, it had seemed logical to Rattray to assume that the mission which had called Valentina away from Salzburg had been to pursue and invalidate this selfsame Professor Anton Krilov. Nowhere in Kim's e-mail was this stated explicitly, but Kim *had* unearthed the information that, from early 1905 to halfway through 1908, Krilov had been permanently on the run, and that after the date of the explosion no more was seen or heard of him. 'Clearly this was a Guardian action,' said the e-mail, 'and all the indications are that, like Krilov, the Guardian or Guardians involved in the invalidation perished too.' And who else could that Guardian, Krilov's pursuer, have been but Valentina?

Rattray recalled what he had said to Cecil the day they had met in the fast-food restaurant, well over a week ago now: *Sometimes things just are what they are.* Adhering to such a philosophy kept you from going insane when your world was one immense labyrinth of subterfuges and counter-subterfuges, façades behind façades, lies wrapped up in truths and truths tucked away inside lies. *Sometimes things just are what they are.*

Except when they were not.

Why had he not been told that Valentina had been killed in 1908? Assuming the best, he had always pictured her surviving the Bolshevik Revolution, the Stalinist purges and all the other political misfortunes that had been visited upon her country, and living to a ripe old age in a dacha by the shores of the Black Sea. She had been in her early thirties when he had known her. Until the late 1950s he had continued to believe that she was alive somewhere, envisaging her, in her latter years, as a wizened, mercurial *grande dame* alternately bewitching and maddening those around her. He had even imagined her married to some lucky fellow, and had often, without a hint of rancour or jealousy, wished the imaginary old couple well. Somehow, thinking that she was alive and that he could always track her down and find her if he wanted to, had been immensely comforting. Equally, by the early 1960s, when all logic told him that she must have passed on, he was able to grieve for her at a distance, as a remote object of loss, and then put her out of his mind (though never forget her – she had been right about that, she would always be remembered as long as he lived).

And this parallel existence that he had dreamed up for her had all been in vain. A delusion.

He knew he should not be surprised, and he knew he should not feel as hurt and as bitterly betrayed as he did. All the same, he could not help but think that the Librans had deliberately kept her death a secret from him. Why? Because to have discovered, only a few years into his career as a Guardian, that the woman who had recruited him and whom he had loved had been killed in action might have given him pause for thought; might have given him reason to question, if only momentarily, the rightness of the cause to which he had so recently allied himself; might have led him to withdraw his services.

There was every possibility that the Librans had decided that it would be best if he found out the truth later, when his loyalty had gained a firmer footing, or, preferably, never.

He could not be sure that this was the case. The Librans moved in mysterious ways, their methods and reasoning ever nebulous. But every sinew in his body, every synapse, seemed to be telling him that what he suspected to be so, was so.

His distractedness throughout the mission had been evident to the others, most especially to Lucretia, who knew him better than any of them. He had managed, he thought, to convince them that the matter of Byrne's son was what had been troubling him. It had, to be honest, given him some cause for concern, but not as much as he had made out at the safe-house.

And on the flight back from America he had resolved to give the Librans the benefit of the doubt. Perhaps Lucretia had been right: they were not human, so was it absolutely fair to saddle them with human motivations, human weaknesses?

All the same, he would be regarding them from now on with a deeply sceptical eye.

And if he were to catch them deceiving him, or the Guardians, once more, just once …

They would pay dearly.

Acknowledgements

I am grateful to Tom Thorne, for applying his huge brain to the science in this book, making some invaluable suggestions and amendments, and spotting one egregious error (phew!); and also to Charlotte Hobson, for helping authenticate the Russian historical references in the Prologue.

– J.M.H.L.

USA Networks' *Sci-Fi Channel* is available in millions of homes worldwide and features a mix of original and classic science fiction, science fact, fantasy and horror. For further information, visit the *Sci-Fi Channel*'s web site – The Dominion – at http://www.scifi.com.